Groupwork Volume 7

In this series

Published Spring 2007

Groupwork: Volume 1
ISBN 9781861770554

Groupwork: Volume 2
ISBN 9781861770561

Groupwork: Volume 3
ISBN 9781861770578

Groupwork: Volume 4
ISBN 9781861770585

Groupwork: Volume 5
ISBN 9781861770592

Groupwork: Volume 6
ISBN 9781861770608

Groupwork: Volume 7
ISBN 9781861770615

Groupwork: Volume 8
ISBN 9781861770622

Groupwork: Volume 9
ISBN 9781861770639

Groupwork: Volume 10
ISBN 9781861770646

Groupwork: Volume 11
ISBN 9781861770653

Groupwork: Volume 12
ISBN 9781861770660

Groupwork: Volume 13
ISBN 9781861770677

To be published Autumn 2007

Groupwork: Volume 14
ISBN 9781861770684

A full contents list for volumes 1-13 will be found at the back of this volume

Groupwork

An Interdisciplinary Journal for Working with Groups

Volume Seven

edited by

Allan Brown & Nano McCaughan

Whiting & Birch Ltd
1994
Reprinted 2007

Notes from the Publisher

Citation

This volume comprises, without any amendment, all material published in *Groupwork* Volume 7, 1994. It is advised that authors citing material in this volume should recognise this original date and journal provenance in the manner indicated by the house style of the publication for which they are writing, either by citing material as the original periodical article, or, if citing this volume, by clearly indicating the original date of publication of the material both in text references and in the bibliography.

Reproduction

For technical reasons, the typesetting files of some early volumes of *Groupwork* are no longer usable. We have therefore scanned early volumes in this series from the original journals. This inevitably results in reproduction which is less than ideal. Material is available in some other formats.

Editorial contact details

We have reproduced volumes in their complete original format including notes to contributors and advertising. It should be remembered that editorial contact details and manuscript preparation requirements have changed. Current contact details and notes for contributors are available at www.whitingbirch.net.

Published by Whiting & Birch Ltd,
Forest Hill, London SE23 3HZ

ISBN 9781861770608
ISSN 0951-824X
Printed in England and the United States by Lightning Source

Groupwork
An Interdisciplinary Journal for Working with Groups

Volume 7, 1994

Contents

Preface

Since its first issue in 1988, much interesting and inspiring material has been published in *Groupwork*. Most of this still says much of use to today's groupworkers. We are therefore delighted that back volumes of Groupwork will in future be readily available in convenient form.

Mark Doel and Pamela Trevithick
Co-Editors *Groupwork*

EDITORIAL

The articles in this issue are mostly connected to one another by a theme of the exploration of cultural difference and a desire to usc that difference creatively and value it as a richness rather than a destructive force. In some of the groups recorded here however, cultural difference occurs in a structural context of oppression and unequal power. This requires group approaches which enhance the individuals' self-belief, and which confront inequality.

Paul Taylor's paper was given as a lecture at the 1993 European Groupwork Symposium. Taylor, an Englishman living and working in Paris, examines the barriers to cross national groupwork. He points out that ethnocentrism is a natural psychological reaction, linked to our identity and feelings of belonging. However, we have sophisticated ways of remaining locked into the deep structure of our cultures, including adopting an over tolerant attitude towards difference - he proposes that this can both be a substitute for a genuine meeting and exchange, and a form of disrespectful cultural tourism.

Taylor provides us with a useful classification to examine differences in cross national groups, and draws on comparative anthropological research to demonstrate how different European countries are ranked on these dimensions.

His thesis that we need to confront and dialogue with each other, or there will be no change is echoed in the article by Jill Reynolds and Jane Shackman. Their focus is the co-working dynamics in running training workshops for people who work with refugees and tortured victims. In an interesting way they hypothesize about the links between what happened to their relations as they worked together with the issues of concern to group members. The paper provides a good model of how to work together with the issues of concern to group members. The paper provides a good model of how to work together with someone with different training, work experience and personality, who responds differently to stress. They accepted the anxiety and envy implicit in perceiving difference, and did not project blame on each other when an error of judgement occurred.

> The problem with crime is a problem with men. To be a man is to need to dominate and control...to demonstrate 'machismo'; to express anger and suppress feelings of pain; hurt and tenderness...

The article written by a group of men working with male offenders at Avon Probation Centre focuses on the link between elements of male gender socialisation and criminal behaviour. John Bensted et al. describe two phases of an intensive groupwork programme with male offenders which included a deliberate and a voluntary aspect; a group experience offering self awareness and exploration of the person and the build up of the macho ethos.

These group members had committed serious offences and practically all had experienced several periods of custody. It is too early yet to learn whether the 80-day programme has had any long term rehabilitative effect, but it could be an innovative alternative to custody. There was a high level of attendance, participation and commitment to the programme.

Geraldine Grindley describes various interventions she has made as a consultant working with female religious communities in Ireland. Perhaps we see here the opposite to the culture which encourages male criminality! These women have faced enormous changes in the mission, organisation and structure of religious life since the impact of the Second Vatican Council in the 1960s; their formation and training has not prepared them for the small group life which now they lead. Dealing with the new autonomy, new experience of having to relate interpersonally and the change from all the aspects including dress, which caused them previously to live a 'life apart' had caused tensions and unhappiness in many communities.

Marie Ni Chorcora, Eddie Jennings and Nuala Lordan also first shared the experience and thoughts contained in their paper at the Third European Groupwork Symposium. Two of the authors are severely disabled, and in essence the work of the Disability Equality Training Group in Cork, with which Nuala is associated, has been to enable members to free themselves, internally and externally from the disempowering and stigmatising bonds which occur because of the disabling culture in which they live. The group found that they had adopted the principles later outlined in Mullender and Ward's 'self directed groupwork' approach. A vital aspect was the grasp of the political challenge, and the need to change existing power relations.

Children who are sexually abused by adults are also certainly an oppressed group. Gary Dixon and Michelle Phillips report on their work with a group of sexually abused boys; a central aim was to build up a culture of hope, trust and communication of feelings. They wanted to break through the barriers created by erroneous guilt and shame. The workers had to learn how to respect the anger these young boys were holding and find ways to allow the expression of it without destructive behaviour, so that the children could feel better about themselves.

Call For Papers

The editors would appreciate some more articles so that the Journal can be planned further in advance and need to rely less on the ebb and flow of papers received. Both practice and theoretical papers will be welcomed.

Nano McCaughan and Allan Brown, Editors

The linguistic and cultural barriers to cross-national groupwork

Paul Taylor

The political, social and cultural mobility of the new Europe makes possible a new form of cross-cultural and cross-national dynamics. Three factors militate against such potentially creative groupwork: cultural tourism, morality and a surfeit of tolerance. Some of the distinguishing characteristics of national identity which are the frontiers or barriers which the groupworker has to cross are identified and their relevance for groupwork practice explained: language, hierarchical distance, individualism, gender roles and the management of risk.

Introduction

The question posed by this Symposium, 'Survival and Success in Groupwork in the 1990s', reflects the enormous political and social changes which have come about in Europe in the last two years and which concern us directly. This Europe of the future will require us more and more to have professional competencies in multi-lingual and multi- cultural groups. Without the frontiers of the past, Europeans have a cultural, social, economic and political mobility which previous generations have never known. We will therefore find ourselves in a new group dynamic, in both social and task groups, where there will be no single, dominant cultural or national norm. It is therefore most opportune that we look carefully behind the jargon of groupwork 'without frontiers' in the new, open Europe which exists, because of or despite Mastricht, since January, 1993.

In proposing this reflection on the barriers to such cross-national work created by the way people speak, by the way they think and the way they behave, it is critically important that I move both beyond simple anecdote and over refined stereotypes to offer a more rigorous analysis of some of the criteria by which we differentiate cultures and national identity.

First, however, we need to consider the more permanent, insidious, blockages that drastically limit or even prevent an approach to creative groupwork.

The most evident of these blockages is cultural tourism. We know

Groupwork Vol. 7(1), 1994, pp.7-22

that a host country or culture often has a vested interest in exploiting what the tourist wants to see (traditional dress, dances, music, recipes), but that this exploitative nostalgia is a collusion in highlighting what is quaint, exotic, historic or folkloric. Both host and tourist know that such cultural stereotyping does not represent the reality of contemporary, ordinary life. As many anti-racism campaigns have discovered, cultural tourism creates a false image of the society or culture because it remains a profoundly ethnocentric way of looking at what is different. It is a voyeurism, a consumerism of the dominant myths, reinforcing prejudice. As Levi-Strauss indicates[1], we cannot respect what we feel to be quaint. Cultural tourism gives us refracted knowledge without responsibility.

Our personal moral system often provides a different form of mind-guarding, a more insidious blockage. Morality substitutes for knowledge: I have no need to know more about the other because I have already decided the degree to which she or he is compatible with my own moral values. Morality is of course important, but it cannot replace understanding. It is in many ways like a frontier: we are morally open or closed, allowing ourselves a more or less restricted passage of values and opinions. Is the Russian or Chinese culture more just or more democratic than the British? Are Scandinavian cultures more permissive or less sexist than the French or German? Are women in Arab cultures less free than women in Europe or North America?

These are not flippant, stereotyped questions. They appear regularly today, for example, in the debates about immigration, the right to asylum, citizenship and the right to vote which are currently occupying many European parliaments in their struggle to define national identity. They represent a view of complex cross-cultural, cross-national problems, seen through the simplifying lens of a certain morality. It is as much a distorting lens as is the third form of blockage - the view from a distance caused by a *surfeit of tolerance*.

At best tolerance is a necessary virtue, at worst it is a refined system of self-defence, a half measure. It is a substitute for real confrontation, a genuine meeting, a going beyond the 'what lies between us'. If we only tolerate, if we each respect the territory of the other, we will never have to cross the barriers or frontiers which divide us.

The plea for more tolerance is often only a political ploy, at a personal or national level, to ensure that there will be no change. Implicit in the statement 'I am willing to tolerate you, I accept you as you are' is the reverse appeal: 'You must accept me as I am, let me be'. I will tolerate you but on condition that I do not have to change.

Tolerance avoids or pre-empts conflict. Yet cross-national groupwork demands that we confront each other (literally, confront means to 'stand face to face with someone'), honestly and authentically, otherwise there will be no group or group life. We need to engage in constructive, cultural opposition which goes far beyond the simplicity of liberal toleration (Demorgon, 1993).

Culture

If the preconditions of cross-national groupwork are that we should not be seduced by the attractiveness of different cultures, should not export our own moral judgments nor import a confining tolerance, then where do we begin? There are two very different ways to start looking at another culture -from the inside as it is lived, or from the outside as it is thought to be lived. Obviously the new arrival who adopts a given culture, who is trying to be culturally integrated, does not see that culture in the same way as someone who has been born and bred into it, for whom it is completely natural, first nature. This is the key 'insider-outsider' analysis of Pike and Harris (Headland et al., 1990) about emics and etics which has so much to offer our discussion. It exposes the differences between what is essential (emic) to a culture and what is changeable (etic), between what is learnt consciously (etic) about a culture and what is acquired subconsciously (emic).

What is fascinating is that the insider's view, the emic analysis, is not necessarily more authentic or accurate than the etic view of the outsider (Reiss, 1990). This is because we learn culture, or at least our primary culture, mostly unconsciously through the acquiring of personal, social and moral values and behaviour.

The groupworker/community worker is most often, almost necessarily from the outside, someone for whom the culture of the group is not a natural, first instinct, but which she or he has to learn by active observation and reflection. How then do we look at such a group, especially when that group is of a different nationality, inhabits a culture which is foreign[2] and even speaks a different language?

Their culture, any culture, is effectively a collective mental programming, a way of thinking and behaving that distinguishes one group from another. Many differing scales (national, regional, local, social group, task group) of programming are possible, all inter-related and more or less mutually coherent.

An etic description of a given culture allows for the discovery of patterns of thinking or behaviour within this collective mental programming which are unavailable to us through emic descriptions. Harris (1979) firmly asserts that the observer's competence (linguistic or cultural fluency) is sufficient to enable him or her to have a valid etic mental understanding of a culture, that is, to be able to identify a rule or principle of that culture. This is not the same as saying, however, that the observer is thereby immediately capable of acting or reacting in accordance with that culture.

An example might be useful here: I might have observed where, how and when the French or the British shake hands. I can formulate a rule that in such or such a circumstance, shaking hands is the correct thing to do, and, given the necessary circumstances, I may be able to behave appropriately and so express my understanding of, and acceptance of, those cultural norms.

In another culture, I may be able to observe with the same correctness and accuracy that the law and social customs of a society require that certain criminals are subjected to a public flogging. However, although the circumstances of a particular crime may be clear and beyond doubt, I may not be able to collude with this form of punishment. At best, my non-conformity would express my understanding of, but rejection of, what others would consider to be normal, acceptable behaviour.

Both these examples, but particularly the latter, expose the fact that both emic and etic perceptions are essentially ethnocentric: in fact, they cannot be otherwise. Ethnocentrism is a natural, psychological reaction, which is inextricably linked to a sense of identity and of belonging. The processes of enculturation, integration and socialisation all seek to provide each individual, group or community with an ethnic or cultural centre. We learn to belong, we learn to centre ourselves on a given culture, to have roots and to recognise those who share those roots and those who do not (Tajfel, 1979).

This acquired, passive ethnocentrism is not the same as the active, exclusive ethnocentrism which lies at the heart of positive xenophobia or conscious racism. It is rather a way of drawing attention to the fact that ethnocentrism is to society what egocentrism is to the individual. I have to start with the fact that I am who I am. I can only look honestly at another culture or another individual if I know genuinely what it means to be Me.

One notes time and time again, therefore, that what happens across the cross-cultural boundaries has more to do with what happens within those national cultures that it has to do with any great spontaneity or dynamic produced at the moment of encounter. The participants of any mixed national group tend[3] overwhelmingly to express themselves on issues of power, control, sexuality, agreement and disagreement based on their normative behaviour within their own separate cultures.

Let us take a light-hearted example. In no matter what culture they find themselves, the English tend to form a queue for anything: the French do not. The Dutch, like the French, greet strangers when they enter the confined spaces, for example, of a shop, a lift or an office: the Belgians do not, be they French or Flemish speaking. Austrians on foot wait for green before crossing a main road: never the Italians. Swiss drivers and even pedestrians are voluble if you mistake a road sign or impede the flow of traffic: Swedish people are much more tolerant and forgiving (Tixier, 1992).

These specific examples of national differences are not in themselves important, but the question which lies behind them is critical: how is it that differing cultures, in situations which are common to all, prefer a particular response which is often quite at odds with that of their neighbour? The striking fact that we need to analyse is that our European neighbours, despite being Europeans, are all very different. That is what makes our reflection on cross-national groupwork exciting. We have no need to hide behind the liberal pluriculturalism which claims that all peoples and all cultures are different and that, therefore, cultural comparisons are odious or useless. On the contrary, we can exploit and better appreciate that diversity and difference: we can observe, as a phenomenon which we have all experienced, that there are specific characteristics which create typologies of national identity. These are founded on the differing cultural, climatic, historic, economic, social and educational variables (which ethnomethodology (Handel, 1982) defines as 'indexical' factors) which give rise to each nation's sense of identity.

The diverse cultural barriers to cross-national groupwork

These typologies, embedded in history, schooling and collective moralities, just as much as in present social, political and commercial behaviour, reveal five barriers which a cross-national group must confront before it can work effectively together: language, hierarchy, individualism, gender and uncertainty.

Language

From Saussure (1974) to Barthes (1986) to Lacan (1977), many anthropologists and linguists, as observers of groups and cultures, have argued that all human beings and all cultures are essentially a product of language. Fascinating then that not all languages have words to describe even ordinary things that human beings might take for granted. Some languages do not have words to distinguish blue from green in a rainbow, others have no word for brown. We describe time differently and accordingly behave differently: 'half-eight' in English is thirty minutes after eight o'clock. In German, it is thirty minutes before eight, that is, half-seven. Some languages do not distinguish 'mother' and 'aunt', reflecting a particular construction of family life, while some Scandinavian languages have separate words to distinguish maternal and paternal grandparents.

As educators or social and community workers, we have to confront the problem created by the fact that, for example, the British idea of Community Education does not translate into German, that the French *Animation* does not translate into English, nor the German *Bildung* into French. Core groupwork concepts like empowerment, leadership, achievement, accountability, and self-assessment cannot easily be expressed, for example, in French. The words do not exist, so what does one do faced with the question of team-building and group identity? We may at least begin to suspect that standard groupwork theory as taught in the U.K., heavily American as it is, cannot be translated sufficiently accurately in order to provide us with a coherent base on which to develop cross-national groupwork.

In some cultures, contrary to Asch (1956) and Milgram (1963) for example, it is more important to be polite than to be seen to be right or forthrightly honest. The Japanese rarely say 'no', with the result that their 'yes' is not necessarily the same as *ja*, *oui, si*, or even *si*. They also do not have a word for 'decision-making', despite their very commercial culture. It is this kind of observation, of which there are numerous examples, which helps us appreciate that cross-national groupwork is not simply a question of translating words which we could all understand by agreeing to some kind of international glossary of useful terms. It is rather the more complex process of interpreting the connotation of words[4] within the cultural context of the other person (Demorgon, 1989, p.127).

An illustration is perhaps useful: if we ask in any given language 'what is the word for inedible?, we can find that word in a simple dictionary. I know of no language that does not have such a word. However, if we ask 'What do they mean by inedible?', the dictionary is no help. We would need to understand the religious, historical, geographic, social and economic context which results in one culture defining as inedible what another culture may think is a great delicacy. One person's poison is another person's fish, just as one person's morality is another's barbarism (Hurstel, 1988).

The translation/interpretation of relationships provides us with another potential stumbling block. English is habituated to a number of extended and restricted codes, often highly nuanced (Bernstein, 1971), but its generic *you* loses the important distinctions of the two forms of you which we find in many European languages, e.g. *tu / vous*, *du / sie*, and which identify both the singular and plural 'you' and a continuum of formal and non-formal relationships. Here, in ordinary everyday language, as in the *thee* and *thou* of yore, much is made implicitly and explicitly of the different degrees of relationship and familiarity, indicating a respect for older people or solidarity with a peer group, the status of an individual, a professional distance, an invitation to a closer relationship or the marking of a solemn moment. The problem for English speakers is how to transit from one culture to another, how to learn to use correctly these complex interpersonal modes of communication which, in English, are not marked by the verb but rather more subtly by the use of adjectives or a particular tone of voice. The converse is that it is not surprising that those whose first language is not English often find the British address them in a style which is cold and lacking in sensitivity. Interesting that *sang froid* might be a product not of heredity but of language ?

Hierarchical distance

No anthropologist has ever found a society that was not marked by inequalities. That is simply another way of saying sociologically that any society that values difference over homogeneity ends up by structuring the disparities which cut society vertically by family and clan and horizontally by status and power.

What interests the cross-national groupworker is how a given society or culture perceives the degrees of inequality or distance between those who hold power and those who are subject to that power. Bollinger and Hofstede (1987, p.73) clearly argue that this perception differs from country to country.

In measuring the continuum of power, establishing the psychological and social dynamic that exists in a given group, we are able to calculate a figure for any country's 'relative hierarchical distance' (RHD).

Within the observed behaviour of a group, we can note the frequency with which leaders consult or value another opinion; whether the group seeks to personalise task activities rather than resting at a functional level where detailed directives would be sufficiently effective; whether the group collectively requests or demands an increased level of participation rather than 'accepting its place' in the hierarchy of things.

The groupworker needs to know how the group interprets the concepts of leadership and hierarchy, and its preference for modes of communication and interaction which are a-autocratic, b-paternalistic, c-consultative or d-democratic. Generally, in countries with a high RHD, that is where differences in hierarchy and power structures are clearly marked, the preference for the group culture is for a-b; in countries where hierarchical status is less evident, (low RHD) the preference is for c-d.

In that the culture of a group will naturally reflect the overall national culture, the consequences of differing RHDs for potential cross-national groupwork are significant. We observe that, generally, the Latin European countries (Italy, France, Spain, Greece) have a high RHD, a tendency confirmed by other countries nearer the equator. Germanic Europe (Germany, Scandinavia and the U.K.) tends towards a low RHD.

Table 1
Relative Hierarchical Distances

Relative ranking of each country		RHD Score*
1	Malaysia	104
14	Brazil	69
16	France	68
19	Turkey	66
20	Belgium	65
27	Greece	60
31	Spain	57
33	Japan	54
34	Italy	50
38	USA	40
40	Holland	38
43	Germany	35
44	UK	35
45	Switzerland	35
48	Sweden	31
52	Israel	13
53	Austria	11

** 110 = high RHD* *0 = low RHD*
(*Source:* Bollinger and Hofstede, *1987)*

Clearly geography and particularly nearness to the equator is an important element, but technology is also an indexical factor.

Countries with a high level of technological culture tend to have low RHD, perhaps because technology is a major equalising, levelling force in society. Conversely, poorer countries tend to distinguish more between the rich and the poor, the powerful and the powerless and this shows in their RHD.

The impact of such culture on the group is clear. Unless the groupworker places the group's preferences for styles of leadership and management within its own cultural context, the standard questions about authoritarian, *laissez faire* or democratic communications within groups will yield only misleading responses. A high RHD, where social stratification and access to power is clearly marked, creates a culture of latent conflict, tension, and competitive rivalry. Power is invested in the individual who leads either because of their charisma or because of their unquestioned role. Power is a pendulum between left and right, and change is founded, therefore, on conflict.

In a group culture of low RHD, change is more evolutionary, even though more slow because of the constant balancing mechanisms which prevent one person power. Power lies in the group, even in the team, where the internal politics tend to disguise or disregard the latent inequalities in the group.

Individualism

Different societies construct the continuum 'society-community-family-individual' in different ways. Anthropologists distinguish those that are dominantly communal societies from those that are individualistic. The former identifies the individual with their personal moral involvement in the society and in a given group. The social unit is the 'we of me', the individual whose place is firmly within a network of intercommunications. Immigration into, or emigration out of, such a group in extremely difficult.

The latter mode prioritises a person's professional contribution in society, their role and function rather than their personality. Individual convictions count more than collective identity. The social unity is the 'me of me', the individual who stands on his or her own two feet, but who is fundamentally no better nor no worse than the next person. Consequently, the tendency to individualise is compensated by tendencies to depersonalise, homogenise. Such 'equality of opportunity' makes immigration fairly easy.

Obviously there is a high correlation between the richness of a country and the value which it places on individualism. The standard americanised, 'Thatcherised' theory is that it is the individual, the entrepreneur, the self-employed who create a thriving economy and individual wealth. However, another ideological explanation may also be possible: that only in the rich countries can one afford to be self-centred and individualistic.

Table 2
Degree of Individualism

Relative ranking of each country		Score*
1	USA	91
3	UK	89
5	Holland	80
7	Italy	76
8	Belgium	75
10	Sweden	71
11	France	71
12	Ireland	70
14	Switzerland	68
15	Germany	67
19	Israel	54
20	Spain	51
22	Japan	46
35	Portugal	27
47	Pakistan	14
50	Venezuela	12
52	Ecuador	8
53	Guatemala	6

** 100 = individualistic society   0 = communal society*
(Source: Bollinger and Hofstede, 1987)

This index is useful in assessing whether a group is more likely to create a culture of cooperation or competition (Ladmiral and Lipiansky, 1989). Communal societies avoid major swings in power and government: for someone to lose face or honour or standing is a collective loss, their failure a collective failure. Relationships are founded on a social morality as they represent an investment in the social fabric in which all gain or lose. Professional life is integrated with personal life.

This is much less true in the *Gemeinschaft* societies where individualism flourishes. The pendulum of power can swing radically as certain individuals become more or less dominant. Relationships are founded on utility, calculated to advantage: useless relationships, familial or social, are discontinued. There is a marked separation between the personal and the professional.

Groupworkers in the U.K. will be used to working with the kind of group which is essentially a collection of individuals, but there are clearly situations, for example with minority ethnic groups, where a sensitive analysis of this indexical factor of individuality would be crucial to the proper functioning of the group.

Gender

It is this kind of setting that highlights another important barrier to groupwork, viz., that sexual differentiation is not the same in all countries. In some countries, high status roles are automatically masculine and, where there is role differentiation, it is nearly always the male who is advantaged. Without entering the sexism/ sexist debate, although it is clearly associated, we can define a masculine culture as one where there is clear male/female role differentiation and a feminine culture as one where there is role equality and interchangeability.

It is interesting to reflect that Catholic countries in Europe are more male dominant than those more influenced by Protestantism. There is a marked correlation between that and the ideologies and style of social policy making, for example, which is itself an indexical factor for evaluating a given culture. Compare, in this light, Italy and Ireland with the Scandinavian countries.

The importance of this barrier for groupwork is that masculine cultures tend to be competitive, status aware, product oriented but technology dependent. Feminine cultures, particularly in small groups, tend to be process oriented, pay more attention to the ambience of the group that will facilitate cooperation and exchange, are competence rather than status aware, and exploit more its human rather than its technological resources. Within this whole debate, it is certainly my experience that British groupworkers express and impose their view about the gendering of culture and of group dynamics much more than their continental European counterparts. This despite the fact that English is not fundamentally a gender differentiated language. The definite article, adjectives, participles, nouns and pronouns do not have to accord in the same way that other languages (*le/la, der/die, el/la*) have to reflect grammatical gender. The paradox is that, in grammatically differentiated language, e.g. French, the dominantly masculine form renders women less visible. British groupworkers may well find that much of what they take for granted as anti-sexist language

Table 3
Degree of Gender Demarcation

Relative ranking of each country		Score*
1	Japan	95
2	Austria	79
4	Italy	70
7	Ireland	68
8	Jamaica	68
9	UK	66
10	Germany	66
18	Greece	57
21	India	56
26	Pakistan	50
27	Brazil	49
29	Israel	47
36	France	43
37	Spain	42
41	S. Korea	39
45	Portugal	31
50	Denmark	16
51	Holland	14
52	Norway	8
53	Sweden	5

** 100 = masculine culture 0 = feminine culture*
(Source: Bollinger and Hofstede, 1987)

does not translate directly into other European languages. Indeed, despite the dominance of English as a language (Lafont, 1991), the exporting of, or the insisting upon, anti-sexist language or codes of practice may well represent a neo-colonial form of cultural invasion. At least English speakers may need to think through the relationship between biological gender and arbitrary grammatical gender.

Managing uncertainty

The final barrier to cross-national groupwork is crucial to any form of change. How do we see the future? How do we cope with uncertainty? These simple questions influence each and every form of communication that goes on with a group, but needless to say, not all countries or cultures respond in the same way.

Table 4
Management of Uncertainty

Relative ranking of each country		Score*
1	Greece	112
2	Portugal	104
5	Belgium	94
7	Japan	92
10	France	86
11	Chile	86
12	Spain	86
19	Israel	81
23	Italy	75
29	Germany	65
33	Switzerland	58
35	Holland	53
43	USA	46
47	UK	35
48	Ireland	35
50	Sweden	39
53	Singapore	8

** 120 = threatened by uncertainty, seeks to control it*
0 = liberated by uncertainty, seeks to exploit it
(Source: Bollinger and Hofstede, 1987)

More than the other three indexical elements which we have already touched upon, the responses to the management of uncertainty are more evidently polarised. Some countries and cultures seek to limit disruptive insecurity by the existence of written constitutions, identity cards for every adult[5], passes, permits, and other controls. No-one is anonymous. Groups, in turn, insist on formal roles, written structures, conventions, rules and clear processes to avoid misunderstanding. Whatever the issue, whatever the context, the first court of appeal is 'What do the regulations say?'

Where countries seek to control uncertainty, there is often a belief that technology can provide safeguards, that rules can define behaviour and that religion and/or politics have access to some form of absolute truth. Complex ritualising curtails uncertainty: meetings are verified by reports and minutes rather than by results; planning prefers clear aims and objectives to preclude the unforeseen; experts and consultants are appointed to control rogue practice; and precise rules define responsibility and limit initiative.

Imagine, therefore, a meeting where participants are from, just for example, the U.K., the United States, France and Germany and we can see immediately why the GATT negotiations were so difficult.

Countries and groups which exploit uncertainty, as in Britain or in America, are more outward looking, less tolerant of aggression within the group, more able to take personal risks and rely on intuition. They are ill at ease within a culture that relies on logic, objectivity and insists on consensus. It is deeply significant that the expression 'non-directive groupwork' has its origins deep within the English speaking world: to many Europeans, it is a contradiction in terms.

Conclusion

Inevitably, language remains the major barrier to cross- national groupwork[6]. Nonetheless, in hoping to bring about change, we know that cultural norms, be they of a group or of a society, change rarely by the adoption of external values but rather because new conditions or situations arise within the group which facilitate necessary change. Cultural change always has more to link it to the known past than to a desired future.

Secondly, in order to change ideas we need to change behaviour. For me that means that we need to have more and more contact with other national groups and cultures, as a result of which our ideas will change. It is no good hoping for a change in patterns of thinking, new ideologies, and new groupwork practice so that, at some future but ill defined date, cross-national groupwork might be possible.

One cannot learn to swim in a library: nor can one learn the theory or the practice of cross-national groupwork in a mono-cultural or mono-national environment.

The values which we cherish as groupworkers have a clear intensity and direction. Our interventions in groups, as in society, are not neutral. We need to avoid the homogenising attraction of 'political correctness' which is often merely a thin disguise for 'cultural cleansing'. Only then can we confront the vibrant cultural differences within our own national and social identities, and push out the frontiers of social work and groupwork. The barriers to cross-national groupwork begin here, this side of the frontier and not in some other far off place. Perhaps the only real barrier to international groupwork is the frontier we build around ourselves.

This article is the substantive text of the paper given at the Third European Groupwork Symposium which was held at Goldsmiths' College, London, 15-16 1993, under the auspices of the publishers Whiting and Birch.

Notes

1. The tension which exists between tourism, ethnology and ordinary life is well explored in Claude Levi- Strauss, *Tristes Tropiques*, Paris, Plon, 1955.
2. Someone who is foreign, a foreigner, is simply someone who, by definition (Latin: *foras, foris* = outside, not at home, from without) regards me, as I regard him or her, from a distance. It is necessarily an etic regard, a view from an 'other' perspective.
3. I have kept the word 'tend' here because, happily, there will always be individuals who do not conform to the norm. However that does not invalidate the norm or the typology. At the individual level, we are all different and inhabit our own specific 'culture'. Nonetheless, the constitutive variables of identity are sufficiently distinguishable for us to recognise national characteristics which give rise, at the macro-level, to verifiable typologies.
4. This point itself is dependent on the particular, indexical language of this article, i.e. the English nuance of the words 'translating' and 'interpreting'. French and German have the same words (*traduire / ubersetzen: interpreter / verdolmetschen*) but not necessarily the same connative or indexical usage.
5. Austria, Belgium, France, Germany, Italy, and Switzerland have identity cards; Denmark, Finland, Holland, Ireland, Norway, Sweden and the UK do not.
6. It is an important illusion of liberal cultural studies that learning a language necessarily helps a person understand the culture of that country. Language that is learnt/taught mechanically, simply as translated information, cannot transmit the qualitative value system of the culture.

References

Asch, S. (1956) 'Studies of independence and conformity', *Psychological Monographs*, 70(9), No.416.

Barthes, R. (1986) *The Rustle of Language*. Oxford: Blackwell.

Bernstein, B. (1971) *Class, Codes, Control*. New York: Routledge & Kegan Paul.

Bollinger, D. and Hofstede, G. (1987) *Les differences culturelles dans le management*. Paris: Editions d'organisation

Demorgon, J. (1989) *L'exploration interculturelle*. Paris: Armand Colin.

Demorgon, J. (1993) 'Un nouvel appareil à penser et à vivre les cultures', *Reperes et Action*, 2. Paris: CEMEA.

Handel, W. (1982) *Ethnomethodology: How People Make Sense*. Englewood Cliffs, NJ: Prentice Hall.

Harris, M. (1979) *Cultural Materialism: The Struggle for a Science of Culture*. New York: Random House.

Headland, T., Pike, K. and Harris, M. (eds.) (1990) *Emics and Etics: the Insider / Outsider Debate*. London: Sage.

Hurstel, J. (1988) *Chroniques culturelles barbares*. Paris: Syron/Alternatives.

Lacan, J. (1977) *Ecrits*. London: Tavistock.
Ladmiral J.-R. and Lipiansky, E.-M. (1989) *La communication interculturelle*. Paris: Armand Colin.
Lafont, R. (1991) *Nous, peuple europeen?*. Paris: Kimé.
Milgram, S. (1963) 'Behavioural study of obedience', *Journal of Abnormal and Social Psychology*, 67(4), pp.371-378.
Reiss, N. (1990) 'The emic-etic distinction as applied to language' in Headland, T., Pike, K. and Harris, M. (eds.) *Emics and Etics: the Insider / Outsider Debate*. London: Sage.
Saussure, F. (1974) *Course in General Linguistics*. Glasgow: Collins.
Tajfel, H. (1979) 'An integrative theory of intergroup conflict' in Austin, W. and Worchel, S. (eds.) *The Social Psychology of Intergroup Relations*. California: Brooks Cole.
Tixier, M. (1992) *Travailler en Europe*. Paris: Liaisons.

Partnership in Training and Practice with Refugees

Jill Reynolds and Jane Shackman

Partnership by co-workers, providing training sessions on refugees and mental health, is explored alongside the partnership that non-refugees and refugees need to achieve in working with refugee communities. Two examples of challenges which the authors met as co-workers with groups in training sessions are presented, with discussion of how these challenges also represented some of the issues of concern to group members. The response of the co-workers, to some extent, reflected what was happening in the group. Partnership is characterised by equality, difference and sharing: these can all be problematic aspirations for co-work involving refugee communities. Non-refugees and refugees seeking to work together in partnership need to accept that things may go wrong at times.

Partnership in training and practice with refugees

At the end of a three day workshop we had been running, one participant commented that seeing us work together was like watching a skilled brain surgeon with an assistant handing the right implement at the precise time it was needed. The additional feature in our case was that we took it in turns to be brain surgeon! This image surprised us: it did not conjure up the relationship of equals which we thought central to our co-work as trainers. It did, however, capture elements of precision, expertise and confidence in each other, to which we would be delighted to lay claim. Our operation was less life-threatening and dramatic than a brain surgeon's, but a demanding one nevertheless. We had been invited to New Zealand for two weeks, by Auckland Institute of Technology under their 'visiting experts' programme, to provide consultation and training workshops on refugee mental health, education and welfare.

We had not thought of our way of working together as a major part of what we set out to teach. It was, we thought, the medium, rather than the message. Yet participants in our workshops were telling us that we had provided good role models for 'working in partnership', one of the themes of our workshops.

Groupwork Vol. 7(1), 1994, pp.23-36

This paper explores how our partnership in working together was highlighted by issues of partnership for practitioners working with refugees, and how we reflected on, reviewed and refined our partnership over the two week period.

Partnership

Partnership is becoming one of the buzz words of the social welfare field. Attempts to pin down this warm and positive word result in lengthy lists of expectations. In addition there is always the fact that each of us has an unspoken notion of what partnership is, against which we test other people's claims to be acting as partners (Daines et al., 1990).

Important components seem to be equality, difference and sharing (Pugh et al., 1987; De'Ath, 1982, cited by Daines et al., 1990). There may be tension between these three components. Partners contribute different skills, knowledge, and aims to their collaboration, with the expectation that their common purpose can only be achieved through their shared efforts.

Partnership in groupwork

In a groupwork context partnership is often referred to as 'co-work' or 'co-leadership'. Tara Mistry and Allan Brown (1991) prefer 'co-work' since in groupwork leadership is shared with all members of a group. We use the term co-work here, although in our training role we expect to take the lead more often than might be required in some other kinds of groupwork.

Co-workers may bring different skills, experience and knowledge, possibly even some different values, but they need to share some common core of agreement, at least as to how they handle their differences. Co-workers are role models for the group and conflict between co-workers which is left unresolved can be mirrored in the process of the group, or hamper group development. Co-working implies a relationship of equals, and it may be difficult for people to work together confidently if there is a disparity of experience or professional status, although it can be a way for a newcomer to groupwork to learn groupwork skills (Preston-Shoot, 1987). Co-work requires careful preparation, and clarity about the different roles the co-workers will take.

There are inherent tensions in developing the partnership of co-workers. Differences in experience or approach can become sources of envy or irritation between co-workers. Group members may respond differently to the groupworkers on the basis of perceived inequalities of skill, experience or authority. If dynamics are not discussed, co-workers may find themselves in competition for the attention of the group.

Partnership in practice with refugees

Partnership is an important theme in work with refugees (Finlay and Reynolds, 1987). Whatever the differing circumstances of those countries receiving them, refugees inevitably arrive as 'strangers in a strange land' (Antonouris, 1987). Service-providers have to forge some sort of partnership with incoming refugee groups in order to begin to meet their needs. Agencies with different remits and agendas for action often find they are competing over what tasks they take on, and indeed for funding: to be effective they need to collaborate and develop partnership. Individual health and welfare workers are often unable to do direct work with refugees on their own. Language and cultural differences invariably mean that interpreters are needed, or health and welfare workers who share language and culture with the refugee group. So for those workers who do not speak the refugee's language, another kind of partnership, with bilingual/bicultural workers is implied.

Sometimes the partnership will involve refugees and non-refugees in direct work together with clients or projects. At other times the partnership is looser, the team-work implied from a multidisciplinary approach or transcultural consultation.

In any of these arenas for partnership there are likely to be considerable obstacles to finding the basis for a shared enterprise which values each partner equally. We consider here the interpersonal level: bicultural workers drawn from the refugee group have a whole new cultural system and language to deal with, and even if they have appropriate professional experience in their own country this may not be recognised as valid in the country of settlement. Those who are new to this kind of work on either side of a working partnership may feel that they reach the limits of their knowledge and skill quite quickly.

Conflict and perceived inequality between refugee and non-refugee workers will have its effects on refugee communities, whose members may try to further divide workers, and will certainly take note of a role model of refugee worker as assistant rather than co-equal.

While partnership may offer advantages in refugee work, a joint approach is not always be a matter of choice: the different parties may be unable to proceed alone. Partnership in groupwork has its tensions too, but co-work is often chosen by groupworkers for the attraction of additional support, help in managing the group process, and complementary approaches. In many circumstances groupworkers can still work on their own if they prefer.

Background to our consultancy and training visit

We chose to work together for the reasons outlined above. Our visit involved meeting with refugee community leaders, workers in organisations which offer support services to refugees, and interested academics. The overall brief included aims of increasing public and professional awareness of the health, mental health, social and educational needs of refugees; fostering multidisciplinary co-operation in clinical activities directed at refugee health and well-being; and enhancing the competence of different occupational groups to work effectively in areas of treatment, rehabilitation, community development and health promotion.

As well as consultancy sessions, we were asked to hold three workshops. A three day intensive workshop on 'Refugee Mental Health and Welfare' (1) was aimed at health and allied professionals in practitioner and teaching roles. A second workshop of one day (2) was to provide an overview of refugee mental health issues for general practitioners, primary health care workers, counsellors and others working with refugees in community settings. The third half day workshop was for community interpreters (3).

Developing our partnership in co-work

Literature on co-work in groups stresses the importance of the development of a good working relationship, familiarity with each other's approaches, careful preparation before groupwork begins, and attention to role definition (see for instance Galinsky and Schopler, 1980; Heap 1985).

We were able to fulfil most of these requirements. We had worked together as practitioners in refugee reception and as trainers on many occasions before. We had some knowledge of each other's strengths and weaknesses, and could give each other feedback on these. We also had a good grasp of each other's approaches, with shared perspectives on some matters as well as some areas of contrasting experience, knowledge and skill. We prepared in some detail in anticipation of our visit: for instance organising material we intended to use in workshops in terms of how to present it, who would introduce topics, lead discussions or take feedback. Our roles would in part be defined by our experience and knowledge. Jane's clinical work at the Medical Foundation for Care of Victims of

Torture would be an important resource to practitioners. As a teacher of social work, Jill would be able to give guidance to teachers and trainers on the development of teaching materials on refugees. We also knew from previous joint work that we would each tend towards different roles in terms of task and process. Jill likes to keep her focus on the aims of a session, while Jane is particularly good at staying in touch with emotions in the group and picking up changes in atmosphere.

Our individual strengths were also the source of some anxiety and envy for us. Jill felt a little distant from her practice in work with refugee communities, and unfamiliar with working with the effects of torture: one of the themes we had been asked to address. While Jane was confident in her practice, she was less sure of her ability to draw out the conceptual frameworks which could help others. It was tempting to leave entirely to the other the areas of which we were less confident, but this would limit our individual contributions considerably. So some of our preparation involved sharing ideas and learning from each other.

Our familiarity in working together meant that we were also aware that we could get upset over misunderstandings, and we agreed that rather than let these escalate 'in public', we would try to acknowledge disagreements at the time but reserve discussion until later. Easier said than done! We are different in our approach to giving feedback. Different too in our pacing and temperaments: Jane gets more enthusiastic and energetic as she engages in work to which she is committed. Jill's enthusiasm is more muted, and she needs time to herself to recharge. We knew we had to respect each other's needs, although Jill might experience Jane's excitement as criticism of her own silence and vice versa.

The planning and preparation that we did was an important foundation to our working partnership. Similar preparation is also a requirement in the partnerships of refugee work, but the need for this is not always acknowledged. A handbook on work with refugees comments on dysfunctional stress in refugee work: 'We have only fleeting contact with our co-workers. Everyone is perhaps highly concentrated - and rushed' (League of Red Cross and Red Crescent Societies, 1991, p.143).

Our co-work planning was also highly concentrated, but we tried not to rush it too much. We saw our own exploration of the evolving programme as an important part of developing our roles as co-workers.

Planning our programme

We had several key objectives for our major workshop (1) which carried us into personal reflections and debates of help to us in all the different groupwork contexts. These were that participants:

1. relate their own experiences of disruption to learning about working to support refugees;
2. examine what they find difficult, distressing, or simply different about working with refugees and torture survivors;
3. recognise issues in refugees and non-refugees working together in partnership, and develop strategies for problem resolution.

Planning a programme with these objectives forced us to recall our own reactions to disruption, loss and change. We thought about what we had ourselves found difficult, distressing or different in our experience of working with refugees. We examined achievements and dissonances in our partnerships with workers from refugee communities, as well as reviewing satisfactions and dissatisfactions in our partnership with each other in previous co-working arrangements.

Slowly programmes for the workshops evolved. The outline for workshop (1) covered most of the material we would hope to use in other contexts. This included exercises and discussion on loss and exile; a framework for making assessments; mental stress and social functioning: working with torture or trauma survivors; the dynamics of asking for help; different methods of working; issues in partnership for refugee and non-refugee workers; approaches to problem solving; developing appropriate teaching resources and mapping your own support system.

Drawing a dream house

We used activities in our workshops which would meet our objectives by drawing on participants' experiences, and which were in themselves experiential. One such activity draws out the elements of co-operation and conflict which arise in efforts to work in partnership. Michael Preston-Shoot (1987) describes the dream house exercise as a technique which can help illuminate the effectiveness of communication between co-workers leading groups. It certainly had application to our own partnership, as we will demonstrate in this article. Our use of it in workshop (1) was to explore partnership in helping refugees.

The activity requires participants to work in pairs, holding one pen together. Without speaking they draw their dream house. Discussion afterwards covers how people experienced the activity, how conflict was resolved, what issues of partnership in a refugee context it highlighted for them.

In our workshop one person, who was something of a draughtsman, thought he would draw a plan of the house. His partner, however, was busy trying to fill in windows and smoke coming out of the chimney. The resulting joint picture was hard to decipher. When concepts and aims are so far apart, the efforts of two people cannot easily be blended. Other pairs in the group were closer in their notion of their dream house, and were able to take turns in leading the pen, giving each other the opportunity to develop and add to the drawing.

Sometimes one person in a pair will take over the pen, leaving the other with nothing to do. Or each competes with the other as they tug wildly in different directions. The activity is a powerful demonstration of how the dynamic creativity of partnership can flourish or be destroyed. A second step involves the pair in individually plotting where they would place their own performance and the other's on a continuum from dominant to passive. The discussion which follows this can take participants some way towards discovering their unarticulated expectations of each other as partners, and even their notions of partnership in general.

Confronting imbalances in the partnership

When workers who are not refugees seek to work in partnership with refugees, both partners need to confront the imbalances in the relationship. Of course, structural inequalities are not dispensed with at the level of individual partnerships. But they need acknowledgement if a joint 'dream house' is to be created. If the house that is pictured is chiefly the work of just one partner, then it may be a house the other would not choose to live in. It is equally problematic if both partners become so inhibited by fear of disagreement that they fail to communicate their own intentions or expectations clearly.

We used an extract of an article by a Vietnamese social worker, Ngo Pham, to illustrate some of the problems in achieving partnership. She describes co-work with American social workers in arranging foster care for unaccompanied Vietnamese children in the USA:

> While working with American co-workers, they often have the feeling of powerlessness because of their lack of social work background...In reality, the American worker is the one in charge. Sometimes ethnic workers are considered as interpreters or case aides. Decisions made by American workers are not always appreciated by ethnic workers...

> Some of us have been on the job for up to five years. We have found out that because we were immersed in the American society it is easier for us to learn about the American laws ... than it is for our American counterpart to learn about our culture (Ngo Pham, quoted by Reynolds and Finlay, 1987, pp.53-54).

Participants had further examples. A difficulty we all faced was that only two of the participants in this workshop were refugees: a result of structural inequality. Most of the workers from refugee backgrounds are on part-time contracts: even if their organisation paid the fees, they would not be paid for their time spent on a three day workshop.

One person working with a newly arrived refugee group was the only worker available from the same ethnic background. Her post was insecure as her employers did not have the funding to make a long term appointment. Her colleagues were conscious that she was bearing the brunt of the refugee group's anxieties more or less on her own. There are demands and burdens on refugees working with their own communities which can mean that it is far more difficult for them to maintain acceptable limits to their involvement in the work.

Sometimes the worker who is a refugee will find that his or her view is marginalised in an organisation which is predominantly made up of white non-refugees, with an unspoken consensus on the correct ways of doing things. He or she may give up raising concerns, or all may get locked in conflicts in which everyone ends up feeling frustrated or guilty.

Difficulties in guiding the pen

Issues of dominance and passivity need confrontation between co-workers in groups too. On the whole, as our discussion of developing our partnership in co-work suggests, we had a good basis for getting a balance. But there were still times when we had difficulty in jointly guiding the pen to achieve our dream house. Sometimes neither of us picked up the pen, more often we were tugging it in different directions.

Not picking up the pen

Our first afternoon of consultancy faced us with a challenge and the need to review. We arrived at a refugee agency expecting to meet informally with a few staff. Instead, delayed by a lunchtime reception, we were to find twenty-four workers and volunteers all waiting for us to run a training session. At this moment either of us would have welcomed the other coming in confidently with a firm approach. In the minute or two while people were taking their seats, we were conscious of panic: did we know anything of help to these people? We started the session without a clear idea of how to proceed. Jane suggested that everyone introduce themselves, and mention an area of their work with which they would like help this afternoon. This gave us some breathing space, and made us feel more connected to the room full of strangers. Various concerns were mentioned: one which recurred was the difficulty of this current period of waiting for a new quota of refugees to arrive. We asked for a moment to confer, and put together a sketchy programme.

We had not fully worked out our time boundaries, or which of us would be responsible for moving us on from one theme to the next. The result was that the session drifted. The concerns that people had raised in their introductions never got adequately addressed. We felt embarrassed by our failure to meet the needs of the group. We had not felt in tune with each other as co-workers. Initially we had no direction at all: each of us was reluctant to take up the pen. As we formed some ideas of how to use the time, we imposed a structure on the group which we were then unable to keep to: we had a firm hold of the pen, but had not worked out how to move it in our agreed direction. Nor were we truly allowing the group some say in how the time was used.

Reviewing the situation

We reviewed our work each day: at times we were able to see reflections of what was happening in the group in our own behaviour.

For instance, there seemed to be some parallels between how we were feeling about the crisis-like aspects of this unplanned workshop, and how the group members were feeling in preparing for and meeting with new refugee arrivals. Refugees' arrival in countries of asylum is often fraught with uncertainties for reception workers, as well, of course, for the refugees (Whitham, 1983). At the time of our visit a group of Somalis were due to be received in New Zealand, but there was as yet no information on who they would be, or when they would come. The workers at the project had to make preparations for people who had no family or settled community in New Zealand. They needed to make links with potential interpreters and other helpers, but could not say when work might begin.

Such uncertainty is often the pattern when quotas of refugees are awaited. Dates of arrival are unknown, preparations can only be tentative. People expected do not arrive, or arrive much later than the intended time. Those who do arrive may not have chosen to be in this distant country. They may have expectations, perhaps around the arrival of members of their families, or the ease with which they will find work, which cannot be met in the short term, and remain uncertain even in the long term.

These circumstances place a good deal of stress on those involved in planning and implementing reception programmes. They inevitably get drawn in to a crisis response to a continuing refugee crisis. This can make workers feel embarrassed, and ineffective, just as we felt in this afternoon session. Crisis responses sometimes involve 'rescue' (O'Hagan, 1986). We had tried to rescue the afternoon's work. We wanted people to go away feeling helped, rather than that due to ineffective liaison the time had been wasted.

On reflection, we wondered why our desire to be useful had led us to take on all responsibility for the consultation session. Consultation usually means that consultees as well as consultants take responsibility for the good use of time spent together. We could have asked the centre's director to take a more active role in chairing the session. Our panic that we might have nothing to offer had led us to try to put together a programme at a moments' notice. Our role as 'visiting experts' had got in the way of our partnership with each other and with the group. Our overall planning of the visit had neglected the need to deal with unexpected contingencies, an important skill for partners to develop.

Since we had a different consultative visit the next day we decided that we would aim on this occasion to share responsibility more fully with the group for how the time was spent. This session felt far more satisfactory to us. Our partnership with each other was more coherent, and our partnership with the group was more relaxed. We had accepted that we were not visiting the project as expert teachers, but as people with skills and experience which might have some relevance and resonance with the work they were doing, and who might also have something to learn from them. There is a similar lesson for people receiving new quotas of refugees. Those engaged in this reception work cannot possibly be expert in all aspects of newly arrived refugees' needs. Part of the skill lies in working towards some partnership with an incoming group.

Tugging in different directions

There were other times when our work felt less harmonious. Our workshop (3) for interpreters had a high attendance of nearly forty people. There has been impressive progress in creating recognised programmes of training and qualifications for interpreters in New Zealand. Yet as in England it remains a rather undervalued activity, with unresolved dilemmas for those engaged in it (Baker et al., 1991; Shackman, 1984; Shackman et al., 1987). Many of the participants in our workshop had jobs as health care or social work professionals, with interpreting duties built in to their job description. Juggling the different roles can cause confusion at times (Reynolds, 1993).

The interpreter often has an uncomfortable role between conflicting parties. There can be misunderstandings or different expectations from service users and professionals. The interpreter has a pivotal position in explaining the constraints of the interpreting role, and averting misunderstandings. At times they may have to call a halt to an interview which is proving unproductive.

We wanted to discuss these issues in the workshop, and had asked participants to exchange ideas in small groups on what they could do in an interview when things appeared to be going wrong. When we asked for feedback, two participants started arguing about a case they had both been involved in. One had been acting as interpreter and had kept back a key piece of information which she only knew because of her other role as social worker to the client concerned.

We had asked participants to think about what to do when things go wrong. Now we seemed to be faced with things going wrong ourselves. Two people were monopolising the discussion with their heated argument, and were asking us to judge which of them was right. Jill was leading this part of the session and hoped to bring this discussion to an end and move on to the next exercise. Jane also wanted to say something. For a moment both facilitators were locked in an ungainly struggle to have the last word. Although this moment passed, it was to be repeated at the end of the session. While Jane was making some closing remarks, Jill passed round the handouts, diverting the focus from Jane, who then needed to regain the attention of the group.

In the context of the whole workshop, these were rather minor hitches, which we hope did not detract from an interesting and lively set of exercises and discussion. However they gave us a sense of disunity, and again drew our attention to the matters with which our participants were working. To be a refugee is to be in conflict with authority: the authority of the home country. Once in exile refugees often see their new communities as marginalised within the new country. The community itself may be split, replicating divisions from home (Melzak 1992). Esma'il Kho'i argues that the political refugee is always 'in between': 'An outsider here, an outcast there. Physically here, mentally there. Not a split personality, but a split person' (Kho'i, 1987, p.13).

Those working with refugee communities may feel pulled in different directions in response to the powerful emotions from communities in dispute. We were not able to recognise and act to counter our own disunity as we dealt with the conflict within the group. Had we done so this could have been a more powerful message towards constructive partnerships between the interpreters in the group.

A shared vision

We have discussed some of the moments when our sense of partnership felt threatened. This has helped us to understand better why and when we worked well together. The powerful image which we gave in our introduction of the brain surgeon and the assistant working together in harmony was most to the fore when we were sufficiently confident of our shared vision for one of us to take the lead, and the other to anticipate her partner's needs and provide support.

The time spent in sharing our ideas about work with refugees and planning how we would work together meant that we had a firm foundation for our dream house. We knew what our objectives were in different sessions of the workshops, and had discussed what teaching points we hoped to make. Such time for reflection is equally important in work with refugees.

Communicating the differences

In general, we had confidence in each other's ability to respond to the requirements of the groups we were working with. It was at times when we were less sure of how to respond to the group that we were more likely to start competing with each other for control of the group. Communication was the key: sometimes we could keep each other informed: 'I know we're running late, can I just make this point before we move on to the next exercise?'. This worked much better than if one of us noticed a need, responded, but failed to let her partner know her intention. Just as interpreters have to keep all parties informed, perhaps explaining to a baffled professional why a translation of a simple sentence is requiring so much discussion with the client, we needed to find ways to keep each other informed. A word was often enough.

We have already mentioned our different approaches to feedback: we had planned to acknowledge conflict without letting it absorb workshop time, yet our personal styles shaped how we did this. Jane was immediate in her responses: it was clear to Jill when she had said or done something with which Jane disagreed. In contrast, Jill tended to hold on to concerns for later discussion: this sometimes came across as stored up resentment. Either approach could unsettle our equilibrium. As with our different paces and energy levels, we had to cope with and respect each other's ways of being, while adapting and learning from each other's style what we could.

Conclusion

Literature on co-work in groups does not minimise its 'inevitable' tensions (Galinsky and Schopler, 1980). Yet it is hard to extract guidance from the literature on how much tension is too much tension. We were often less conscious of the 'smooth and seamless collaboration' noted by one workshop participant of our co-work, than of joint panic when something unexpected happened, little tussles of will as we developed our programme in action, and envy of the skills and knowledge each thought the other to possess. We suspect this may often be the reality of creative partnerships, whether between co-workers in groups, or those working with refugees. The good working relationship survives these moments and errors of judgment can sometimes be retrieved to create good outcomes.

There are limitations to the analogy between our own co-working partnership and those we sought to encourage amongst people working with refugees. We are both white, as were the majority of the people in the first two workshop groups. We did not have to deal with major differences of culture, outlook or aspirations between ourselves, but we did need to be sensitive to difference within the groups if we were to promote equality and sharing in our partnership with group members.

Assisting refugees in their settlement in a new country is difficult and demanding work. People working in this area often feel isolated and marginalised. They may feel that they are the only one who cares, that 'mainstream' society is hostile or at best indifferent to the cause they have espoused. If they are themselves refugees, they are even more likely to feel exposed to the demands or expectations of their communities.

Effective partnership in co-work and collaborative efforts across different occupations are urgent requirements for those engaged in work with refugees. Such partnerships are, however, fraught with difficulties because of inequality, ignorance and institutional racism: to embark on partnership can seem a risky business. We have learnt more about our own partnership by reflecting upon the necessity for partnership in work with refugees. We hope that this account of a partnership in which sometimes things went wrong, encourages others in their different kinds of partnerships: whether as co-workers in groupwork and training contexts, or as practitioners with refugee communities.

References

Antonouris, G. (1987) 'Strangers in a strange land', *Youth in Society*, Sept.

Baker, P. with Hussain, Z. and Saunders, J. (1991) *Interpreters in Public Services: Policy and Training*. Birmingham: Venture Press.

Daines, R, Lyon, K. and Parsloe, P. (1990) *Aiming for Partnership*. Ilford: Barnado's.

Finlay, R. and Reynolds, J. (1987) *Social Work and Refugees: a Handbook on Working with People in Exile in the UK*. Cambridge: National Extension College/Refugee Action.

Galinsky, M. and Schopler, J.H. (1980) 'Structuring co-leadership in social work training', *Social Work with Groups*, 3(4).

Heap, K. (1985) *The Practice of Social Work with Groups: a Systematic Approach*. London: Allen and Unwin.

Kho'i, E. (1987) 'People in between' in Finlay, R. and Reynolds, J. (eds.) *Children from Refugee Communities: A Question of Identity, Uprooting, Integration or Dual Culture?* Derby: Refugee Action.

Melzak, S. (1992) 'Secrecy, privacy, survival, repressive regimes and growing up', *Bulletin: Anna Freud Centre*, 15.

League of Red Cross and Red Crescent Societies (1991) *Working with Refugees and Asylum Seekers*. Geneva.

Mistry, T. and Brown, A. (1991) 'Black/white co-working in groups', *Groupwork*, 4(2).

O'Hagan, K. (1986) *Crisis Intervention in Social Services*. Basingstoke: Macmillan.

Preston-Shoot, M. (1987) *Effective Groupwork*. Basingstoke: Macmillan.

Reynolds, J. (1993) 'Words apart', *The Health Service Journal*, 8 August.

Reynolds, J. and Finlay, R. (1987) *Making the Links: A Training Workshop on Social Work and Refugees*. Derby: Refugee Action.

Shackman, J. (1984) *The Right to be Understood: A Handbook on Working With, Employing and Training Community Interpreters*. Cambridge: National Extension College.

Shackman, J., Reynolds, J., Greenwell, S. and Chin, R. (1987) *The Right to be Understood*. A Training Video on Working with Community Interpreters Cambridge: National Extension College.

Whitham, R. (1983) 'A health visitor's view of reception and resettlement of Indo-Chinese refugees in the UK' in Baker, R. (ed.) *The Psychosocial Problems of Refugees*. London: British Refugee Council.

Men working with men in groups: masculinity and crime

John Bensted, Allan Brown, Carlton Forbes and Rick Wall

Crime is predominantly a male activity and male problem. Moreover, the connection between male crime and notions of masculinity is well established. Yet very little attention has been given to the crime-masculinity link in groupwork with offenders, other than in some of the work with sexual and other violent offenders.

This paper briefly examines some of the possible explanations for this apparent contradiction, and goes on to describe and conceptualise the evolution of a men's group in a probation centre in Bristol, England. The features of an unstructured approach are discussed, and the personally challenging nature of this type of groupwork for male workers is emphasised.

Crime is predominantly a male problem

In England and Wales in 1991, 88% of all the people convicted of indictable offences were men. Of those convicted of burglary, 97% were men. At any one time, approximately 50,000 people are held in prison, and of those about 48,000, or 96%, are male (HMSO, 1992). There is no doubt that for the most part: 'The problem with crime is a problem with men' (Coote, 1993). This is certainly not a reason for marginalising women offenders (Heidensohn, 1987), rather the reverse, making it essential that women are not subjected to male-dominated penal programmes. However, it is a reason for examining those characteristics of being male that lead to so much criminal activity, and for putting that at the forefront of work with male offenders, whilst not losing sight of the impact of the socio-economic-political climate.

This huge differential between male and female offending may be largely explained by the way in which masculinity and male behaviour have been socially defined (see for example, Chapman and Rutherford, 1988; Seidler, 1989; Segal, 1990; Phillips, 1993). To be a man is to need to dominate and control (things and people, especially women and children); to demonstrate 'machismo'; to express anger and to suppress feelings of pain and hurt and tenderness; to show bravado with peers; to be like father was; to use physical force to resolve conflict; to be heterosexist, sexist and (for white men) racist. Not all these characteristics are true for every man, but one of the things working in men's groups has taught us, is that more of them are true for more of us than we care to admit.

The reluctance to focus on the crime-masculinity link

Given the established links between masculinity and crime, why until very recently has the agenda of social work with male offenders, and particularly groupwork, not addressed this area as a central concern? We cannot prove anything about the reasons, but we can put forward some ideas drawn from our own experiences and observations. We suggest four possible interconnected factors:

1. The lack of theoretical interest in the 70s and 80s, at least in Britain. The discourse, in a roughly chronological order, has been about marxism (class), feminism (gender) and racism ('race'). Feminism has largely concentrated on the position of women, and what they experience in the face of male power and domination. To give much attention to the needs of men - albeit to try and change their oppressive characteristics - has been seen as suspect. Significantly, male theorists have mostly avoided the subject. Furthermore, whereas women and black people have led the moves to articulate and counteract sexism and racism respectively, there is no such clearly defined and distinguishable 'victim' of the oppression of masculinity motivated crime.
2. The domination of the criminal justice system by men, many of whom - whether judiciary, police, prison staff or probation - share many of the same masculinity characteristics as the male offenders. This is demonstrated in the 'macho' ethos and methods used, for example by the police (Reiner, 1985; Campbell, 1993), and in prison regimes. It is also central to the current policies and polemic of the male-dominated government and Home Office politicians in Britain.
3. The trends in social work and groupwork with offenders in the last two decades. There has been a clear shift from person-centred to task-centred and cognitive/behavioural approaches to intervention, which has been documented elsewhere (Brown and Caddick, 1993). Other examples of this are seen in the Intermediate Treatment developments of the 70s and 80s (Thorpe et al., 1980; Denman, 1982); the preoccupation with

outcomes and evaluation rather than process and methods; and the popularity of standardised 'packages' of intervention for tackling offending in groups.

4. The resistance of male workers to taking the risks involved in facing up to the issues and holding a mirror to what goes on within ourselves. Some probation officers, including some of us, have got close in our groupwork over the years, for example with sexual and other violent offenders, but then drawn back from masculinity issues as the core. This resistance has been further exacerbated by problems of engaging colleagues, and finding an appropriate medium and language for the work.

The awakening of interest in a masculinity focus in work with male offenders

There is some evidence (Burnham et al., 1990; Senior and Woodhill, 1992) of a growing interest in this subject in recent years. Before describing how that developed for us, it is interesting to speculate - and it is no more than speculation - on possible reasons. We suggest the following possibilities:

1. The impact of the anti-oppressive emphasis in social work training, especially on male practitioners. It is possible that, for example, the work on anti-racism has transferable features to other oppressions and has sensitised workers to the dominant culture of white masculinity.
2. The development of carefully planned sophisticated groupwork with violent and other sexual offenders (Canton et al., 1992; Cowburn, 1993), revealing content - including the extent of childhood abuse among offenders - on the influence of masculine socialisation and brutalisation on a wide range of crimes.
3. A reaction in groupwork generally, and specifically in groupwork with offenders, against the ubiquity of highly structured groupwork packages and predetermined programmes. Some of these may be quite effective (Raynor and Vanstone, 1993), but they have the limitation of fitting the person to the programme rather than vice-versa. We detect a possible revival of interest in responsive, 'person-centred' approaches to groupwork with offenders.
4. The proportionately large intake of women probation officers in recent years has changed the sex balance in the composition of many probation teams, and the ethos of the approach to the work. This may well have impacted on those male workers prepared to listen.

We now move from speculation to a description and analysis of the evolution of our groupwork approach with male offenders with serious and prolonged criminal records.

The men's group

Evolution of the approach

In 1991 a new probation centre was established in Bristol with the aim of providing an intensive 40 day/three month programme for adult offenders (male and female), who had committed serious offences and were in danger of going to prison. A small staff group was appointed with the task of planning and developing a multi-faceted programme which would capture the imagination of both the courts and the participants.

The 80 x half day programme had four main elements. The core element was the 35 session cognitive 'Reasoning and Rehabilitation' (R & R) groupwork package developed at the University of Ottawa (Ross et al., 1986). This group was co-led by rotating pairs of the three (two male, one female) probation officers on the staff. The second element was another group (12 x weekly sessions), split on a gender basis. The primary aim was to provide separate space for the very few women on the programme to meet with other women offenders from the area and with the woman probation officer. The parallel group for men was run initially by the two male probation officers, and entitled 'Lifestyles'. It was structured and pre-programmed to cover specific topics including discrimination, substance abuse, victim awareness and personal relationships. The third and fourth elements in the programme were respectively 12 one-to-one counselling sessions; and various activities e.g. woodwork, drama, photography, art, literacy (25 sessions).

All four elements are essential parts of the integrated programme, which has two distinct phases. Participants can start the programme at any time, but may have to wait up to three months before starting the 12 week intensive groupwork programme which is run four times a year. Whilst waiting they attend for activity sessions and individual counselling. However, it is with the evolution of the gender-based men's group that we are concerned here.

Group model 1: 'Lifestyles' (June 1991-Sept 1992)

It was during the initial year of 'Lifestyles' that recurring themes of masculinity surfaced in the discussions, irrespective of the designated topic and the membership of that particular group. Away from the highly structured 'R & R' sessions (3 per week), the men used this more traditional groupwork setting to talk openly about their personal histories, including relationships with parents, experience of the care system, and growing up as boys and young men in 'machismo' street cultures. Inevitably they also spoke about present and past relationships with girlfriends and partners, often interweaving their reasons for offending. Thus for example the role of 'provider' for a wife and children was used to legitimise their offending. It became increasingly clear that many of these disclosures revealed specific links between men's patterns of offending and the culture of masculinity into which they had been socialised.

One man, a 35 year old fraudster, declared towards the end of his Lifestyles group that what he really needed was 'to understand how I have come to be the man I am'. This desire to talk about his 'masculinisation' and the effects of this on his offending behaviour, was echoed by other men in the group. On another occasion when the men's group was meeting at the same time as the women's group, the men became intrigued about what was 'going on' in the room next door. Envious of what appeared to be a lively and involving discussion, one of the men suggested that 'what we need is a men's group'! This incident was one of the factors leading to our review of the group format and title.

In the Lifestyles group model, although most of the sessions were highly structured with the agenda predetermined, those that focused on male identity and relationships were relatively unstructured. In these the (then) two male workers relied both on their understanding of the development of their own male identity, and on a useful board game 'It's a man's world' which addresses many aspects of the culture of masculinity. These 'identity' sessions seemed increasingly important in helping men begin to explore aspects of themselves as men, broadening their understanding of the need for personal change - an aspiration that was common to nearly all group members. In taking the decision to move away from a rather directive approach to a more open and democratic style we found that we were 'listening' more to how the men perceived themselves as men and as offenders. This led us to the crucial decision to try running the whole 12 x two hour weekly sessions on an essentially unstructured basis, albeit in an overall framework with very clear aims and methods.

Group model 2: 'The Men's Group' (Sept 1992 to date)

The 'new' model is based on the assumption that 'somewhere' in most men is the need to talk about their 'masculinisation', and that in doing so, within a reflective and challenging setting, they may acquire a deeper understanding of themselves, which in turn may contribute to a change in their offending behaviour. Each group, and even each session, has its own unique culture. However, the workers' heightened awareness of masculinity/offending links, means that whatever incidents or experiences are presented by group members, the workers can help them to see them in a new light.

Rarely, if ever, have they had the opportunity to discuss critically and explore with other men their lives, their views, their relationships, their hopes and fears. Often the simple expression of thoughts and ideas can help them become more coherent about their experience, and listening to the views and attitudes of others helps to develop alternative perspectives.

The men's past 'brutalisation' has disabled many forms of communication, and they appear to be locked into cycles of destructive and self-destructive behaviour. M. (26) spoke for the first time of his experience of being the victim of ritualistic bullying when at approved school, and how this led to him becoming the bully himself. For F. (28) the whole experience of developing a 'hard man' image took many years and had become part of him: the anxieties and fears that he expressed in the group about 'letting go' of that image appeared to reflect a genuine struggle.

The model and the methods

In the new mostly unstructured model the members have much more ownership of the agenda and process than they had in Lifestyles. It is held together by several strands: the clearly understood purpose of clarifying and understanding masculinisation/offending links as a basis for making choices involving change; an explicitly negotiated and agreed agenda; clear groundrules; the use of carefully thought out 'triggers' to start each session; and the capacity of the workers to cope with the risks and uncertainty inherent in an unstructured approach. It is also important to remember that the group is run in parallel with the highly structured R & R groups.

In the current model of the men's group the links between a whole range of crimes and masculinity are made explicit from the outset. Nearly all the men have experienced several periods in custody, and their offences include persistent driving offences, theft, burglary, assault and robbery. None of them are convicted sex offenders and none have attended for offences of domestic violence. There are specialist groups for both these types of offence, though domestic violence is very much on the agenda of this group, as both witnessed

Diagram 1

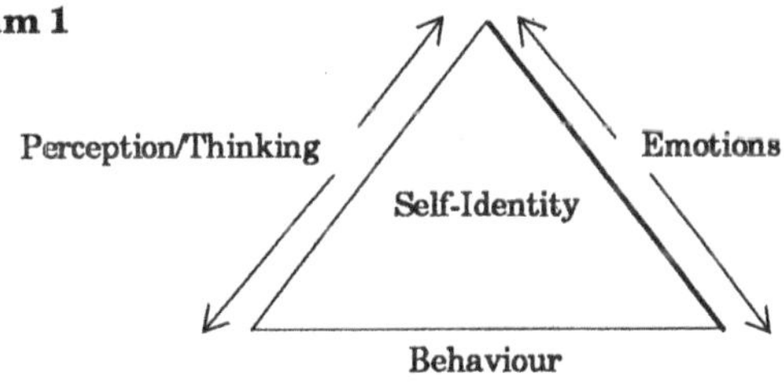

The 'Self-Identity' Diagram

Diagram 2

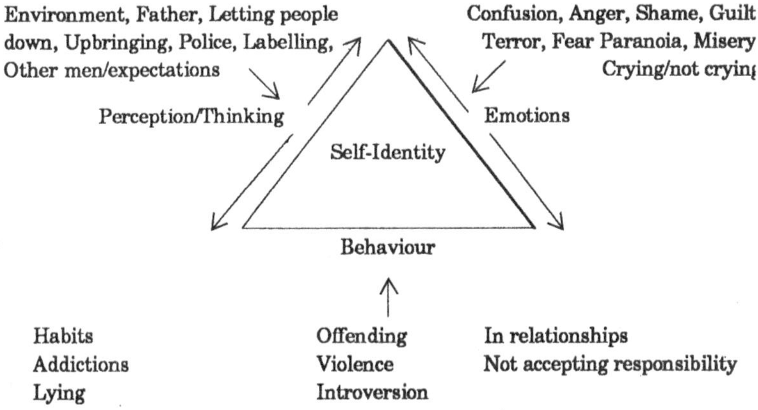

and perpetrated by some of the men. For many of them long-term substance abuse is a highly significant factor in their criminality.

One of the trigger exercises used in the first session to help generate the agenda, is asking group members to respond to the quote already mentioned, 'the problem with crime is the problem with men' (Coote, 1993). The responses range from quite personal statements about an individual's history to more general comments about 'men needing to be the earner'. Very quickly the discussion moves on to issues of masculine identity and how men learn to become men: 'fathers', 'the area we grew up in', 'learning to survive on my own', are typical comments.

To help make sense of the wide range of confusing and often contradictory factors involved in establishing identities, a simple cognitive model is also used in the first session. The 'self-identity triangle' (see Diagram 1) is explained, and group members contribute their personal responses (see Diagram 2). This is a quick way of recognising the most important factors in their identity formation.

Significantly, the emotions of anger, rage, guilt and fear predominate, as distinct from more positive emotions. For example, T. (55), ex-army, rigid, racist and with a strong belief that to show any emotion was a sign of weakness, said that he had not cried since he was five years old. Over three sessions he began to express very real emotions in interaction with one of the workers. The fact that the other group members encouraged him in this 'letting go', allowed him to change his perceptions in this way. Behaviour is discussed not only in the direct context of offending, but also in the associated areas of relationships with children, partners and friends. The men's perceptions of the world of men, not surprisingly have been influenced by their father's behaviour, experience in school and street, care, prison, and by various 'heroes and villains'.

This initial orientation to the group is preparing the ground for the agenda for the subsequent sessions. For example, one member, M. 29), was arrested and released on bail whilst a member of the group. He recounted to the group how when he went home and saw his wife's face as she opened the door he was startled and said to himself 'enough is enough'. At first he thought it was his wife that had changed, but group feedback confirmed to him that it was his perception that had changed: he was now more open and aware of the impact of his behaviour on others. This incident became the trigger for discussion at the next meeting.

The 'self-identity triangle' exercise also prepares agendas which are about the connections between the different dimensions. For example, G. (25), who had grown up as a 'hard man', made a knife attack on a policeman after the break-up of his marriage. With the assistance of a press cutting, the group helped him to see that it was his emotional anger with his wife that contributed quite inappropriately to his violent behaviour towards the policeman.

In one group, the triangle exercise led to a group decision to have a session on 'fear': fear on the streets, fear in prison, fear of never managing to break away from crime — all concerns the men themselves had raised. During this session the discussion moved on from 'fear' to 'hope'. For men who have been in the criminal justice system for many years, the notion of hope has faded and yet every one of them clings to the belief that 'one day I might be able to change'.

Discussions about the future are inextricably linked to the past, and a crucial function of the group is exploring the idea of myth and its influence on behaviour. The following quote has been found very useful as a trigger in the group:

> The task of any individual who wants to be free is to demythologise and demystify the authority of myth that has unconsciously informed his or her life. We gain personal authority and find our unique sense of self only when we learn to distinguish between our own story - and autobiographical truths - and the official myths that have previously governed our minds, feelings and actions. This begins when we ask: 'What story have I been living? What myth has captivated me? It ends only when we tell our own story, and authorise our own life rather than accept the official view of things (Sam Keen, 1991, pp.33-34).

Many different triggers have been used in the present group model, including press cuttings and other visual material (photos, pictures, TV plays and documentaries). However what seem to be the most important factors in this approach are no different from almost any good groupwork practice: establishing trust; clear communication of purpose; and a confidence and belief in groupwork as an effective way of surfacing personal and/or pertinent issues. One extra ingredient in this group is a commitment from the workers that they are involved in the group almost as much as participants as they are as facilitators - a point to which we return.

Other oppressions

By definition in a men's group of this kind issues of gender and sexism are central themes. But other oppressions have to be addressed, both as important issues in their own right (the Centre has a strong anti-discriminatory policy which applies to all activities), and because of their direct links with criminal behaviour.

Racism

These groups are composed almost entirely of white men (The non-referral of black offenders to the Centre is a matter of great concern that we cannot address in this article). In Lifestyles there was a specific session on racism/anti-racism, and it was noticed that racism was openly expressed when there were white co-workers, but suppressed with the (then) black worker. In the current 'unstructured' model, the one black and two white workers are developing skills in bringing racism/anti-racism onto the overt agenda of at least one meeting of each group, and this is supplemented by work done in individual sessions.

Homophobia

It is well known that homophobia is almost invariably a facet of the masculinisation that is associated with offending. This was borne out in Lifestyles where homophobia was a set topic, and heterosexist attitudes were openly expressed, challenged and discussed. It is only recently when preparing this paper that we have realised that homophobia has unwittingly been a 'hidden' topic in the unstructured model. This exposes a potential weakness in a model which relies on worker skills to create group conditions which bring out the crucial issues in ways that can be worked with. It also demonstrates the value of consultancy and writing up group experience, for sharpening up practice - we are now making homophobia a high priority.

Issues for the workers: in the team

In the preparatory phase before the Centre opened the staff were in the fortunate position of having time together to share personal and professional histories, motivations and personal philosophies. This process enabled us to become very aware of each other, a factor that can be critical when working in a small staff team running an intensive groupwork programme. One crucial aspect of this preparation was inclusion of all team members including workshop supervisor (male), sessional art worker (female) and administrative staff (all women), together with the three probation officers, under the facilitative leadership of the (female) senior probation officer. The relationships formed during that time have been significant in how we have managed the issues arising from the evolution of the men's group.

The model for the women's group had its roots in the recognition that some of the core issues facing women could and should be best addressed in an all women group. Feminism had reached a clarity of direction and understanding which produced a clear and articulate voice. The same could not be said of the men in the team, who struggled to find the language to explain to their women colleagues - and indeed to each other - what was evolving as we moved from a structured approach to the current model.

This initial inability of the male workers to communicate adequately about what they were doing contributed to feelings of confusion, fear, frustration and at times anger. With the change to the unstructured model, it was agreed that external consultation was necessary. The male workers felt - rightly or wrongly - that they would prefer to have a male consultant initially: firstly to work at the personal issues they were being confronted with as men; and secondly to consider developmental issues arising from the group. The prospective consultant attended a team meeting at which a consultancy contract was drawn up. This was fully supported by men and women colleagues on the understanding that after four months there would be a team review with the consultant, and that a woman consultant would be introduced at the next stage.

The consultancy resulted not only in the male co-workers developing increased clarity about the masculinity/crime relationship, but also an improved capacity to communicate about process and content to others, and particularly to their women colleagues. This was most important in helping:

1. to have the work supported and recognised;
2. to alleviate fears about male collusion and negative spillover into other elements of the programme;
3. to raise and discuss team strategies to counteract concerns about the possible undermining of women colleagues in male-female co-working in other parts of the programme.

A central paradox of men working effectively with men in a mixed gender context can be a replication of disempowerment of women in another guise. As one (external) woman colleague put it, only partly tongue in cheek, 'bloody men taking over again'!

Issues for the workers: co-working, and personal impact

For this model there have been three male co-workers, one black and two white; from different class, ethnic, cultural, and personal backgrounds. We think the special features of the group, and the mix of worker skills and experience including black and ex-offender perspectives, justifies the use of three male workers. However this combination only works because it is based on much hard effort and sharing of - often difficult and painful - personal experiences. It also depends on the willingness of each to disclose and share much of ourselves in the group, as male oppressors who also (between us) have personal experience of racism, discrimination against the ex-offender, repression and brutalisation. This helps to create an atmosphere that enables group members to feel safe in taking risks and working at their own personal issues.

The group has had a major impact on the male workers as individuals, holding up a mirror to our own behaviour and the destructive aspects of our own masculinisation. Disclosure in the group about what we think and feel personally as men, is a matter of skill and judgement, with a fine line to be drawn between facilitation of change in others and male collusion. Sharing of our own experiences as sons, boys, men, fathers and partners, as we try to redefine our own masculinity involves risk and 'mistakes'. It is however our view that unless male workers are prepared to take risks and question and seek to understand their own masculine experience and how it affects their behaviour, then it is perhaps better not to undertake this kind of groupwork.

Evaluation and conclusion

No formal evaluation has been undertaken of the model to date, as the first step has been to establish as clearly as possible the parameters as these have evolved. There are also difficult methodological problems, not least because the men's group is one of several elements in an integrated programme, all contributing in their different ways to the overall aims of the Centre.

There are however some encouraging indicators including:

1. the high level of attendance, participation and commitment of men with long-term patterns of serious offending;
2. the willingness of most men to work hard in the group and persevere with a personally challenging agenda;
3. the positive impact on the men's use of the other components of the programme;
4. the provision of a safe (but not protective) space to share difficult things;
5. positive feedback in the evaluation sessions at the end of each programme;
6. positive impact on worker skills which transfer to initial assessments of suitability for the programme, one-to-one counselling sessions, and the rest of the work.

One former member said, two years after the group had finished, 'Tell Rick I've grown up, I'm trying for change'.

A criticism voiced occasionally is that the group pushes members to go 'too deep too soon'. We are acutely aware of this danger, and of the fact that the intensive group programme only lasts 3 months. The men then have to return to personal, social and institutional environments in which the destructive aspects of masculinisation are still rife and constantly around them to undermine the start which many have made with great seriousness whilst at the Centre. As in many other types of group, there are also issues about the possible effects on external personal relationships of both group members and workers. This whole 'move-on' issue poses new challenges about how to establish supportive structures to reinforce the start that has been made, without perpetuating dependence on Centre staff.

Note on the roles of the authors

John and Rick (both probation officers) have worked with these groups since the Centre opened. Carlton (a sessional social worker) joined them as co-worker after the change to the current model. Allan (university lecturer) became consultant to all three a little later.

References

Brown, A. and Caddick, B. (eds.) (1993) *Groupwork with Offenders*. London: Whiting & Birch.

Burnham, D. et al. (1990) 'Offending and masculinity: working with males', *Probation Journal*, 37(3).

Campbell, B. (1993) *Goliath: Britain's Dangerous Places*. London: Methuen.

Canton, R., Mack, C. and Smith, J. (1992) 'Handling conflict: groupwork with violent offenders', *Groupwork*, 5(2).

Chapman, R. and Rutherford, J. (eds.) (1988) *Male Order: Unwrapping Masculinity*. London: Lawrence & Wishart.

Coote, A. (1993) Article, *The Independent*, 16 February.

Cowburn, M. (1992) 'Groupwork programme for male sex offenders: establishing principles for practice' in Brown, A. and Caddick, B. (eds.) (1993) *Groupwork with Offenders*. London: Whiting & Birch.

Denman, G. (1982) *Intensive Intermediate Treatment with Juvenile Offenders*. Lancaster University.

Heidensohn, F. (1987) 'Women and crime: questions for criminology' in Carlen, P. and Worrall, A. (eds.) (1987) *Gender, Crime and Justice*. Milton Keynes: Open University.

Home Office (1992) *Criminal Statistics, England and Wales 1991*. London: HMSO.

Keen, S. (1991) *Fire in the Belly: On Being a Man*. Bantam Books.

Phillips, A. (1993) *The Trouble with Boys*. London: Pandora.

Raynor, P. and Vanstone, M. (1993) 'STOP: does it work', *Probation Journal*, 40(3).

Reiner, R. (1985) *The Politics of the Police*. Brighton: Harvester Press.

Ross, R.R., Fabiano, E. and Ross, R.D. (1986) *Reasoning and Rehabilitation: A Handbook for Teaching Cognitive Skills*. Ottawa Cognitive Centre.

Segal, L. (1990) *Slow Motion: Changing Masculinities, Changing Men*. London: Virago.

Seidler, V. (1989) *Rediscovering Masculinity*. London: Routledge.

Senior, V. and Woodhill, D. (eds.) (1992) *Gender, Crime and Probation Practice*. Sheffield: PAVIC Publications.

Thorpe, D., Smith, D., Green, C. and Paley, J. (1980) *Out of Care: The Community Support of Juvenile Offenders*. London: Allen & Unwin.

Working with religious communities

Geraldine Grindley

This paper describes the background to the writer's work with groups of religious in Ireland. It discusses the context within which this work is carried out, at a time of enormous and radical change in the form of religious life. It outlines some of the problems presented by groups of religious looking for professional groupwork interventions, attempts to clarify the types of intervention made by reviewing the literature on the subject. It includes a brief description of some work done with one religious congregation of women over a period of one year and it presents an analysis of the findings of a survey conducted some time later to assess the effectiveness of the intervention.

Background

Religious communities are groups of men or women who live and work together in such a way as to give witness to the values of the gospel. They have taken vows of chastity, poverty and obedience and they are generally involved in some form of public ministry in the service of the church. Up to the Second Vatican Council, which ended in 1965, religious lived a life set *apart from the world* in large institutions. As a result of the recommendations of the Council, religious orders underwent considerable change and renewal. They were exhorted to adapt their way of life to the times and the places in which they existed. These changes in religious life amounted to a revolution, particularly in women's congregations. Instead of setting themselves apart by wearing a habit and living in convents and monasteries, religious began to try to find ways of being religious *in the world*, working closely with lay people and with institutions of state. Sisters particularly gave up wearing a habit and veil, preferring instead to dress as the people with whom they worked. The liberation of religious had several far-reaching effects. These are demonstrated in the tables below. The columns for Diocesan Priests are included for comparison

Groupwork Vol. 7(1), 1994, pp.50-62

Vocations to religious life in Ireland

	Total vocations	Female religious	Male religious	Diocesan priests
1989	320	75	108	139
1985	471	123	179	169
1980	608	181	232	195

Source: Statistics Office, St Patrick's College, Maynooth

This shows a percentage decrease in total vocations in the period 1980-1989 of 47%, a 58% decrease in the number of women being finally professed, compared with 53% for male religious and 28.7% for Diocesan Priests:

> The annual number of new priests has declined by two-thirds since the mid-1960s, according to the Church's own figures. Church data also reveals that the total number of Christian Brothers in Ireland has dropped by almost half in less than 20 years... (Dawson, 1989)

Departures after Ordination to the priesthood or final profession as religious

	Female religious	Male religious	Diocesan priests
1989	10	9	
1985	27	210	2
1980	38	Not available	6
1970	83	62	6

Source: Statistics Office, St Patrick's College, Maynooth

This table shows the dramatic number leaving religious life in 1970 and the relatively large number still doing so today.

A third effect of the Council recommendations has been that religious orders have reconsidered their commitment to education, social services, and nursing. Many sisters are involved in low-paid, low-status work, which professional lay people would not be prepared to do. Religious orders have been forced to sell off their large properties and lands, because they do not have the income to maintain such institutions, nor the personnel to justify them. Many women in congregations which were concerned mainly with the provision of education, hospitals and social services have moved out of those professions into low-paid, low-status work with the poor and underprivileged, operating at the margins of society. They have moved from large institutional convent buildings into small private houses, apartments and public housing to live among the people they serve. 'Historically, the periphery or the desert or the frontier is the place where religious congregations were founded' (Leddy, 1990, p.102)

So religious orders began the long, slow process of change from a hierarchical, institutional model to one that is democratic, person-centred and liberating . This process of change tends to be more advanced among women's orders than among men's and so we intend to focus specifically on female congregations in this paper.

With very few young women joining religious congregations, most orders are top-heavy with sisters over 60, retired or ill or infirm, and these are supported by ever-decreasing numbers of middle-aged women. '....close to 50% of Ireland's nuns are now aged over 60' (Dawson, 1989). They tend to live in small communities of five or six. Those who can earn a salary do so; others work voluntarily in parishes, prisons, adult education and community development.

Living in a small community demands a great deal of interaction, collaboration and intimacy. For sisters trained in the religious life at a time when communities were large and professional, when there were domestic staff to look after the sisters, when the spiritual life of the nuns was governed by strict procedures and where the life of the religious was highly structured and controlled by others, the change is often difficult:

> The move of religious into the world was momentous. Many religious recall the anxieties of that time associated with the move out of enclosed spaces, habitual ways of dressing, and defined modes of service. We no longer set the terms for meeting the world (Leddy, 1990, p.16).

The problems

The kind of problems identified by congregations and communities which leads them to the point where they engage a 'facilitator' to come and work with them may be grouped under three headings:

1. vision and models of community;
2. leadership;
3. interpersonal relationships.

Vision and models of community

Hammett and Sofield (1981, p.6ff) claim that communities are groups and that 'the dynamics that occur in any group also occur in communities'. They also argue that groups are powerful agents of change, for good or for bad, and that community life can be productive if those in it understand and use group dynamics in such a way as to make the community more healthy and life-giving for its members. They say that community groups are 'hybrids', having some of the characteristics of a family, support groups and peer groups, and that the tensions in community life spring from the attempts of members to meet their personal needs in the group. For most religious today, the struggle is to find ways of living in community that foster authentic relationships, enable intimacy, encourage personal responsibility and at the same time provide support to members in the carrying out of their mission. Fiand (1990) says that in this way religious communities must not be like families, but more like friendship and support groups. Boyd (1991) provides a conceptual framework for a small group, in which he suggests that three systems operate in a group. These are the social, the cultural and the personal systems, which are constantly in development and in a state of interaction with one another. He argues that any group provides its members with opportunities to grow and develop and to accomplish 'reality-adaptive tasks' through the dynamic set up by the interaction of the three systems.

Religious generally are not in a position to choose the people with whom they live and work. Communities are usually set up in response to a need, either for a service in an area, or for sisters to be able to live and work. Some see community as a rich and valuable resource, providing them with love and friendship, professional and spiritual support, and material and financial means to live a life of dignity. Others see it as a place to sleep when the important work of the day is done. These represent two extremes of vision. Those whose view leans more towards the former idealistic picture of community, experience hurt and frustration when it does not work. The more cynical, who adopt something closer to the latter view, have as their priority the minimising of conflict, pain and intimacy, so that community life is as painless as possible. These are often lonely, isolated women (and men) whose need to defend themselves in a community can lead to even greater difficulty and conflict for everyone.

Leadership

The concept of leadership in women's congregations has had to be examined in the light of these changes. Experiments are being carried out to try to find ways of exercising leadership which empower people and encourage them to take responsibility for themselves. In the past, religious orders had hierarchical structures and each level of that structure had an appointed 'Superior'. Most congregations are now trying to change their organisation to a more democratic one. Some congregations and communities operate a system of elected or selected leaders, or rotated leadership. Communities may elect one of their own members, others have a leader who lives outside the community - perhaps in another small community. Leaders are no longer referred to as 'superiors' in most religious orders, and a proliferation of new names has appeared - co-ordinator, facilitator, animator being just a few.

Interpersonal relationships

One of the commonest presenting problems of religious is that of dealing with conflict. In our work with sisters, we have done considerable research into perceptions of the concept. In all groups of religious we have found that their perception of conflict is largely negative. Sisters find it difficult to confront their colleagues, difficult to deal with negative emotions and difficult to confront destructive behaviour. Hammett and Sofield (1981, p.23) make the following point:

> If our past has taught us to think of anger as wrong, then feeling angry may be perceived as being a bad religious. To avoid being bad, we believe we must avoid any situation that might produce anger. Since disagreement, conflict and confrontation arouse anger, we believe we must avoid them.

Formerly, sisters were expected to spiritualise their conflict, maintain long periods of silence, and were actively discouraged from forming close relationships. After the Second Vatican Council, many religious:

> ...greeted the changes with great optimism. There was a promise of a new style of community living that emphasised the human dimension of life in the community. Many religious felt revitalised by the emphasis on a communal life with greater intimacy and better relationships among those living in it (Hammett and Sofield, 1981, pp.5-6)

However, since the Council, many religious have become

discouraged and disillusioned about community life, which has been 'the neglected piece, the stepchild...of renewal..' (Fiand, 1990, p.76). According to Hammett and Sofield (1981) this disillusionment has been the cause of some leaving religious life.

Types of intervention

There are many consultants, or 'facilitators', as they are called, working with religious in Ireland today. What they do varies infinitely. Some of these consultants are themselves religious and others are lay people. It is difficult to define the types of interventions made and while there has been one attempt to convene a group of about 100 so-called facilitators, so that a register could be compiled and the types of interventions identified, this was only partly successful because there are so many different interpretations of the term 'facilitator'. The writer has, therefore, attempted to scan the literature in search of some clarity about the meaning of the word.

Hope and Timmel (1984, p.49), whose training manual is based on the philosophy of adult education developed by the Brazilian adult educator, Paulo Freire, have defined the role of the facilitator as follows:

> ...the role of the facilitator is to provide a process which will help the group to discuss their own content in the most satisfactory and productive way possible. The facilitator is neutral about the content of the meeting, and has no stake in the decisions that are taken. The facilitator is totally concerned with process, not at all with content. The facilitator's responsibility is to ensure that there is good communication in the group and that all the members are satisfied with, and fully committed to, the decisions taken.

This is the role played by 'facilitators' who are invited in to help a community discuss some issue related to its work which is difficult or contentious, such as the closing of a convent, or the relocation of personnel. This function may also be carried out by those who help to run Chapter meetings, at Congregational level, during which major policy decisions are made and future direction decided.

However there is another role, which has been defined by Hope and Timmel (1984, p.49) as that of an 'animator' - a word also used widely in France and other parts of mainland Europe. They say that this role is:

> ...to help the community discover and use all its potential for creative and constructive teamwork. An animator needs all the

skills of a facilitator but ...also has a special responsibility to stimulate people:
to think critically
to identify problems
to find new solutions
The animator provides a process in which people can share their concerns, their information, their opinions
set goals
make decisions
plan action.
The animator needs to understand the different forces operating in a group.

Brown (1979, p.4) defines the roles of a social group worker in terms of the principal aim or focus of the group. If the principal aims of a religious community are a combination of individual, group and community change and support, then the person who is making the intervention can be defined as 'therapist, social educator, enabler, trainer, facilitator, negotiator, and mediator'.

Bion (1987, p.11) says that:

> The term 'group therapy' can have two meanings. It can refer to the treatment of a number of individuals assembled for special therapeutic sessions, or it can refer to a planned endeavour to develop in a group the forces that lead to smoothly running co-operative activity.

If the intervention of the groupworker in religious communities is to help them to work more effectively as a team or a group, then according to Bion's definition, the consultant acts as a group therapist.

Benson (1987, p.11) sees groupwork practice as:

> ...(a) conscious, disciplined, and systematic use of knowledge about the process of collective human interaction, in order to intervene in an informed way, or promote some desired objective in a group setting.

Like Boyd, and Bion, Benson sees the role of the groupworker as in some way transformative or therapeutic.

Thompson and Kahn (1970) distinguish between three types of work in groups, classifying them as:

1. group therapy, the aim of which is to bring about change in the personality of each member of the group

2. group counselling which is designed to bring about changes in attitudes and relationships, and
3. group discussion, the primary aim of which is educational.

These writers point out that from group discussion, insights and understanding will be developed which may in turn affect behaviour or personality, but that the primary purpose of the groupworker in such groups is not therapeutic but educational.

Douglas (1978) also recognises these three types of intervention in groups and seems to imply that the same techniques and skills are required for all three. Yalom (1970) refers to the blurring of the boundaries between therapy and personal growth groups, such as self-help and encounter groups. This writer also discusses the difference between a training group and a therapy group. He claims that to a great extent the goals of both groups overlap. This is an interesting point for consultants working with religious, who are often asked to conduct training groups for superiors. Yalom (1970, p.527) clarifies the difference as follows:

> In a therapy group, the intensive group experience, the expression and integration of affect, the recognition of here-and-now process, are all essential but secondary considerations to the primary goal of individual therapeutic change. In a training group...the reverse is true.

A brief account of work with one religious community

The writer deals here with a systematically planned series of interventions with one religious order of women, which took place in the year July 92-July 93. The congregation in question was one which was introducing some radical changes in the way religious life was organised in community and the way in which leadership was exercised. At its Chapter, some three years previously, the order had agreed to experiment with small communities and 'shared responsibility'. After discussion with the General Council of the congregation it was decided to expose as large a number of sisters as possible to an experience of groups which would be liberating and empowering. A number of two-day workshops was organised for this purpose. The design of the days was based on the model described in the programme of Training for Transformation (Hope and Timmel, 1984).

The day began with the sisters carrying out a listening survey in pairs, interviewing one another about the concerns they had about their lives in community. These concerns were synthesised and categorised in small groups. They were then used as the basis for the design of the workshop. They included problems of communication, painful community meetings, difficulties in dealing with conflict, loneliness and isolation, and general concerns about people who opted out of the group in any way, either by silence, apathy or aggression.

Because communication is a fundamental need, not only in the community, but also in the training group, the sisters did an exercise in triads, practising the five techniques for listening and responding - questions of clarification, paraphrasing, neutral responses, reflective listening and summarising. It is useful, when working with a group who are very familiar with one another, to do some exercise which helps to break established patterns of ineffective communication.

Using the 'praxis' model (Freire, 1972) (action, review, reflection, relation to theory), exercises were set up, the sisters participated and this was followed by a reflection on how a group could work in a collaborative and creative way, with the help of an effective 'animator'.

The group looked at meetings, using a fishbowl technique, with one-to-one observation. They were given a simple decision-making task to do and observers were asked to note what their observee did which contributed to the work of the group. This kind of observation is very affirming and helps to build up the self-esteem of the sisters, raising the level of trust in the group and generally improving morale.

Using another simulation as a consciousness-raising exercise, the group explored how it worked at making decisions, identifying its strengths and weaknesses, and suggesting ways for making meetings more satisfying and productive. Conflict is a major problem in religious communities. In brainstorming on the word, it became apparent that the perception of these groups was that conflict was almost always negative. In the discussion that followed the sisters talked about attitudes and values in religious life which made it difficult to allow anger, to confront or to be assertive about one's own needs.

Following this experience, many of those responsible for animation, leadership, or facilitation in communities requested a training course to help them to develop the knowledge, skills and attitudes which would enable them to work in this way with their groups. The General Council agreed, and allocated finance and other resources to allow two groups of sisters to attend weekend workshops, which used experiential methods to allow them to learn and practice the skills and to begin to understand the process.

The difference between the workshops for the congregation in general and these training weekends was that in the first case, the aim was to provide an experience of open, collaborative, empowering groups, whereas in the second it was to teach or enable others to do the same. This process is similar in the first two stages - carrying out exercises and reflecting on them in a structured way. But in a training course it is necessary for participants to be able to conceptualise their experiences and to fit them into some kind of theoretical framework. For example, what leaders of communities describe as 'difficult behaviour' is often a series of defence mechanisms operating in an unhealthy way. A leader can learn how to handle the specific behaviour in one situation, but in training it is important that she learns about defence mechanisms in general, what they are, how they operate and why they come into play, so that she can deal with other types of destructive behaviour when it arises in another group.

Another difference between the 'experience' workshop and the training one is the level of self-awareness required. Over and over again, sisters say that they have difficulty confronting one another. When one explores this statement, it is usually clear that the problem arises because people blame one another for their feelings. An understanding of personal responsibility helps sisters deal with conflict and negative emotions in a much more healthy way, and enables the facilitator/animator to be more objective and therefore more effective.

This is just a small sample of the kind of issues which arise, the techniques used and the philosophy behind the interventions. While there are common topics in all groups, each group may have different priorities, and each group requires a different approach from the trainer.

Some of the sisters, in a situation where there was no appointed leader, asked for a direct intervention at community level. This community was experiencing great difficulty in working together as a team. The intervention here consisted of helping the group to identify the problems, and then looking at ways in which they might deal more constructively with the conflict in their group. While the intervention began as an 'animation', it became clear that some of the problems were associated with events which had taken place long before this community was formed, and the intervention made by the groupworker moved into the realm of group therapy as she dealt with the repressed and suppressed material, which was unconsciously influencing the way in which the sisters related to one another.

This kind of intervention cannot be planned and structured in the same way as other types of interventions. Techniques which helped people to get in touch with their here-and-now feelings, their deeply held attitudes and beliefs, were used. Methods of accessing the unconscious, such as visualisation, and the use of symbols were employed. At one stage some people were saying that the group was divided. The groupworker requested that they show her, physically, how it was divided. This became a turning point in the process. The main aim of this intervention was to enable the group to articulate its problem clearly, identify possible causes for the problem and look for ways of improving the situation. As it turned out, the third phase of the process required the intervention of the Superior General, who represented authority and leadership in the congregation as a whole, which had contributed to the problem in the first place by the way in which certain decisions had been taken about this group.

These three interventions by one consultant with one congregation formed an interesting experiment because they gave the consultant an opportunity to operate at all three levels of group interaction - the task (intellectual) or cognitive element of the group; the socio-emotional (Bales, 1950) (relationships and feelings) or affective element of the group; and the unconscious (the pre-conscious - suppressed and repressed material and the personal unconscious) in the group (Jung, 1959).

The last intervention took place in March 1993. In June-July 1993 the sisters who took part were surveyed, in an attempt to discover the effectiveness of the intervention. An analysis of the responses is included here.

Twenty sisters completed the survey questionnaire. In questions where a qualitative analysis is possible the answers are given as percentages. Of the respondents, 65% had attended two one-day workshops at intervals of about one month; 55% had attended an 18-hour weekend training workshop.

One of the questions asked was to what extent had the sisters been helped by the workshops personally, as a member of a community, and as a leader\facilitator\superior of a community or other group. The answers were analysed as follows:

	Greatly	To some extent	A little	Not at all
	%	%	%	%
Personally	45	40	10	5
As a member of a community	25	50	0	10
As leader, superior, facilitator	35	25	10	5

The reasons given for these answers were that listening was better and that sisters felt more self-confident about participating, asserting their points of view and differing with others. They said that they had become more aware of and sensitive to others in their groups, were more aware of themselves and more objective. Some sensed an increased respect for other people's opinions and a greater sense of solidarity and belonging. Those for whom it was not helpful in any way said that this was because of the nature of their community meetings or, in one case, the total absence of any such meetings and consequently the inability to put into practice what was learned at the workshops.

Have the workshops changed the way you deal with

	Yes	No
	%	%
Conflict	75	15
Other people's emotions	60	20
Your own emotions	65	20
Silence and other difficult behaviour	50	30
Confronting others	50	30

Of the sisters, 65% said that the workshops had had an impact on their community meetings in that there was better listening, that facilitators were more confident and skilled, better at organising the meetings or clearer about their role, and able to give feedback to the group. Some 35% who said that the workshops had not helped explained that they either had only 'business' meetings or else none.

Of those who took part in the workshops, 75% thought that the methods used were very good, encouraging and non-threatening, challenging, provoking, enjoyable and interesting, while 25% expressed discomfort with the artificial nature of some of the exercises, while one person thought that the sessions were too long and too 'heavy'. Overall, 65% thought that the workshops had been very effective, 20% deemed them effective to some extent and 15% said that they were not effective at all.

In terms of follow-up, sisters said that they would like leadership training for leaders of communities; help with building up the community, developing better relationships and methods for helping those who find community life particularly difficult; more training in listening and communication skills, decision-making and general facilitation skills; more training in dealing with conflict and difficult behaviour in general; and exploration of the concept of power in groups.

At the end of each workshop a written evaluation was completed by the participants. The questions used were practically the same as those used in the survey which was carried out several months after the event. It is interesting to compare the two. The evaluations tended to be a little euphoric in tone or more enthusiastic in the degree of the responses. But it was heartening to note that even six months later, the general tone of the responses was much the same, and the general consensus was that the workshops were worthwhile and effective.

References

Bales, R.F. (1950) *Interaction Process Analysis*. USA: Addison Wesley.

Benson, J.F. (1987) *Working More Creatively with Groups*. London: Tavistock.

Bion, W.R. (1961) *Experiences in Groups*. London: Tavistock.

Boyd, R.D. (1991) *Personal Transformations in Small Groups*. London: Tavistock/Routledge.

Brown, A. (1979) *Groupwork*. London: Heinemann.

Dawson, K. (1989) 'Challenge to Church as vocations plummet', *The Sunday Tribune*, 27 August.

Douglas, T. (1978) *Basic Groupwork*. London: Routledge.

Fiand, B. (1990) *Living the Vision*. USA: Crossroad.

Freire, P. (1972) *Pedagogy of the Oppressed*. UK: Sheed and Ward.

Hammett, R. and Sofield, L. (1981) *Inside Christian Community*. USA: Le Jacq.

Hope, A. and Timmel, S. (1984) *Training for Transformation*. South Africa: Mambo Press.

Jung, C.G. (1959) *Collected Works*. New York: Pantheon Books.

Leddy, M.J. (1990) *Reweaving Religious Life*. USA: Twenty-Third Publications.

Thompson, S. and Kahn, J.H. (1970) *The Group Process as a Helping Technique*. Oxford: Pergamon Press.

Yalom, I.D. (1970) *The Theory and Practice of Group Psychotherapy*. 3rd Edition. USA: Basic Books.

ISSUES OF EMPOWERMENT:

ANTI-OPPRESSIVE GROUPWORK BY DISABLED PEOPLE IN IRELAND

MAIRE NI CHORCORA, EDDIE JENNINGS AND NUALA LORDAN
CARTOONS BY S. O' SHAUGHNESSY

This article examines the dilemmas inherent in working to empower marginalised groups. It seeks to analyse the difficulties of a groupwork model which views empowerment as a political process. The authors discuss their experience as disabled people in the development of a group, where members concern and commitment was to overcome their feelings of powerlessness. This group sets out to learn new ways of dealing with their oppressors; and to create societal structures where people, who are most affected by decision making, can have a meaningful impact on policy making. The barriers to participation and powersharing are considered and an effort is made to understand how the power structures of society operate. The paper concludes by identifying key issues in the groupwork process which facilitated empowerment, and enabled members to take control and begin to challenge their oppressors.

The focus of this paper is on a model of groupwork intervention which seeks to challenge oppression, moving from identifying personal experience to understanding the political forces which create and maintain the status quo. The approach is closely aligned to Mullender and Ward's 'self directed approach' (1991) to groupwork. It acknowledges a clear value base, which views empowerment not merely as an enabling process, but a political position which has as its goal the changing of existing power relations. Challenging the status quo and finding ways and means to negotiate new structures, which provide for real dialogue and partnership in the decision-making organisations of our society, is central to power sharing.

The analysis of our experiences in the development of a group of disabled persons whose initial concern was the marginalisation of people with disability in Irish society highlights many of the dilemmas inherent in this model. We believe that the issues which this process has raised are not unique but relevant to all groups of marginalised people. Although every group has its own dynamic forces, the context and cultural stimuli play a major role, in determining the central issues of concern.

Anti-oppressive practice and empowerment.

The concept of anti-oppressive practice has come very much to the forefront of the social work agenda. British theoreticians and practitioners have done much to highlight the key challenges facing groupworkers who work to empower marginalised groups; but the question, of whether it is possible to develop partnerships with user groups within structures which by their very nature seek to maintain the equilibrium of the power structure, still needs to be addressed. Much of our thesis has been said before, and there is already a substantial literature on power and empowering practice. Why does it need to be repeated? We believe it needs repeating because in our experience it does not often happen. It is we realise a very difficult process: our wish is to create a forum for dialogue regarding the reality of the dilemmas inherent in empowering practice.

The word empowerment slips easily off the tongue, anti-oppressive practice is a little more difficult. Both have become the 'fashionable' words for social work practice. Empowerment has 'power' as its centrepiece an attribute crucial to its understanding and use. It has to do with enhancing people's power, (Preston-Shoot, 1992), and through non-hierarchical working, empowerment sees users as subjects rather than objects in the social work process. When we talk about working toward empowerment, we are talking about developing ways of creating a transfer of power, so that people can become involved in the processes which produce plans and decisions which affect their lives.

It is worth asking the questions:

Who are the experts on knowing what it is like to live with a disability?
Who plans the services?
Why?

We are talking of moving from the personal to the political. The issue of participation, or lack of it, is forcing its way onto national and international agendas. Notably, at a time when in Europe decision making structures are getting further and further away. Some structures of our society allow people to be represented in the decision making process. However almost all of these structures do not provide genuine participation for most people affected by their decisions. Take the allocation of European funding, in the area of disability: decisions are taken in Brussels, in consultation with a national agency of non-disabled people, although there does exist in Ireland a forum of disabled people.

It is interesting to note that the language of anti-oppressive practice and empowerment is now being used by social workers. This is occurring during a time when on the political agenda and other power fronts, those with rightwing conservative policies have gained ground world wide. Mandates are being sent from Europe about the importance of user participation, and the mobilisation of selfhelp is a key issue in the obtaining of funding. However it is clear that the interest in the corridors of power is in people becoming more self reliant, self supporting, employable. However laudable this aspiration is, it does not take into account the experience of marginalised groups; their involvement at this level has not even been considered, genuine participation is not on the agenda.

Limited information is given on the decision making process. Groups are put in competition with each other in their efforts to obtain limited funding, and it would appear that the well tried techniques of control are operant in the form of 'divide and then conquer and rule'.

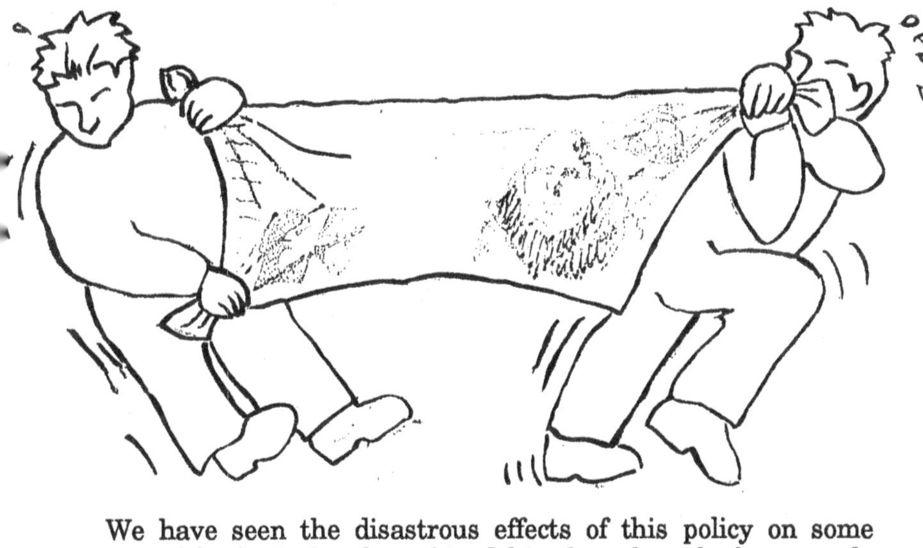

We have seen the disastrous effects of this policy on some communities in Cork, where friendships have been broken, people divided, in their scramble to obtain resources. Indeed there is now a belief among many that the continual need to compete for funding is just a strategy of those in powerful positions to keep the poor busy preparing proposals, diluting their strength and motivation to band together in opposition to the faceless controllers of resources.

There are many aspects to powerlessness. Sennett and Cobb (1972) and Conway (1979) list these as being; economic insecurity, absence of fiscal support, lack of training in critical and abstract thought, and physical and emotional stress. One thing all marginalised and oppressed groups have in common is poverty. This includes: a lack of money; a lack of rights; lack of entitlements; and a lack of access to opportunities. Speaking from their personal experience of poverty, reports from women's groups in Ireland (Daly, 1988) have stated that poverty is about feelings, how one regards oneself, and how one is regarded by others. It is about feelings of powerlessness; experiencing exclusion; rejection; being treated as inferior; lacking in status or being in some way inadequate. Members of our group report a very similar encounter, they constantly experience exclusion, being on the outside, and they are made to feel inadequate, helpless, and dependent. These feelings are central to the experience of marginalised groups.

Solomon (1976), identified three potential sources of powerlessness:

1. the negative self evaluation attitudes of oppressed people themselves;
2. negative experiences in the interaction between the victims of oppression and the outside systems which impinge on them;
3. larger environmental systems which consistently block and deny effective action taking by powerless groups.

This has indeed been the experience of all our disabled group members, who constantly encounter these levels of powerlessness. Empowerment is about gaining power and in doing so, the above mentioned areas need to be addressed. People need to develop self confidence, self esteem and control of their situation. They need to learn to be assertive regarding their rights, and to challenge the structures which oppress them. For us working in an empowering way means that group members have real power.

They control the finance.
They make the decisions.
Each member has a role to play.

- TAKING CONTROL -

Croft and Beresford (1989) talked in terms of three dimensions to empowerment: they suggested that social service agencies must be committed to the concept of empowerment; this will necessarily involve offering its users a say in the control and management of the agency, and enabling people to take up opportunities for a say in the agencies' functioning whenever possible. It is our experience that agencies do not give away their power, unless of course they want the job done on the cheap. Usually they will stay in a position of sufficient power to claim the credits. Mullender and Ward (1991) added another crucial dimension to those already mentioned. It is the importance of developing a way of working, which in its foundations, its techniques and style of operation, empowers those who experience its use. It is this aspect of empowerment we hope to address here. How can a real change of power take place in an environment which as Pernell (1989) so aptly points out:

> When the powerless stir and begin to seek some equity, the system shakes and the powerful move to restore the equilibrium, giving a little perhaps, but substantially retaining power. The social worker, then engaged in the process and goal of empowerment of the disadvantaged group or individual, may stand exposed and vulnerable to the efforts of those in power to hold the line' (p.110.).

From its origins, the function of groupwork has been seen not only as the accomplishment of (individual) personal goals, but also through group exchanges and networking as a means for achieving social change. However, in Ireland there has been a great resistance at agency level to groups that do anything other than individualise problems. Much of the groupwork which is done focuses on personal development and individual coping, and although this is very valuable, there is great difficulty moving beyond this level to becoming involved in structural change issues.

Sabotage

Efforts to establish groups to address structural issues are in fact actively sabotaged by those in positions of power, as in the following example:

A group of parents of autistic children came together due to their frustration with the lack of services. They wanted to demand better services for themselves and their children. Many of them were regarded by professionals as very disturbed families whose anger was largely a symptom of their pathology. These professionals joined them, praised them, and directed their efforts toward fund-raising, to gather money on a voluntary basis for more services. Thus the present service was not challenged, the rights of these families were not considered. The professionals maintained the equilibrium, where they continue to define the agenda.

Similarly when Combat Poverty Agency placed its first workers in Cork, to work in a particular neighbourhood, the local statutory authority (the equivalent to social services) put their workers into the same area to work in competition and make sure they would be kept informed of any developments taking place.

Yet another example is when the voluntarily run Family Centres came together (there are five in different neighbourhoods in the city) and wished to negotiate with the statutory authorities as a group, in an organised planned fashion. They were informed individually that they would do much better financially if they negotiated by themselves.

These vignettes all demonstrate quite clearly that the establishment is not supportive of group initiatives which are about to create change. After all those in the establishment do not want to lose their position in the pecking order of the power structure.

Disability in Ireland

Let us now look at the question of disability in Ireland. It is not an exaggeration to say that disabled people are one of the most marginalised groups in Irish society. They are hidden and dealt with behind closed doors. Their position in society is that of second class citizenship. This is best illustrated by the depiction of 'the collection box mentality' where people with disabilities are objects to be pitied, patronised, prayed for, and seen to be in need of nothing more than a few pounds tossed into a collection box. This money is then to be managed and spent by 'do gooders' out to save their souls in the provision of services for the disabled. These attitudes have definitely kept people with disabilities in their place. *'Grateful'*.

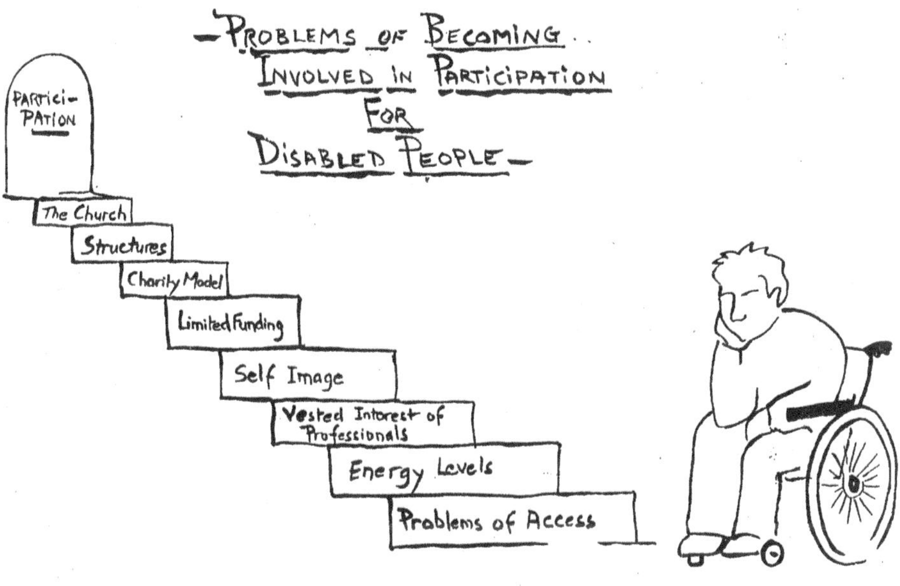

The Green Paper on Services for Disabled People (Department of Health, 1983) examined the introduction of legislation on the rights of people with disabilities. The Green paper decided against the introduction of legislation, preferring instead to rely on 'goodwill and understanding', thus leaving disabled people very much the victims of charity. There have been murmurings of consultations about how best the rights of disabled people can be promoted, but little attention has been paid to the problems of becoming involved in real participation for disabled people. Issues have been identified by members of our group as being:

Problems of access.
Energy levels.
Vested interest of professionals.
Self image.
Limited funding.
Charity model.
Structures.
The church.

The motivation to start the group.

It was the felt need of disabled people which created the group, which started when about six like minded individuals came together. Their concern was about the level of ignorance regarding the realities of disability, and the need to get the issue of Disability on the political agenda as a rights issue. They felt that it was time people with disabilities made themselves heard. *But how?* Many voices were necessary, group members lacked the know how, their experiences heretofore had not equipped them for this task, and indeed had left them feeling helpless and frustrated. Thus it was decided that the best place to start was with training. Some of the members were aware of the excellent training initiatives in Britain, but felt that being disabled in Ireland was a different experience. Little is written about being disabled in Ireland, the collective experience is unknown. The first task of the group was to network with other people with disabilities. Since the group had as its catchment all disabilities, members found themselves very ignorant about each others needs. Much of the groups beginnings were taken up with information exchange and learning about each others experiences. Members wrestled with understanding and developing action plans to combat the many encounters of discrimination that individuals brought to the group.

The group at this stage is made up of about 20 members, who

meet on a regular basis. This group forms a steering committee where policy decisions are made. The group have received financial aid, from the European Union under the horizon programme, in partnership with the Adult Education Department of University College Cork, to launch a training program for 12 disabled persons to become disability equality trainers. Various sub-groups have been established as the need arises to get on with the work of the committee. They report on a fortnightly basis. There is a commitment to keeping everyone as informed and involved as possible. There is an action group of five members, who carry on the work of the group between meetings. This action group rotates its membership on a regular basis so that everyone gains experience at this level.

The personal experiences of two group members.

The following accounts of our experience give a factual picture of the reality of life with a disability and the ways in which we have been marginalised. It also outlines the significance of this group, and its meaning for us. Let us begin with Eddie's story:

> I was diagnosed with Multiple Sclerosis when I was 22 years old -that was nearly ten years ago. What is Multiple Sclerosis?...it's a disease of the brain and the spinal cord, central nervous system. MS interferes with the brain's ability to control such functions as seeing, walking, and talking. It's called multiple because many scattered areas of the brain and spinal cord may be affected. The symptoms can be mild or severe, and come or go unpredictably. It is called Sclerosis because the disease involves sclerosed or hardened tissue in damaged areas of the brain and the spinal cord. MS is not a mental illness, it is not contagious and is not preventable or curable yet.
>
> When I was first diagnosed I was working as a technician / buyer in an electronic plant in Shannon which is in the west of Ireland. I had recently been made a permanent member of staff, although I had not been working with this company for long. I was enjoying my time, I received a good salary, I liked the opportunity to work away from home, I had no worries, my social life was excellent.
>
> I really had no concept on diagnosis what MS was all about save what I had been told by the doctors. I hadn't met others with it so I didn't really understand what to expect. I went back to work shortly after being diagnosed as I didn't feel very physically sick. I did have double vision and I knew I dragged my foot a bit. But I felt alright, I wasn't ready to talk about it yet to any of my colleagues until I was sure of the answers. I did tell my immediate

boss whom I felt would support me because he was always telling me to be sure and come to him about any problems I may have had. I did confide in him feeling it was the right thing to do. This was a mistake as I found to my peril. Not long afterwards, I was made redundant.

I felt that my life had ended...Now everything was up for grabs including my future job prospects. I soon realised I would never again pass another medical examination, for I would have to disclose everything about my MS to other employers. It was a dreadful shock for me, I felt let down. Who would have confidence in me again? When I enquired about the redundancy, I was told that it was outside local control who was to be laid off. But later I found out that I had been betrayed, information about my medical condition became known, soon after I informed my boss.

When I had worked out my notice, I felt that I had no option but to return home to Cork. I loved my independence, I loved the kind of life I had and the choices I could make because of it. I went home reluctantly without much prospects. I languished there for about a year without doing very much but getting used to my MS and getting more depressed.

I was signing on the dole but I was soon advised that I wasn't really available for work, and therefore I should go on a disability payment and be certified sick and unable for work. I was told that I should register with the National Training Agency for disabled people if I wanted a job or training of any kind. I was extremely excited about the prospect of working again. At the same time, they told me about the uncertainty of finding an employer to take me on. My opportunities were very limited.

My placement officer picked me up from my home on a Monday morning. He arrived in a beautiful tan coloured Alfa Romeo car something akin to the one I had sold the week previously as I couldn't afford it any more. We were going to visit a training centre. This was my first introduction to sheltered workshops. All the 'so called' trainees were in one room. They were people with all different kinds of disability. I felt I needed to get out of this place fast. I also felt angry that this was the only option to be presented to me. There had to be more. I never went back to see that particular placement officer. Anyway I felt he talked too much and nicely about all the great things he could do for me.

Next, I got involved in voluntary work and self-help initiatives locally and nationally. This gave me an opportunity to develop skills in community work. I eventually decided, having received professional guidance, to pursue full time education and training in Community and Youth Work at Maynooth College.

I got involved in this Disability Equality group from the very beginning, in fact I was a founding member. For a long time now we have had professionals in all kinds of areas speaking about disability, whereas we the people with disabilities are the experts. This programme is about training people with disabilities to be able to speak for themselves. It is a unique group. From the beginning people have gained loads of confidence by being part of a group which is willing to be tolerant and listen. Never before have they had such an opportunity, People just do not hear disabled people or do not give them the chance. Group members have a sense of possible power to change their own situation and circumstances. For my part, as a newly trained Youth and Community worker I have been extremely interested in disability equality training, so this project provided me with plenty of scope to develop this skill. It added a definite focus and direction to my life for which I had been looking.

Maire's experience

I am a disabled woman working in a full time post, living with my partner and two daughters. My main dilemma in life has been my struggle to be 'normal' and knowing in my heart that I had to acknowledge the fact that I am disabled.

My story began when I contracted Polio at fifteen months. It impaired my mobility in my lower spine and legs. I was immediately isolated physically and emotionally from everyone and everything that was familiar to me. I was hospitalised. For the first three months of my hospitalisation my parents were only able to view me through clear glass for fear they would catch or carry the virus outside the fever ward. So the only contact I had was with nurses and doctors and my uncle, who because he was a Roman Catholic Priest was allowed to stand beside my cot. I learned through my parents at a young age that mystique either medical or spiritual held a lot of keys. I was eventually discharged after one year, unable to walk and with my callipers on back to front. This was the beginning for me of not quite fitting in - either outside the hospital or inside. During hospital stays I knew that I had to be a 'good girl', a 'good patient', a good polio victim, and in order to acquire the tag of 'good' I had to stifle the positive and negative emotions and do what others, the professionals expected a good girl to do.

At home my Mam and Dad desperately tried to make me normal

despite the fact that I had a major mobility impairment. But they always stated the only chance I had was if I was to become as normal as possible. Being disabled for them meant that I had no future educationally, financially and sure as hell I wasn't going to be happy. So they did everything as the hopeful parents they were, in order for me not to fall into the disabled 'bracket'.

The downside for me was that even though I tried and succeeded in the normal world I was never true to myself. I am only now acknowledging that I am disabled by the social attitudes of the society we live in and the environmental barriers I hassle with everyday of my life.

Society's view is hardly one where a disabled person is economically independent - not just on a state pension but fully employed - not just a token, but a fully active sexual member of that society. Disabled people are generally disadvantaged in relation to the above assumptions and one has to ask why? I speak as a woman and I believe disabled women are even more disadvantaged. Our image of disabled women is hardly one that includes being sexually active, whatever your sexual preference. Rearing children, feeding them or caring for them is not part of the picture, and again one has to ask why not. The answer for me is that disabled people, both men and women and children, have no choices, no decision making powers. Because we are not in the position or the places where choices and decisions are made, so therefore we are forgotten, only to become more isolated and alienated than we already are.

I believe it is not until 'abilist' people in society, face the possible vulnerability of old age, or the personal fears and prospect of a disability for oneself or for a loved one, that disabled people will be welcomed as part of the human race.

For years I have swung from wanting to be seen as normal to wanting to have my disability acknowledged as part of me, But if I gave into this I would have become invisible, lonely, and genderless. These are my fears and they are real because up to now I as a disabled person have not been spoken to or listened to. My needs have not been met in the society of which I am a part. However society does manage subtly, to deal with me at some level by putting the penny in the box, or buying the odd piece of art, or being a member of the committee that is doing such 'good work'. Charity has been as easy option for everyone. Pay lip service and forget all about us. I am learning that charity does not any longer serve to absolve society of all responsibility, charity will no longer buy our gratitude. It will serve to create a greater divide. I am now in my 40th year and only now hearing the voices of my fellow disabled, the real story of their lives and I am learning to say I will not go away and be normal. I am learning to say I want to be part of this society and a disabled part at that.

Key issues in the group

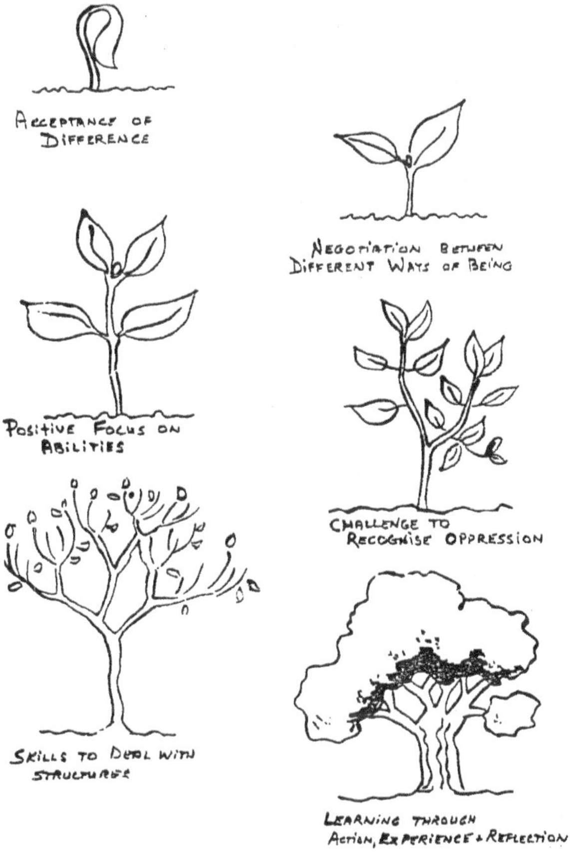

The key issues in this group which have facilitated the empowering process are:

1. Recognition and acceptance of difference,
   a. Everybody has a right to be themselves, they are OK.
   b. Everyone is different.
   c. Everyone has a way of being.

This aspect of the group was greatly facilitated by the fact that everybody was so totally different. We all had quite different experiences of disability and thus could not presume to understand each other.

2. The group's commitment to negotiating between different ways of being. Great effort was put into meeting each others needs. Be it difficulties in communication or concentration, ways were sought to facilitate all members: for example because it is difficult for some people to concentrate for any lengthy period the group takes a break and coffee, tea and cakes are provided to recharge member's energy levels.
3. Positive focus on people's abilities. We always focus on what members can do and can contribute to the process, involving everybody as much as possible.
4. The challenging of oppression. The focus of the group has been to learn actively how to gain and to keep our own power. One of our main ground rules was the right to challenge ourselves and to recognise our oppression, as most of us were often not even aware of this oppression.
5. The development of knowledge and skills to deal with the structures of society. This is an ongoing process with each new task demanding knowledge and skills not in the repertoire of our previous experience. We opted to develop a partnership

with the University, recognising that alone we would not qualify for EC funding. nor would we have a Certificate to Award. Our dealings in this partnership highlight the many issues facing groups who do not want to be taken over by the well organised and functioning elite.

For example they constantly choose one member of the group to negotiate with them. This has the effect of divide and rule in the group by influencing peoples perceived status with each other. Similarly organisations want to take power for themselves so they then get to make the decisions which will eventually only suit their own needs, giving them the prestige and reinforcing the global ethos that disabled people have not the personal resources to organise their own lives.

6. Learning through action, experience and reflection. At committee level the rotation of roles has facilitated the learning of different skills and expertise, using our own creativity, acknowledging and having our needs respected. Everybody gets the opportunity to carry out tasks on behalf of the group and to experience all this involves, such as facing the panic of what to do, and the feeling of achievement in a task well done.

These aspects of the group have been positive in enabling group members to grow in confidence, knowledge and expertise. Through this experience they have recognised that they have abilities and can make things happen, they can move from dependence to taking control of their lives.

Summary and evaluation

- Challenging the Status Quo -

In this paper we have endeavoured to highlight the issues and dilemmas facing any marginalised group who wish to challenge the status quo. Change does not come easily, power is not usually given away. However as we have discovered through our experience, it is through the ongoing analysis of encounters with the establishment that the group members learn the power game. In doing so they grow in strength within themselves, as can be seen from this sample of quotes we collected from group members.

> The group is about confidence, pride in your disability and not having to hide it.
>
> I see it as a liberating group coming from the grass roots with individualistic experience.
>
> I feel equal.
>
> The group provides a platform to achieve specific goals and remove obstacles for all people with disabilities.
>
> I have developed new meaningful relationships which I feel enormously comfortable with, which I know will outlive the life of the project.

Each new action brings with it new questioning, new reflections and it takes strength and determination to succeed. The continual problem is to sustain the group in the face of such adversity. This can only be done through recognising the gains made, however small, and the acknowledgement of each others support in understanding and fighting oppression.

References

Conway, M. (1979) *Rise Gonna Rise*. New York: Anchor.

Croft, S. and Beresford, P. (1989) 'User involvement, citizenship and social policy', *Critical Social Policy*, 26.9(2)

Daly, M. (ed.) (1988) *Women Together Against Poverty*. Dublin: Combat Poverty Agency.

Department of Health (1983) *Towards a Full Life. Green Paper on Services for Disabled People*. Dublin: Stationery Office.

Mullender, A. and Ward, D. (1991) *Self Directed Groupwork: Users Take Action for Empowerment*. London: Whiting and Birch.

Pernell, R.B. (1989) 'Empowerment and social groupwork' in Parnes, M. (ed.) *Innovations in Social Groupwork: Feedback from Practice to Theory*. New York: Haworth Press.

Preston-Shoot, M. (1992) 'On empowerment, partnership and authority: a training contribution', *Groupwork*, 5(2) pp.5-30.

Sennett, R. and Cobb, J. (1972) *The Hidden Injuries of Class*. Garden City, NY: Vintage.

Solomon, B. (1976) *Black Empowerment: Social Work in Oppressed Communities*. New York: Columbia University Press.

A PSYCHOTHERAPEUTIC GROUP FOR BOYS WHO HAVE BEEN SEXUALLY ABUSED

Gary Dixon and Michelle Phillips

This paper describes the authors' experiences facilitating a psychotherapeutic group for boys who have been sexually abused. Different aspects of the group are explored, including preparation for the group; the therapeutic relationship; group themes; the boys progress within the group; and consultation / supervision.

Introduction

The first Child Sexual Abuse (CSA) group for boys - held between July 1991 and April 1992 - was a joint venture between Camberwell Child Guidance Centre and South London Family Service Unit (FSU). Children living in Lambeth and Southwark, who have been sexually abused, are referred to these two centres, which offer family work, groupwork and individual work.

The group had male-female co-leaders, one from each centre, and was held at the FSU. The boys referred for the group had experienced different forms of sexual abuse; by paedophiles, strangers, and family members. The abuse had ceased 6-12 months before the group started. There were no court cases outstanding. One perpetrator had been successfully prosecuted and was in prison.

Prior to the group

The following areas were worked out before the group commenced: objectives; philosophy; practicalities; and appropriate referrals:

Objectives

1. To help children realise they are not alone in their experiences and feelings.
2. To enable communication of feelings experienced: guilt; anger/ frustration; sadness/loss; fear; loneliness.
3. To introduce the idea of hope and looking to the future.
4. To help children to seek protection from adults where needed (thus helping to prevent further abuse).
5. To help develop appropriate trust.
6. To help develop confidence and self esteem.

Groupwork Vol. 7(1), 1994, pp.79-95

7. To improve peer relationships.
8. To provide appropriate caring role models: male and female.

Philosophy

In the UK, there have been few long term psychotherapeutic groups specifically for boys who have been sexually abused. The workers thought it was essential to develop a philosophy based on their shared beliefs. Two important elements within the group were considered fundamental in effecting change:

1. group leader-child relationships;
2. relationships between the children.

The following aspects of these relationships were thought to be particularly helpful:

1. Showing an openness and a wish to understand each child's feelings evoked from past and present experiences.
2. Showing genuine interest in each child; providing a stimulating environment.
3. Appreciating each child's struggles and difficulties; showing patience regarding change and remaining hopeful even amidst the children's despair; supporting each child's strengths and acknowledging their struggles.
4. Providing a safe containing environment; demonstrating an ability to be concise and clear about boundaries, being flexible where necessary; tolerating misbehaviour without condoning it.
5. Reflecting upon issues that arise with the children; considering feelings evoked in the group in order to understand group process and to separate this from the group leaders' own personal issues.
6. Providing an opportunity for the boys to share their thoughts, feelings, memories about the abuse.
7. Providing opportunities for the children to develop and practice ways of relating to each other in the group, and to help them develop new ways of relating outside the group.

Practicalities

These included: one and a quarter hour weekly group meetings; three quarters of an hour weekly preparation/planning sessions; groupwork consultation for co-leaders every three to four weeks; transportation to and from the group (the group leaders shared this task); petty cash for drinks, snacks, outings etc.; a suitable room for the group.

Appropriate referrals

The referral process consisted of three stages:

1. Information gathering - group leaders discussing referrals with the referrers.
2. Acceptance of referrals for the group - group leaders deciding on suitability of each boy for the group, taking into consideration the group 'mix'.
   Age range 8-11 yrs.
   The child's race, colour, cultural background, and developmental level were taken into account.
3. Preparatory meetings: between groupworkers, referred child, his family and his social worker (if allocated one).

Preparatory meetings

The group leaders' objectives for these meetings were:

1. To engage with parent/s and referred child.
2. To find out parents' main worries about their child and how they felt the sexual abuse affected him. The child's emotional state questionnaire was completed (see Appendix I).
3. To explore how open the issue of sexual abuse was in the family. To help families realise that they were not the only ones. To help make sexual abuse 'alright' to talk about.
4. To give details about the group; what happens, its aims and how other children had benefited from the group.
5. To explore possible fears, anxiety and reluctance to attend the group (parent/s or child's).
6. To negotiate whether the child would like to attend and whether his parent/s would agree to him attending the group.
7. To discuss practicalities, transport, sickness, holidays etc.
8. To discuss further family contact, review meetings and the possibility of family work at FSU.

The meetings required skilful, delicate handling by the group leaders. Joining with the families was an arduous task. The workers had to be extremely receptive to the parent/s' feelings of guilt, shame and anger, and to try and understand their 'hurt', before they were able to allow their child to make a choice about coming to the group. Most of the parents struggled to understand their child's behaviour. The meeting offered an opportunity to explore how their child felt and enabled the necessary communication about feelings. Parents were helped to listen to their children. With much empathy, a judgemental, negative atmosphere changed into one of sadness and compassion.

Using the 'Child's Emotional State' questionnaires it was evident that parents had noticed differences in their children since the sexual abuse. This was obviously very worrying for them, and all reported that their children were having difficulties at school. They were described as: naughty, difficult, rude, oppositional, and unable to concentrate on school work. All the boys were described as being more moody and prone to aggressive outbursts at home and at school. Since the abuse, all the boys were experiencing difficulties being with friends, both in making and sustaining friendships. Most of the parents thought their child felt bad about himself and lacked confidence. Some boys however, were perceived to be lacking in confidence prior to the abuse. Every child was described in some way as more isolated, distant, withdrawn or less cuddly. Other differences noticed by parents were 'fears of going out' and nightmares.

The completion of the form in itself facilitated discussion about the sexual abuse. Mrs Dale, Peter's mother, said it was the first time she had been able to talk to her son about how worried she was.

When meeting with Mr and Mrs Jones, Allan and Garth's parents, there was an unexpected difficulty. The co-workers realised there were child protection issues. Allan and Garth (brothers) were still having contact with their abuser, a cousin who kept coming to the house. Communication of concerns to the social services dept. resulted in assessments of the level of risk to these two boys. The group leaders informed the children's social worker that they were not prepared to accept the two children whilst they were still in fear of further abuse. The situation was complex. Various social services departments were involved. Eventually the social worker was able to ensure that the perpetrator had no access, and the parents agreed to allow the boys to attend.

Six boys were invited to the group; an ethnic mix of four white boys and two black Afro-Caribbean boys. Unfortunately, after the first meeting two dropped out, leaving four in the group: Peter (aged 9, white); Simon (aged 10, black); Garth (aged 9, white) and Allan (aged 8, white)

Themes of the group

Developing trust

The boys understandably found it difficult to trust the group leaders, who quickly discovered that working with sexually abused children required a slow and gentle pace. The boys seemed to be trying to work out whether they would be treated well or whether this would be another abusive experience. It was as if they could not believe the workers would be interested in them, and they would constantly test to see if they were being listened to.

Children can feel worthless or 'tainted' as a direct result of abuse. This negative sense of self can be increased further by other peoples' (family and friends) responses to the abuse.

The boys often made threats about not coming to a group. Simon regularly hid from the minibus to test whether the leaders would seek him out. Garth and Allan initially presented with an 'I don't care, you can't hurt me' attitude. This tough front appeared to protect them from their painful feelings and memories. It very gradually receded when the leaders remained responsive and caring, as did Simon's habit of hiding.

During the first few groups the workers helped the boys to devise a rule system. A list of rules was placed on the wall, clearly visible. One example of a rule was 'No hitting, biting, punching or kicking'. The setting of boundaries enabled the boys to trust they would be protected and helped to control their behaviour.

The leaders found it useful to provide the boys with an outing every three or four weeks, which helped to establish relationships in the group. Fun and games also offered some relief from what was initially felt to be a threatening experience.

Sometimes the boys would appear blank and 'feelingless'. Throughout the group they were helped to externalise feelings, directly through conversation, play, and art. Charts were also used, e.g. 'The feeling faces' which illustrates children with different feelings. The boys appeared surprised to have someone so interested in, and accepting of, their feelings, let alone someone who was able to bear hearing about the effects of the abuse.

Very gradually the boys started to show their feelings. Some responded to playing with puppets in a very direct and telling way. By week five, Peter had collaborated with the others in an elaborate metaphorical story of his own abuse - complete with kings, queens, an abused prince, and the local police (puppets). The performance was videoed and the group discussed how the abused prince might feel. For Peter, this was clearly a more tolerable form of exploring abuse than talking about what he had experienced within a paedophile ring.

Food and trust were linked in the group. During the first meeting all four boys resolutely refused to eat or drink any of the snacks provided by the group leaders (crisps, peanuts, fruit, fizzy drinks etc). It was as if they feared that the leaders were involved in some sort of trickery, some sort of bribes to make them eat 'poison food'. Of course food as a bribe or reward for engaging in unwanted sexual activity is a well known ploy used by perpetrators. Peter, Allan and Garth indicated later that they had accepted sweets from their abusers. They felt that they had in some way given permission for the abuse, so causing them to experience tremendous guilt.

Only after much discussion could the boys question their responsibility for the abuse. This, coupled with their growing trust of the workers, meant food was able to take on a more pleasurable meaning. As their fears subsided they developed almost insatiable appetites. Sometimes they were unable to set their own limits, and if given the chance, they would have eaten until they were literally sick. They seemed to be communicating how easily an experience can flip from nurturing to abusive without these limits.

Developing power

The theme of power ran through the whole of the group. Each of the boys had been overpowered by an adult male or older adolescent, and they understandably struggled with the issue of 'appropriate power'. At times, this led to some identification with the aggressor. At other times the boys clearly felt 'powerless' and 'victims'. They were wary and passive, reluctant to assert their wishes or needs. They discussed incidents of having been bullied or bullying others.

It was quite moving when they chose to name their group THE POWER GROUP. Each boy glued their individual and group polaroid snapshots on the group poster, with individually cut out letters forming the words THE POWER GROUP. Although they were at a low ebb they seemed to be expressing a hope for something different.

For the leaders to help the boys develop appropriate power, it was essential to talk about it, including their wish to misuse it (see anger section for details). The boys conveyed their feeling that they lacked experience of having choices at home and school. This belief coupled with the abuse seemed to increase their sense of powerlessness. Through being given choice in the group (even for the smallest decisions) the boys realised they could influence events.

Choice was a key issue. One of the most successful outings involved going to a local go-kart track. Each boy was given the choice to drive the go-kart on their own or with an accompanying adult. With a short explanation from the trackworker they were launched onto the track for 20 laps. Initially each boy drove around the track waving to the others, whilst the workers stood aside like anxious parents. After several laps the boys became more engrossed in the pleasure of the driving. Peter had felt worthless and inadequate for two years, and he was ecstatic as he drove around the track. This new experience of power, control and competence seemed to be an essential part of the development of his self-esteem.

As the boys developed an awareness of the group's boundaries and gained an appropriate sense of control, a safer atmosphere was established. They were then able to begin to face their fears.

Fears

All the boys were fearful and isolated. They had experienced frequent nightmares. They no longer sought cuddles and comfort from their parent/s because of their fears of intimacy, hurt and rejection. There was a great reluctance to discuss 'feeling fearful' as if this might be seen as evidence of weakness and would put them in touch with vulnerable feelings.

Children who had attended previous sexual abuse groups, had compiled a list of their fears (see Appendix II). The boys in this group were dominated by some of those fears, some more noticeably than others.

All the boys to some extent, had a continual fear of how abusive the leaders might be with them. It also seemed that in the early part of the group the boys believed they were going to face some elaborate form of interrogation about the abuse they suffered and their part in it. The workers were sensitive to the boys' fears and worries, and helped them to put words to them. An environment was encouraged where it was 'OK' to be afraid. Being fearful was hard, but all of the boys were able to express fear at different points and were able to receive the support they so desperately wanted. On the go-kart outing Allan, who had previously been very outwardly 'tough', was brave enough to say he didn't feel able to go on by himself; one of the workers drove with him, commending him on his bravery.

In week twenty, the boys quite unexpectedly talked directly about their abusive experiences. The session began with an activity in which they were making masks. Simon and Peter made a mask of the male leader which seemed to have malevolent and fearful qualities. A discussion followed about the links with the boys' abusers. Simon, the black boy, spoke negatively about the 'blackness' of his mask. The workers raised the issue of how some children experience adults using abusive language. Simon then began to talk about the abusive and racist language that was directed at him by his abuser. He had been horrified by what had been said to him, and felt humiliated and denigrated.

It was not the first time the issue of racism had been raised. There had been previous discussions about the anti-racist and equal opportunities policy poster on the wall. It seemed that Simon feared how he would be treated in the group. The leaders were able to talk about the awful reality of racism, and appreciate his feelings. The group was able to look more closely at differences and prejudice. Peter, who had a mixed race brother, was able to empathise with Simon.

There were discussions between Garth and Allan about whether they could share their experiences of abuse or not. Allan convinced his brother that it was good to tell. What followed was a description of how his older cousin, the abuser, had started a fire in a dustbin and locked the door to the bedroom. He had apparently threatened to set the house on fire if they ever told their secret. Other disclosures of fears and threats followed. When these revelations came to light there was an atmosphere of relief. It had taken twenty sessions for the boys to feel safe to share these previously harboured fears and feelings. They had wanted to share the specific details of insults etc., showing compassion to each other.

The group leaders were able to listen and bear the awful stories they were hearing. In doing so they helped the boys to feel they were worth being with. There was a reluctance to continue talking about the abuse in subsequent group meetings, but the boys' relationships with each other and with the workers were much less guarded.

Anger

Much has been written about how anger is experienced by boys and girls who have been sexually abused. The boys in this group were angry - angry at fathers, mothers, siblings, perpetrators, teachers at school, angry at each other and angry at the group leaders. Simon and Peter were pre-occupied by a murderous fantasy towards the abuser. All of the boys found that their daily lives were dominated by aggression, especially towards adults who made them 'do things'. Simon demonstrated a particular defiance towards his physical education teacher at school, refusing to put his body in some positions when exercising with his class. Garth seemed to withdraw from contact with his family, lapsing into sullen and angry silences at regular intervals - enraging his parents.

It was difficult at times for the leaders to understand how much this anger could be linked directly to the sexual abuse and how much it was a result of general life experience.

Early in the group the smallest and youngest boy, Allan, was bullied and scapegoated by the other three (including his brother).

The workers worried that Allan would leave the group altogether, and they intervened at an early stage to prevent the bullying, whilst addressing the issue of displaced anger and its real causes. Situations that enraged the boys at school and home were discussed at length. It took them some time to learn to verbalise, rather than act out, their strong feelings and frustrations. Puppet play, table football, art work, and pounding clay, all seemed to be helpful in giving some expression to the rage and sense of betrayal that they experienced.

On occasions the leaders had to calm potentially explosive situations. Whilst maintaining limits on behaviour, they provided a model of someone who could be angry without destroying the relationship, losing control, or becoming violent.

Towards the end of the group the boys expressed considerable anger towards the workers. The imminent ending triggered strong feelings of being rejected. The boys realised it was okay to be angry and were confident that they would be listened to. The workers' task was both to bear the anger and explore whether the boys could believe in the good caring experience of the group even if it had to end.

Loss

Loss was an important theme throughout. When the group started, the worry about losing it was apparent. There was a preoccupation with 'time'. How long would the group continue? How long would each meeting last? How could everything the boys wanted to do (e.g. activities) be fitted in?

This whole area was addressed concretely and symbolically. A group calendar was made outlining the length of the group, leaving space on it for outings, activities of choice etc. This gave the boys some visual idea of how long they would be coming and helped them to prepare for an eventual ending.

The group leaders were providing what they thought was a fairly long group (40 weeks). However, the boys did not perceive it this way. After four group meetings, Simon expressed disappointment that it had to end 'so soon'. Peter said: 'Can't it go on for 99 years?'. The feelings of disappointment were addressed and acknowledged by the workers, and connections were made with the impact of other losses in the boys' lives.

The children were noticeably more volatile before holiday breaks and there were often feelings of abandonment, rejection and isolation. They seemed to fear that the workers lost sight of them during breaks and they could not imagine that they might be remembered and not rejected. At times they were able to admit feeling that the leaders didn't really care, because they had holidays and the group would not continue forever. This perception was gradually and sensitively challenged by the workers.

The leaders sent letters to the group members after breaks, reminding them of the group. The boys would help to make cards if one of them was ill, or if someone had a birthday - all significant ways of helping a child not to feel forgotten. There was less compassion when a group leader was ill. They felt angry and rejected, which was understandable, given their vulnerabilities.

The leaders had not envisaged the issue of loss to be so dominant, though in many ways it was healthy and reflected the reality. The strength of emotion may have resulted from previous losses. Simon and Peter experienced pain and loss acutely, and were able to let the group be important to them. Garth and Allan struggled more, defending against experiencing something good, and perhaps highlighting what was less available to them away from the group. These brothers missed three consecutive groups very near to the end, and the workers feared they would not return. Amazingly, with letters of encouragement, they did come for the final two meetings. Perhaps it was easier to face an ending over which they had had some control.

The pain of the group ending reached some extreme levels in the last few weeks. The boys were furious with the group leaders, and tried to rubbish the group generally. At the same time they would ask whether they would be replaced by other children. Their pain/anger that other children might get what they wanted was obvious, resulting in an escalation of their own rejecting, angry and distraught behaviour.

For two weeks the workers literally had to hold the boys near the door as they continually tried to run out of the room. They seemed to want to be held as they half-heartedly said 'let me go'. Once held, they didn't struggle hard but it was quite an effort to catch them as they took turns to try and leave, locked toilets and hid throughout the building. They felt rejected and were 'rejecting' but kept returning to the group each week.

It is important to add that the leaders were very careful and thoughtful in their use of physical contact when keeping the children from running away. They kept physical contact to a minimum and were acutely aware of their intervention being possibly perceived as abusive. It did not feel to the workers like a reliving of an abusive situation, more one where the children were indirectly asking 'how much will you bother and care about me if I struggle against you'. At times the boys would almost run into the arms of the leaders, gently shoving. It seemed the only way they dared ask for affection, but not surprisingly they denied this suggestion. The workers, appreciating the boys' difficulties discussing the ending, continued with the 'holding', physically and psychologically.

As the group neared its end, the struggles, regressions and running away subsided into an atmosphere of sadness, which by then they could tolerate and didn't need to cover up with activity or aggressive bullying behaviour. It was very painful for these boys to be sad, and at times the workers felt excruciatingly anxious about 'allowing' it, acknowledging that they partly wanted the 'sadness and loss to go away'. At the end, the boys developed a way of just being content to be with each other, playing gently and sharing memories of their time together as a group.

Benefits for the group

The evaluation of the group incorporated discussion with the group supervisor, with families and in some cases the schools. The workers felt they had generally met their objectives, some in more depth than others. It was clear that the relationships that had developed during the group had been the fundamental component in helping the children to change.

Simon

Simon changed significantly at home, at school and in the group. His self esteem had developed substantially. He had been able to explore his feelings of anger and rejection during the group, and now seemed able to believe he was worth caring for. Although Simon himself was reluctant to admit any change or progress, his mother and the school confirmed that there were considerable improvements. He was no longer truanting, nor was he being rude to the teachers. He was achieving certificates of excellence in his subjects. He now had a close group of friends. His mother described him as being much more affectionate and open, happier and more confident. She thought he was better behaved, especially as he was no longer bullying his brother.

The group had not been able to address all the issues of what it was like to be a young black boy in this society. However, the open discussion with Simon about the pain of racism, generally and in relation to his perpetrator, combined with the workers' positive acceptance of him did seem to help him to view himself more positively.

Peter

Peter seemed to 'blossom' in the group. It became an important part of his life. When he started he had looked miserable, spoke little and rarely smiled. As the group progressed he laughed and joked, showing his beaming smile. He was now much happier with life, he valued the group and found its ending difficult to bear. He was however, able to express his disappointment and anger openly with the group leaders.

His stammer, which had been quite noticeable at the beginning of the group almost disappeared. Before leaving, his compassion for other children who had been sexually abused, resulted in him making a short video telling other children about the value of the group.

The school were impressed with the changes in Peter. His attendance, previously poor was now almost perfect. The most noticeable changes reported were his increased assertiveness, happiness and his integration with other children. His academic work also improved.

Peter's mother confirmed these changes. Her perception was that he was a bit 'stroppier' and more argumentative. She was pleased and said this was more like the old Peter. He no longer had nightmares and was mixing with other local boys of his age.

Garth and Allan

In comparison to Simon and Peter, Garth and Allan made less progress. They never appeared to feel they had complete permission to use the group, and sometimes it appeared difficult for them to admit even wanting to attend. Their parents struggled to allow them to do so, and were often hostile and suspicious, at times appearing to envy what their sons had. With hindsight, the workers believed more preparatory work was necessary to engage positively with this very untrusting family, which had declined family work at FSU. Despite this far from ideal situation, Allan and Garth both made some progress.

Garth

Garth had gradually let some of his barriers down and had talked about some of his feelings. He had been very wary of others initially, both children and adults. He had been reluctant to discuss openly any area of his life, and the leaders sensed his fear that talking was being disloyal to his family. He appeared quite anxious when the group started and didn't talk a great deal. He would spend his time playing in isolation or worrying about his younger brother, Allan. As the group progressed he became friendlier to the other boys and wanted to be included in group activities. He seemed less protective of Allan and more able to state his own wants. He worried less and was much more playful.

The leaders did not have permission to contact the school and thus were unclear about his presentation there, or his progress. His parents were reluctant to consider any change having taken place as a result of the group. The workers were concerned about levels of negativity towards Garth. There was a great deal of discontent within the family. This was reported to the social worker after the group's completion, and she was considering other forms of help for them.

Allan

Allan had been described as selfish by his parents. They had complained about his fighting with his brothers and sisters. When the group started he had been extremely preoccupied with thoughts of food, drink and 'what he could have'. He felt very deprived and would frequently take other peoples' food, resulting in numerous confrontations. This gradually changed. The workers' ability not to be punitive towards Allan and to acknowledge and allow his neediness gradually seemed to help him want to share.

Allan showed some sadness about the group ending, and he was desperate to give to the other children and for his generous gestures to be praised. He seemed more free to express his feelings. He challenged the others assertively, no longer needing his brother's or the group leaders' protection. He had been very brave talking about his abusive experiences, even encouraging his brother to do likewise. The frequent nightmares reported at the beginning were rare by the time the group ended.

Group consultations

The co-workers had a groupwork consultation every three or four weeks, with the following aims:

1. To explore group process and themes.
2. To develop understanding of each child's emotional state.
3. To discuss possible groupwork interventions and plan appropriate activities.
4. To explore the co-working relationship, and the feelings evoked towards each other and towards children.

Some key areas were explored in detail in these sessions:

- The workers feared losing the boys from the group if they were not kept amused or if the group became too emotionally difficult. This fear was thought to be similar to the one the boys were experiencing 'Will I cope if there isn't an activity or if I have to think about how I feel?'. Discussion took place about the need to balance structure and choice. The workers closely monitored their feelings of wanting to protect the boys, acknowledging how much the boys could cope with.
- There was a struggle to set limits on food quantities eaten and the number of outings. Consultation explored the leaders' attempts to make things better for the boys materially as they became aware of their distress. The resulting awareness enabled the setting of necessary limits.
- The female worker quite often felt 'pushed out' when she made attempts to explore feelings. The male worker at this time felt more identified with the boys. He struggled not to collude with the strong denial and an 'everything's OK' atmosphere. There was much discussion about the two polarised positions. Consultation helped the leaders to see both of these positions in the boys, and the need to work slowly at introducing feelings was highlighted.
- Deprivation was another area discussed. The experiences of the brothers, Allan and Garth, were examined. As well as their sexual abuse, they had suffered from a range of deprivations throughout their life, e.g. chronic poverty, marital discord, and emotional abuse. Their parents seemed envious/jealous of any pleasure that the boys were experiencing in the group, and this undoubtedly affected the boys' self-presentation. The leaders found this enormously distressing and frustrating. Consultation helped them to develop realistic expectations about how much they could expect the boys to change when their parents felt so deprived and resentful.
- The theme of hopelessness emerged regularly. The group leaders would lose hope at the prospect of finding ways to help the boys. They also experienced feelings of shock, disbelief, anger and protection towards them. Consultation sessions were a time to reflect on these powerful emotions and to understand their meaning and origins. Much of the hopelessness was thought to have belonged to the boys. The consultant provided containment which enabled the workers

to continue to believe in their work and renew their hope. Without consultation they felt they could have easily become demoralised and could not have been so receptive to the boys' emotional needs.

Differences in the male and female leader's background and style of working became apparent during the group:

Female (White, British)	Male (White, American)
First group specifically for survivors of sexual abuse	Sixth CSA group
Group based outside own agency	Group based in own agency
Psychodynamic orientation	Social groupwork orientation.
Experience in individual work/-family work.	Experience in groupwork/ family therapy.
Worked in hospital/clinical settings.	Worked in community-based settings.
Stressed importance of expression of feelings, verbally and through art work	Stressed importance of activity/creativity as a means of helping

Consultation ensured that each worker's beliefs, concerns, ideas, and worries were heard. Both believed that open discussion about difference/conflict (within the safety of consultation) prevented resentments building up. It enabled them to maintain a good co-working relationship. This development of openness and trust enabled them to feel safe enough to explore difficult areas with the children, giving them a 'good experience'.

Bibliography (sources drawn on, not referenced in the article)

Bentovim, A., Elton, A., Hildebrand, J.H., Tranter, A. and Vizard, E. (1988) *Child Sexual Abuse within the Family*. London: Wright.

Brown, A. (1986) *Groupwork*. Second Edition. Aldershot: Gower

Glaser, D. and Frosh, S. (1988) *Child Sexual Abuse* London: Macmillan.

Hollows, A. and Armstrong, H. (eds.) 1989) *Working with Sexually Abused Boys*. London: National Children's Bureau.

Lebacq, M. and Shah, Z. (1989) 'A group for black and white sexually abused children', *Groupwork*, 2(2), pp.123-133.

Mandell, J.G. and Damon, L. (1989) *Group Treatment for Sexually Abused Children*. London: The Guildford Press.

Peake, A. (1989) 'Planning groupwork for boys' in Hollows, A. and Armstrong,

H. (eds.) *Working with Sexually Abused Boys*. London: National Children's Bureau.
Preston-Shoot, M. (1987) *Effective Groupwork*. London: BASW/Macmillan.

Appendix I

QUESTIONS FOR FAMILIES WHERE CHILDREN HAVE BEEN SEXUALLY ABUSED

1a. Did your child make/keep friends readily before the abuse?
Great difficulty O________________________5 No problems
1b. Now ? Great difficulty O____________________5 No problems

2a. How do you think your child felt about himself before the abuse?
Worthless O______________________________5 Confident
2b. Now ? Worthless O___________________________5 Confident

3a. How fearful was he of other adults and children before the abuse?
Petrified O_______________________________5 Fearless
3b. Now ? Petrified O___________________________5 Fearless

4a. Generally how aggressive was your child before the abuse?
Not aggressive O_________________________5 Very aggressive
4b. Now ? Not aggressive O_____________________5 Very aggressive

APPENDIX II

CHILDREN'S FEARS FOLLOWING SEXUAL ABUSE

Social

Fear of leaving home/going into care
Fear of loss of family/other relationships
Fear of men/boys
Fear of adults disappointing them
Fear of sexual assault
Fear of strangers
Fear of abandonment/isolation
Fear of breaking up families/causing shame

Identity

Fear of never trusting again/being intimate again
Fear of never being the same again
Fear of labels, ridicule
Fear of loss of identity
Fear of lack of personal controls
Fear of death

Situational

Fear of medical examination
Fear of secrets, whispers etc
Fear of night time/nightmares
Fears triggered by places, situations, sights, smells
Fears of being cornered, entrapped

Sexuality

Fear of 'imprinted' identity
Fear of pregnancy, giving birth, genetic defects
Fear of touch
Fear of sexual arousal
Fear of being soiled, secondhand, used

REVIEWS

Groupwork With Children And Adolescents: A Handbook
KEDAR NATH DWIVEDI (ED.)
London, Jessica Kingsley, 1993, 368pp, price £19.95 (pbk)

In my book, 'a handbook' tells you what to do while 'a sourcebook' directs you to various sources of knowledge. This extensive volume is closer to being a sourcebook.

The sources all spring from cross fertilisation between the Ken Stewart Family Centre in Northampton and the Midland Course in groupwork in Britain. The editor rightly points out the absence of written material about therapeutic groupwork with children, particularly in Britain. This book seems to be a contribution towards helping trainees and practitioners find most of the sources they need in one place. As such, the work is commendable. Five parts comprise this compilation. Part 1, 'Theoretical and Practical Issues', concentrates on conceptual frameworks and the practicalities of setting up groups. Part 2, 'Developmental Perspectives', is two brief comments about child development, an extended essay about the relevance of empathy to prosocial development, and a review of the development of group psychotherapy. Part 3, 'Tools and Techniques', presents an array of methods for working with children in groups. Play, activities, exercises, and games, as well as art, visualisation, drama, and even interpretation are described. Part 4, 'Subjects and Themes', focuses on specific issues presented by children: bereavement, encopresis, sexual abuse, offending, and racial identity. Part 5, 'Contexts and Settings', concludes the book with case studies of groupwork in various work settings: schools, residential child care, child mental health service, youth service, and a therapeutic community.

Arriving at a single view of this book is extremely difficult. Twenty two people contributed, and many wrote jointly with the editor. Merely coordinating all these efforts must have been a most taxing task. Ensuring uniformity of quality and coherence throughout such a book is probably a Herculean one. Indeed, the quality varies considerably. There are real gems here, such as Chapter 10 on art psychotherapy with its lively pictures; and Chapter 11; on relaxation, visualisation, and nourishment. There are also very clearly written and informative ones; for example, Chapter 15 on encopresis, and particularly Chapter 17 on groupwork with young offenders. Chapter 18 makes an independent contribution to understanding the phases through which cultural and racial identity develops, with special reference to black children. The chapters of Part 5; about organising groupwork in different work settings, are mostly clear, practical, and helpful.

Where this book may lose readers is mainly in its theoretical parts. The approach is described as 'eclectic' - '...utilising the principles derived from Therapeutic Communities, Group Analysis, (Multiple) Family Therapy, Behaviour Therapy and so forth'. (p.xi). Like other eclectic, rather than integrative, approaches, there are so may trees in this book that it is virtually impossible to see the wood. Conflicting approaches to child development; for example, Erickson's vs Sterm's, are mentioned as if they simply differ. Awareness of the social context in which children develop is disturbingly mixed with psychopathological terms such as 'narcissistic and animistic perception of reality' (p.119), and with a moralistic stance about 'bad language' (p.187). Some extremely complex and subtle issues, such as interpretation (pp.183-92), are discussed far too briefly. Less experienced readers may begin to believe that once they know the correct interpretation they may just as well deliver it: regardless of the children's pace, awareness, and readiness to absorb the message and use it to change. I trust the author did not intend this to happen.

In view of media coverage, I was looking for the contribution that groupwork may make to overcoming bullying at school; a subject I have long considered overdue. Neither is there any clear reference to overcoming discrimination in its various forms. I can see how the length itself might have prevented these additions. So, it might have been better to divide this sourcebook into two: one about the implications of child development, and the other about direct practice.

Still, here is a rich source of ideas about groupwork with children. It will probably be used to best effect as part of a continuous course, such as the one offered at Northampton. With groupworkers retreating to a merely cognitive-behavioural stance nowadays, it seems important to uphold the full range high.

Oded Manor, Principal Lecturer in Social Work, Middlesex University

The Metaphoric body. Guide to Expressive Therapy through Images and Archetypes
LEAH BARTAL AND NIRA NE'EMAN
London, Jessica Kingsley Publishers, price £13.99 (pbk)
ISBN: 1-85302-152-0

This book is based on metaphorical ways of working with the body, mainly through movement, but also incorporating to a lesser extent other expressive arts, such as painting, drawing, poetry and music.

There are several prologues before the book gets underway with the main introduction, which introduces the concepts of 'mythic' as pertaining to internal perception, and 'metaphoric' as relating to the external senses. The introduction also lays the ground for the main body of the book, which starts with movement exercises to explore the physical aspects of the body. It then uses this as a basis to move on to Taoist, Biblical and Greek frameworks and stories to highlight different aspects of the body and relationships in a metaphorical way.

The authors grew up in Israel (but now work worldwide, including London, where one of them currently lives), and have drawn on the 'melting pot of cultures' they experienced there. They were among the first in the West to learn T'ai Chi, and their scholarship is evident from the many references to texts on eastern mysticism, the Qabala, Greek mythology and modern links with psychology. The bibliography is impressive, and the selection of illustrations fascinating. Occasionally the language and links are a bit abstruse and difficult to follow, unless one is already familiar with the ideas being discussed.

It is written mostly as a 'how to' book, with a statement in the introduction that 'it is a resource book which allows readers directly to experience transformation' (p.1). Although I did try one of the visualisation exercises on my own, with interesting results, I did not feel I could do the movement exercises in that way - it is difficult to get wholeheartedly involved in body movement, clasping the book in one hand! I also felt that some of the material was potentially quite deep, and would need a skilled facilitator/therapist, qualified in dance/movement therapy. Most of the exercises also seemed most suited to a group, and the text suggests this is the way in which the authors usually use the material.

The exercises using movement were the most explicitly worked out, and left the strongest impression. The exercises in other arts, such as the painting and drawing ones, seemed very sketchy by comparison. This is not surprising, given the backgrounds of the authors. Nevertheless, it was refreshing to see workshops using several different art forms, and this could be enhanced by collaboration with other arts therapists to develop them further.

Some of the personal stories from workshop participants were very moving, especially some of the poems, and it is clear that the workshops offer an experience that is difficult to achieve in any other way. Some of these stories were difficult to follow, or to connect to the original exercise; this may be partly due to the difficulty of 'translating' a non-verbal experience into words.

Several layout features made the book more difficult to follow than necessary. There were no numbers for chapters, sections or illustrations, and there were too many different types of heading to see the structure. The bibliography was very inclusive, but the arrangement in two sections, referring to text and notes separately, was confusing; they would be better as one section. The notes on mythology were interesting but confusingly arranged. The lack of index was a sad omission in a book containing such a wealth of information.

Most of the examples were drawn from women, which may reflect what is the case for the workshops run by the authors. There were a few examples from men, but all the photographs showed women. This may be inevitable, but seemed a pity, as there are now more men interested in dance, movement and therapy. This kind of work has a great deal to offer everyone.

Despite these drawbacks, this book has a strong contribution to make, especially in demonstrating how to develop themes imaginatively in many directions and in several art forms. There are some striking metaphors, and the emotional relevance of ancient myths to our times and problems is made clear. This book will be useful to workshop leaders and therapists, especially of dance/movement, and also other arts therapists. For those used to working with mythology, and those in physical healing professions, it will suggest a new approach to explore - but they should go and experience such workshops themselves before using the material.

Marian Liebmann, Art Therapist/Probation Officer/Mediation Worker

Playback - A Guide to Reviewing Activities
ROGER GREENAWAY
Windsor, Berks, The Duke of Edinburgh's Award, price £7.99 (pbk) ISBN 0 905425 09 X

By 'playback' the author means learning from experiences; particularly those which arise during group activities. Many groupworkers call this 'processing' or 'reviewing'. In spite of what it claims, this book seems to have been written to a specific reader: the youth worker who engages young people in shared, usually outdoor, activities. Not being a youth worker myself, it took me some time to enter this world. The work seems to involve offering young people exciting shared activities. Presumably, these experiences are meant to convince them that they can have fun and excitement without breaking the law. It then seems necessary to convince youth workers that the youngsters need also to reflect upon those experiences; a point many mainstream groupworkers may find rather obvious.

The first chapter introduces the idea of reviewing shared activities. It includes a brief introduction to the work of Kolb and Juch, work which I too regard as highly relevant to education. Enabling learning cycles which address as many of our faculties as possible has a recognisable value.

The second chapter is dedicated to helping youth workers find the specific purpose of their involvement in reviewing.

The third chapter is the bulk of this book. After explaining his major technical terms, the author offers an alphabetical list of about 80 ways of reviewing shared activities. Each suggestion is given two pages, and most lack a specific definition, not to mention any reference to what has happened to the group during the activity. Although some of these 'methods' will be known to groupworkers from a variety of sources, no written sources are offered either. On page 29 there is an interesting analysis of the learning styles emphasised in each of the reviewing methods, but no further use is made of it during the rest of the book. The fourth chapter is entitled 'Settings'. Presumably, it is designed to explore how shared activities could be reviewed within different work settings. Yet, I must admit to getting very little sense of these from the flitting comments offered.

'Issues' is the title of the fifth chapter. Again, it seems to aim at helping workers overcome blocks to reviewing, but the rather laconic and brief paragraphs do not convince me that groupworkers will see a real group when reading them.

Chapter 6, about 'Skills', contains hints about the choice of reviewing methods. Again, for a mainstream groupworker these may come across as rather haphazard in view of the extensive study of the impact of various activities on the groups dynamics. A helpful list of resources is offered in Chapter 7; articles, books, and addresses for further contact.

All in all, I must admit to being quite puzzled by this book. It seems to contain many good ideas. The trouble is that these are presented as if the author was conducting a workshop with people and could clarify the ideas with many explanations. Yet, this is merely a written book. As such, the gaps in the text confuse.

I was left with a distinct feeling of a cookbook, loaded with samples of delicious dishes which, in untrained hands, can turn out very sour indeed.

At the back the book was described as 'in no way academic, heavy, or fussy'. It certainly is none of those, but is this really a recommendation?

Oded Manor, Principal Lecturer in Social Work, Middlesex University

A Theory of Groupwork Practice
TOM DOUGLAS
London, Macmillan, price £35.00 (hbk) £9.99 (pbk).

September was probably not a propitious time for this academic to read and review a new book. The prospect of a new academic year, with teaching preparation followed by the influx of new students, not to mention writing for publication with a view to forthcoming quality assessment and research selectivity exercises makes for long and stressful days. This description is offered not so as to elicit sympathy but to offer one potential explanation why I found this book difficult to engage with. Perhaps it was me; but then, if so, how might even more hard-pressed students and practitioners find it?

The book's title is enticing - a theory for practice. The book's jacket cover makes the bold claim that the book will present a theory which can form the basis for all forms of groupwork practice. I remain only partially convinced or, perhaps more accurately, left with unanswered questions. The aim of the book is to demonstrate that all groupwork follows a very simple pattern, and to define and connect into relationship the central factors, purposes and actions in working with groups. The key propositions, which are helpfully summarised periodically within the book, are that there are two definable forms of groupwork groups, namely created groups and adapted (from existing groups) groups; then, that either of these two forms may be further defined by where, at any one time, they rest on a continuum of associative patterns. These patterns range from instrumental - discovering and using the collective resources of groupwork members - to contextual - accessing and using a scarce individual resource. Douglas further proposes that the inherent value of groups lies in the resources available to and/or created by groups. Put another way, the basis of groupwork is to generate resource systems to meet the needs of group members, if necessary by removing obstacles to the use of such resources. It is, in essence, a resource theory of groupwork, the implications of which are developed in chapters which focus on group design, and on teaching and practising groupwork.

Two obstacles for me in reading this book were the continual use of the masculine when referring to groupworkers and group members, and language which I experienced as either mystifying or impenetrable. I found the terms 'group as context' and 'group as instrument', for instance, less than helpful when attempting to discern and follow Douglas's central propositions and to apply these to groups with which I work.

Among the unanswered questions for me were ones concerned with how resources are used, the purposes for which groups might be used, and how to manage situations where constraints beyond the group affect the groups ability to proceed. There is within social work practice, and mirrored by the requirements which qualifying students must achieve, a fudge between a radical, anti-oppressive agenda, a more humanistic anti-discriminatory agenda, and an emphasis on and mandate for social control. To what use should group resources be put? For what purposes might social workers and probation officers be asked to work with groups, and how should they, and those with whom they work, negotiate the conflicting imperatives which are expressed, inter alia, in legal and professional mandates? I missed the fact that the book did not take a critical look, in my view, at 'resources' - what they are, for what they might be used, and by whom? I suppose that what I was hoping to find was an explicit link between Douglas's propositions and a commitment to empowerment, user self-direction, partnership and anti-oppressive practice, the more so because I was thinking about the book just as the Conservative Party conference set a 'right' agenda, and following newspaper attacks upon CCETSW and its anti-racist commitments.

However, there were sections within the book with which I did connect. The chapters on group design, and the introductory chapter's analysis of the dangers and confusions arising from social work's use of theories, generally and in relation to groupwork specifically, were two such instances. Likewise, the chapter on techniques which groupworkers use, and the discussion of teaching groupwork contained both basics of which it was helpful to be reminded once again, and ideas which took my thinking forward. Here I was left wanting more, especially how to teach groupwork within a Diploma in Social Work programme where there is limited scope for tackling any method of intervention is depth. I found that Douglas's discussion of obstacles to resource use highly relevant, but was left wondering about how groupworkers should tackle, and enable groups to tackle those obstacles which lie in the group's environment: other systems can be oppressive, and any theory of groupwork practice must empower groupworkers and members to address how power is used and experienced.

I will put this on the reading list for groupwork students but I suspect that it will be less attractive than 'how to do it' books and Douglas's recent *Handbook of Common Groupwork Problems* (Routledge, 1991). That may be a danger which Douglas was addressing in this book, when he refers to the confusion between theories of behaviour and theories of groupwork practice. It may be a further example of the divide between theory and practice. Whatever else may be certain, practice realities frequently discourage the use of theory.

Overall, I am reminded of the quotation attributed to Perls: if by chance we should meet, that will be wonderful; if not, it is no one's fault. Somehow this book and I missed each other, but I shall return to it. Your experience may be different. Try it and see.

Michael Preston-Shoot, Senior Lecturer in Social Work, and Head of the Social Work School, University of Manchester

NOTES ON CONTRIBUTORS

John Bensted has recently been appointed Senior Probation Officer in Gloucester. He has worked in a wide range of social work settings, including work with offenders in fieldwork, in prison and at the Avon Probation Centre.

Allan Brown is a Senior Lecturer in Social Work, Bristol University, and has done research and consultancy at the Avon Probation Centre. He is co-editor with Brian Caddick of *Groupwork with Offenders* (Whiting & Birch, 1993).

Maire Ni Chorcora has a longterm disability. She is a founder member of DET, working in the area of disability.

Gary Dixon has 'practised' groupwork at the Henderson Hospital, the London Borough of Camden, and the South London FSU (whilst writing this paper). His interests lie in school nurturance groups, CSA groups, training and consultancy, multicultural groupwork and family therapy. He currently resides in the USA

Carlton Forbes is a qualified social and community worker, with experience in a wide range of voluntary and statutory settings. He currently works as a sessional groupworker at the Avon Probation Centre, and is Development Manager of COMOCCO, a Bristol agency working with people who have a crack/cocaine problem.

Geraldine Grindley has worked as a trainer and consultant in the field of group dynamics for the past16 years. She was awarded a Masters Degree by Dublin City University for a major thesis on the management of non-profit organisations. She also holds a professional qualification in groupwork which she completed in France, in addition to a post-graduate qualification in education from London University. She teaches undergraduate and postgraduate modules in group dynamics in St. Patrick's College, Maynooth (Postgraduate Diploma in Adult Education), All Hallow's College, Drumcondra (BA and Postgraduate Diplomas) and Dublin City University (MBA Programme). She is also retained as a trainer/consultant with various groups in the semi-private and public sectors.

Eddie Jennings is a founder member of DET, Freelance consultant, Youth and Community Worker. He is a person with MS.

Nuala Lordan is Lecturer in Social Work, University College Cork. She pioneered the development of social work education in this University. She now teaches courses on groupwork, and social work practice. She is a founder member of DET and Programme Director for a Certificate Course in Disability Equality Training.

Michelle Phillips currently works as a Clinical Nurse Specialist, Camberwell Child Guidance Centre, South East London. She developed her groupwork skills facilitating a variety of therapeutic groups for children and adolescents, whilst working on a children's inpatient psychiatric unit at the Hospital for Sick Children, Great Ormond Street, London.

Jill Reynolds is a Lecturer in the School of Health, Welfare and Community Education, Open University. Her previous experience includes providing training for para-social workers and community workers from Vietnam and other refugee groups. She has developed teaching programmes on refugees in social work professional training.

Jane Shackman is a Social Worker, The Medical Foundation for Care of Victims of Torture. She does clinical work with individuals and families, groupwork and community development, and co-ordinates the work of the interpreters. She has developed training on refugees for different local authorities, aimed at social work staff and teachers.

Paul Taylor is currently Senior Lecturer in Community Education (*Animation socio-culturelle*), University of Tours, France. With practical experience of cross-national groupwork throughout Europe and West Africa, he has particular responsibility for the management of several international exchange/research programmes.

Rick Wall was convicted of his last criminal offence in 1974, following which he was employed as a 'new careers' Social Worker. He qualified as a Probation Officer in 1982, and has extensive experience of developing and facilitating groupwork with offenders. He is currently working at the Avon Probation Centre.

NOTES FOR CONTRIBUTORS

Articles are welcome from all who have an interest in work with groups (whether as practitioner, trainer, researcher, user or consultant) and who wish to contribute to the development of groupwork theory and practice.

Types of Articles

The journal will publish two main types of articles:

i. PRACTICE-BASED PAPERS

These articles will be based directly on groupwork practice experience, but written in a way which is evaluative as well as descriptive. We recognise that many practitioners may not be familiar with writing for journals, and we wish to suggest the following guidelines to assist in this process:

(a) A brief summary of the contents of the article (100-150 words), drawing attention to any particular theme or emphasis.

(b) Background to the group, the context, e.g. agency setting, type of group, workers and members; group aims and objectives; and the theoretical/philosophical perspectives i.e. any particular principles or values central to the approach taken.

(c) A brief review of the group, content, methods and process.

(d) Outcome and analysis, specific topics of interest relevant to the focus of the article, e.g. key issues arising from this piece of practice; and evaluation of the group drawing out learning points for other practitioners.

ii. THEORY-BUILDING PAPERS

Each issue will carry several theoretical papers ranging over groupwork concepts, theory, research, issues and values. Papers on the following topics would be especially welcomed:

(a) The current 'state of the art' of groupwork.

(b) Papers analysing the significance for the groupwork process of race, gender, class, culture and other social factors.

(c) Papers analysing key group concepts and issues.

(d) Papers from different countries, sharing current developments and theoretical concerns and preoccupations likely to be significant for groupwork practice in Britain and elsewhere.

(e) New sources of research evidence.

(f) Groupwork training and skill development, consultation/supervision.

Length of papers

The normal range will be 2,500-4,000 words, with practice accounts normally not longer than 3,000 words. Exceptionally, longer articles will be accepted and there will be a place for briefer contributions on new developments, responses to previous articles and other material of special interest.

Form of Submission

Articles should be submitted in one of two ways:

i. typed on A4 paper, 3 copies, double-spaced with wide margins

ii. on computer disc. Authors who have prepared their material by word processor are asked to provide a copy of the computer file on disk. Most Macintosh, IBM-PC compatible and Amstrad word processing programs can be read.

References

These should be quoted in the text by giving in brackets the author's name and year of publication. They should then be listed in alphabetical order at the end of the article as follows. *Books* - author's surname, initials, date, title of book, place of publication, publisher's name, page if relevant.

Articles - author's surname, initials, date, title of article, title of journal, volume and number. Only those references which occur in the text should be listed. Where appropriate, additional resources may be listed separately as further reading.

Assessment for publication

Articles submitted will normally be passed to members of the journal's panel of assessors, and decisions as to publication made by the editors in the light of the assessors' comments.

Enquiries

Allan Brown, Dept of Social Work, University of Bristol, 8 Woodland Road, Bristol BS8 1TN. Tel: 0272-303030, ext.853/Nano McCaughan, 12 Barr Beacons, Canonbie Road, London SE23. Tel: 081 699 8438

GROUPWORK

Volume 7 Number 2 1994
Guest Editor: Claire Wintram

SUBSCRIPTION, ADVERTISING AND BUSINESS ENQUIRIES
Should be addressed to the publishers, WHITING & BIRCH LTD, PO Box 872, Forest Hill, London SE23 3HL. TEL: 081-244-2421 (Int'l +4481 244-2421). FAX: 081-244-2448 (Int'l. +4481-244-2448)

SUBSCRIPTION RATES
British Isles £35.00, North America US$80, Elsewhere £45.00
Special reduced rates apply as follows: Individuals to private address:
£19.00 British Isles, North America, US$35 Elsewhere £22.00.
Special reductions for members of AASWG and Groupwork Exchange Network.
Groupwork is published three times a year.

PAYMENT
Should accompany order. Cheque or banker's draft (made payable to WHITING & BIRCH LTD) may be in any convertible currency to the relevant amount. Direct transfer can be made to our Girobank account (no. 5440564). The following credit cards are also accepted: Access/Mastercard, Visa, Diners Club, American Express. Quote card number, expiry date and give cardholder's name and address if different from delivery address.

GROUPWORK is cited in: *Applied Social Sciences Index & Abstracts, Sociological Abstracts, Bibliographie Zeitscriftenliteratur aus allen Gebieten des Wissens, Social Care Update, Social Work Research & Abstracts, Special Educational Needs Abstracts*. and *Studies on Women Abstracts.*

PUBLISHED BY WHITING & BIRCH LTD, LONDON. ISSN 0951-824X
Printed by Antony Rowe Ltd, Chippenham, UK

EDITORIAL

Why a special edition on working with women? This question has been put to me by several women friends and colleagues when I've canvassed them for ideas and articles for this edition. The question brings me face to face with my own commitment to publicising in every available space, the multi-faceted experiences, struggles and triumphs that women survive everyday. It was argued that this edition reinforces the marginalisation of women, that writing about women should take place in the mainstream only - any other approach is capitulation to notions of women as second best, needing special pleading.

I had not a moment's doubt. I believe that writing about (and singing and shouting about) women needs to happen in all spheres, and prefer not to make the distinction between specialist and mainstream: this journal is mainstream, and this edition is mainstream. Everything that women have written about that appears here concerns issues of survival, of facing up to loneliness and fear, uncertainty and poverty, discrimination and violence in their many, many forms. Every article offers hope and support to the women who participated in and facilitated the groups, to all the women reading the journal, and to all the women whose lives those readers touch in their turn. There is pain here, but inspiration too, and constant reminders of the absolute essential need for women only space. Every article validates women's demands and rights for time for ourselves, recognition as full members of the human race, time to share the impact of common experience, time to write and rewrite our own version of these experiences as they happen to us and not to accept other peoples need to pathologise.

This edition is timely. Every era in history offers accounts of womens resistance to oppression, whether on a public or private scale or both. It is vital that there are constant reminders that things are not rosy and bright, that Equal Opportunities legislation has left many womens lives untouched.

This relates to women service users, to women carers, women professionals. There is recognition of the necessary blurring of those boundaries for the group to function properly for all participants. The complexity of relationships where some women have more privileges than others is scrutinised and there is recognition that there are no easy answers. It is vital that this complexity is acknowledged and addressed with no hiding behind statements such as 'we're all the same'. This edition interweaves, graphically and dramatically, the great need for work with women in women-only space, (and the fact that that need does not diminish, despite protestations to the contrary), and the great liberating and educating force that groupwork can be.

At the first European Groupwork Symposium in 1991, Ken Heap spoke with passion about his experiences of groupwork in Scandinavia, about diversity and success. I was inspired by this speech to become involved again with groupwork with women and to make connections with other women doing similar work. I have not looked back for a second and have been saddened, moved and elated at being involved in the changes and blossoming that take place in women's lives.

This edition gives us clear visions of the ways in which some women in Britain and in North America, Black women and white women, Jewish women, women with different physical disabilities, women on their own or in partnerships, are coming together to learn to break down the barriers of their own prejudices and fears, to learn about solidarity and difference, to learn where to take responsibility for dealing with the damaging experiences they have survived, but not to blame themselves or each other for what has happened. Women in these groups show tremendous courage, determination and creativity, demonstrating time and time again the power of collectivity and the way in which the group offers a safe but challenging haven in the midst of an alien environment.

Claire Wintram
Guest Editor

GROUPWORK AND BLACK WOMEN

VIEWING NETWORKS AS GROUPS: BLACK WOMEN MEETING TOGETHER FOR AFFIRMATION AND EMPOWERMENT

MARCIA FRANCIS-SPENCE

This paper comments on the interaction between Black women from various social groups and suggests that groupwork needs to be defined in very broad terms if it is to have any meaning to Black women. Many of their experiences whilst unique to them as a group go unacknowledged, consequently unvalued and therefore unrecorded. My aim here is simply to acknowledge, value and record.

Introduction

This paper is not about an actual groupwork session but rather raises wider groupwork issues for discussion. What I aim to do is offer a personal, reflective (and reflexive) account of the relationship between Black women and groupwork. In so doing, I use a wide interpretation of groupwork. I will look at whether counselling or therapy plays a part in Black women's lives and, again, I will be interpreting counselling and therapy in very wide terms. For the purpose of this paper, Black women in the UK are taken as one with an acknowledgement, but no close analysis of, for example, social class differences. This is because, however successful or powerful Black women are in this society, many still carry an inner longing for affirmation of their worth and for respect, which is habitually denied them. The commonality of this experience gives Black women a shared bond, which in groups and networks may act more powerfully than the differences between them.

The intention in this paper is to raise awareness amongst practitioners to help them to understand not only why Black women can never forget about racism but also why the majority of Black women refuse to be confined by it and how this is achieved. It will consider some of the day-to-day actions that Black women use as a safety valve to combat racism. Racism is alive and well and there is little doubt it is a growing industry. Nevertheless, the chief highlight here will be on empowerment and affirmation, and on reminding readers that - contrary to popular belief - the majority of Black people (and certainly Black women) do not sit around and allow their lives to be confined by racism. Unfortunately, practice accounts and student essays alike too often choose to focus on the negative aspects of being Black, portraying Black people as passive dependent victims who are merely done to and take no control over their own lives. This paper will attempt to provide a counter-balance to this perspective.

Why groupwork is important to Black women

Usually when groupwork is mentioned, the tendency is to view it in relation to clients and practitioners. Rarely do we think of it in terms of professional groups or individuals who simply want support. Black practitioners have only fairly recently started to become involved in groupwork and my experience as a practitioner has been that Black women (as are Black people generally) are reluctant to become involved in 'organised' groupwork with practitioners. However, it is not unusual to see groups of Black women talking regularly together and offering support to each other, be they social work/probation clients, unemployed women, women in mundane jobs, or professional women.

I would argue that groupwork is of utmost importance to Black women, in particular Black women who are raising children alone or undertaking other caring roles. This usually results in women adopting dual roles, which entails juggling caring responsibilities and full-time employment as well as, in some cases, part-time study as they try to provide a better future for themselves and their dependents. This inevitably leaves very little spare time and can lead to isolation. The double *day* has, however, long been an established feature of Black women's working life (Bryan et al., 1985, p.18). Many Black women it would appear exist by recreating the networks which have been a feature of the history of their families in Africa, the Caribbean and Asia.

According to Bell hooks, the vast majority of Black women in this society receive substantial care from other Black women, and she states that she is not talking about only lesbian women (hooks, 1992, p.42). Black women tend not to have a history of seeking therapy or counselling, in the formal sense, but I would argue that they do receive therapy and counselling through their interaction with other Black women.

This therapy can take several forms, for example, the grooming of hair is an important feature of Black women's lives. Many Black women choose to wear their hair in plaits - sitting for 8 or 9 hours whilst this is done is not unusual. For those who choose chemically-treated styles, it still takes about half this time. These hours for the majority represent the only space they have that is totally theirs and it is a time when they have the opportunity to discuss issues with other Black women. These issues could be to do with their children, partners, politics, aspirations, parents, their health problems - in fact, anything. More recently an increasing number of Black women have become economically independent and therefore reached a position whereby they have the luxury of acting on the recognition that stress is a danger to their lives. My experience has been that many women now take advantage of leisure centres, enjoying for example Turkish baths or saunas on weekends or evenings and engaging in similar discussion to that at the hairdressers. These women would be appalled if anyone tried to suggest that they were in effect participating in groupwork.

Black women have long recognised the damage that stress does to their lives. To be in a position whereby you are able to do anything about the pressures in your life is quite a privilege for the majority of women even more so for Black women. The pressure remains the same be they part of the so-called underclass or part of a more economically advantaged group. As we look towards the professions, we see Black women making strides, in spite of the barriers, so much so that reports abound of how they are leaving Black men behind and how White women feel threatened by their rapid progress. The presence of stress is not a new phenomenon to Black women's lives but for a long time they did not have the history of recognising or naming it as affecting their lives. 'Getting on', however, does not reduce the stress suffered by Black women; in fact it can be argued that the stress and isolation is increased the higher up the ladder they climb. In many cases this is the result of trying to straddle two worlds.

To cope with stress and isolation, Black women, in particular those who move from their community, often draw on the support of other Black women. For professional women the 'phone often becomes a life-line resulting in enormous bills as they reach out to other Black women for support. This support provides them with a safety-valve by enabling them to air and discuss issues they cannot share with others in the arena they are working in.

Black women's groups as a source of empowerment

'... self empowerment is the most deeply political work there is, and the most difficult' (Lorde 1984, p.170). Audre Lorde therefore advocates that Black women should seek empowerment. The majority of Black women are in agreement and are actually engaged in doing just that. Black women's 'groups' can and do provide an opportunity for empowerment, enabling participants to look at their situation from their own perspective and as a result discover strategies to empower each other to improve their situation. We live in a world that does not respect people who do not fight for what is rightfully theirs. Black women's survival in a hostile environment has been a result of such a fight. Black women need to continue to use the opportunities to learn about and share their different experiences, in effect to drop the outer layer and get to the core of themselves.

We cannot make radical interventions that will fundamentally alter our situation unless we do this. We do, however, need the support of each other. It is when we get together as Black women that the other oppressions affecting us are addressed, because usually we are confined to responding only to racism. A feature of Black women's groups is that they allow women to articulate the differences between women, for example by age, class and sexual identity. When Black women come together, either by letters, the 'phone, or face to face, that is when we begin to acknowledge the other oppressions which are so much a feature of our lives. For example, homophobia, which is endemic in wider society, also has roots in the Black community, thus hindering lesbian women from being frank and open about their lives. The plight of elders is also a cause of concern for Black women. A large number of Black elders have arrived at retirement with the unfulfilled dream of returning 'home', having never had enough disposable income to make it financially viable for them to do so. Children are also a source of concern, in particular the way their future is blighted by the unfair treatment many of them receive in school. There are concerns as to the numbers being forced into under-achievement while others are absenting themselves from the employment market, perceiving their prospects as so dire they see little point in trying. They see failure as inevitable and try to cushion themselves from the humiliation of rejection by opting out altogether. It appears the only time these issues can be discussed constructively is when Black women come together.

Black women are starting to transform the images of Blackness;

the ways of looking at themselves, of being seen. Many Black women are busy trying to ensure that a truer image of Black womanhood is presented to society. There are, however, many barriers. Even those of us who are committed - who feel we have decolonised our minds - often find it hard to speak our experiences. Indeed '... the more painful the issues we confront the greater our inarticulateness' (hooks, 1992, p.2). Fighting against white culture which does not accept the unique experiences of Black women and continues to impose its standards and values, ensures that what we really want only emerges when we get into groups. We are only able to articulate this when we come together in groups.

Meeting and coming together in whatever way is a great source of support; being there for each other when things get difficult or appear impossible as they invariably do. It is not uncommon to see Black women nurturing each other, providing encouragement to continue the struggle, reminding each other to hold on to their dreams and goals.

When I was offered my current job, I was overwhelmed with apprehension about the area I was entering but friends told me 'don't worry, we want you to go; in fact we need you to go and we will provide you with the necessary support to enable you to at least give it a try'. At the time I was sceptical and could not see how they could give me the support I was convinced I would require given that I was going so far. To their credit, I can honestly say that they have kept their promise. It is that support, in the shape of 'phone calls, letters, cards, visits, which has kept me going and two years later still keeps me going. I know my situation is far from unique. I, as well as my friends, provide the same support for others; this support is not confined to a national basis but works equally well on an international level.

As stated earlier, it is my belief that groupwork is part of many Black women's culture. The interaction they have is, however, not called or viewed as groupwork, but only by understanding this history of interaction can practitioners understand how to approach groupwork with Black women. Like so many other aspects of life in the Black communities, for example volunteering, we do it without necessarily putting a name to it. One reason for this is that, often, what we bring is not seen as valuable, we abandon it and try to adopt the more formal style familiar to this society rather than adapt what we bring to fit in with and complement what is already present. An analogy can be drawn here with Black social work trainees. Social work programmes have for some time recognised the need to ensure the barriers are removed to enable Black students to take up training. However, as there is little value placed on what they bring they are usually required to discard the values and beliefs they hold and instead adopt what is in effect a Eurocentric perspective, which leaves them in a situation where they are unable to draw on their inner resources and areas of greatest strength.

Implications for practice

Practitioners must question not only their own practice but also that of their departments if they are to recognise the importance of Black people coming together. The experience of living in a predominantly white society has a detrimental effect on most Black women's lives, both at the personal and professional levels. Their thoughts and ideas are more likely to be dismissed than acknowledged. In order to redress this, practitioners must listen to Black women and enable them to define their experience. Recognition should be given to the fact that Black women are not just consumers of services. Dominant culture does not allow for individuality between Black women and fails to recognise that they do not all have the same needs. Differences need to be acknowledged but must not be used to divide us.

If we accept that talking about our problems can lead to strategies for curing them, and that it is important that those listening understand, then we must appreciate that Black women need the opportunity to talk to each other. This talking together is necessary for well-being and becomes more so for those caught up in the system as clients of social services departments, the criminal justice system, or mental health services. These women often have multiple issues impinging on their lives - issues which they cannot easily explain - and the opportunity to share with each other by drawing from each other's experience could help to make sense of it all.

The opportunity for creative dialogue is already available for many groups: for example within the probation service it is not unusual for there to be various groups meeting, for example young offenders, and groups for women offenders. Given that Black people are the ones denied power, however, it is paramount that they are given space to examine their realities which includes naming their pain, expressing their grief as well as asserting their strength - in a forum where understanding and consequently healing can begin to take place. Practitioners often underestimate the impact of racism and how, for example, it inhibits Black and white women from sharing fully in groupwork together. The nature of racism ensures skin colour has an overwhelming impact on both Black and white people. It is not unusual to witness the latter benefiting, while for the former the experience is a painful one as they attempt to share with individuals who are afraid to witness their pain. As a result, Black women in these groups tend to remain silent.

Support does not necessarily have to come from someone of the same gender or race. Black and white women can and do provide and offer support to each other. This happens all the time and, living in a society where they are outnumbered, Black women could not continue to function adequately without also having some support from white women. It can, however, be more meaningful, and especially affirming for individuals to share with someone who is like them. After all, racism and sexism hurt.

Practitioners therefore need to be aware of these factors and to act on them when working with Black women. In the probation service, for example, consideration needs to be given as to whether one-to-one work is always the most appropriate method or whether joint groupwork with Black and white women is necessarily the best way to work on female offending behaviour. Practitioners may benefit from re-examining the way they approach their work. This, in turn, may result in their looking service-wide and being prepared to co-ordinate groups for Black women offenders addressing a wide range of issues if they are to arrive at the root of their offending. In the mental health field, if Black women have been diagnosed as mentally ill, again they should have the opportunity to come together to discuss their problems, which could lead them to examine their route to their present situation and develop strategies to deal with the root of their problems.

What hinders groupwork with Black and white women from developing and being productive for both sets of participants is usually the issues being discussed. Some of the issues may appear identical but their impact, and consequently the importance placed on them differs. Black women have different experiences and thus interpret situations differently. For many of them their lives are ingrained with stress for reasons which may have additional and more complex causes to them than that experienced by white women.

Conclusion

Above all, we should never underestimate the stress that is generated by living in a society that does not appreciate you, that tells you in so many ways that you are unimportant, that you are not valued, that you do not have a stake here - implying over and over again that it does not matter where or how you live or how your children are brought up. The stress of being denied the opportunity to achieve your potential can lead directly to an absorption of the hostility and of the racist values on which it is grounded. Bell hooks states that 'Militancy is an alternative to madness. And many of us are daily entering the realm of the insane' (hooks, 1992, p.6). In an attempt to avoid the latter, Black women *are* reasserting themselves in a myriad of hidden groups and networks.

References

Bryan, B., Dadzie, S. and Scafe, S. (1985) *The Heart of the Race: Black Women's Lives in Britain*. London: Virago Press.

hooks, B, (1992) *Black Looks: Race and Representation*. London: Turnaround.

hooks, B. (1993) *Sisters of the Yam: Black Women and Self-Recovery*. London: Turnaround.

Lorde, A. (1984) *Sister Outsider*. The Crossing Press. Feminist Series.

STAYING ALIVE IN DIFFICULT TIMES: THE EXPERIENCE OF GROUPWORK WITH MOTHERS OF CHILDREN WHO HAVE BEEN SEXUALLY ABUSED

DEB DOBBIN AND SARAH EVANS

This article is about the rewards and excitement of working with mothers of children who have been sexually abused, despite the pain and devastation of the content of discussion. The work took place because of perceived need of the women within a social work context. The authors of the article also consider how women workers are able to enter into different relationships with service-users within this type of groupwork, because of shared experiences.

This article is ostensibly about an experience of groupwork with mothers of children who had been sexually abused. In fact it is about the rewards and excitement of that work despite the pain and devastation of the content. The work took place within the context of a local authority social services department. It arose out of social work contact with these and other mothers, as well as experience of groupwork with their daughters and other abused adolescents. The article will also explore ways in which this sort of work allows for some shifting of barriers between women who are clients and their social workers, and offers possibilities for different relationships between them based on shared experience.

In a women's group in whatever setting, group members have readily to hand two sorts of shared experience: global - that of being a woman in a society in which functions, expectations and interactions are still largely defined by gender; and specific - the experience of the group. These are still to hand in a social work group setting provided the workers are all women and provided they can walk the line between openness and an acknowledgement of common experience without the kind of self disclosure which impinges on group members and effectively steals their time.

The two groups on which this is based were primarily intended for women whose children were abused within the family: in practice this meant the woman's partner in almost every referral, although somctimes the partner was no longer current and in one he was still

Groupwork Vol. 7(2), 1994, pp.117-124

prospective. In some cases the abusing partner was the child's natural father, in others not. The groups were focused on women in this situation as a response to needs observed, as well as an understanding that a woman who comes to believe that her child has been sexually abused by her partner, or another trusted person, is likely to experience an emotional process similar to a grief cycle, marked by disorientation, internal conflict, intensity of emotion, and the need to work towards a new reality. The groupworkers wanted to offer help in this process by providing an opportunity for sharing experiences and for thinking together about what had happened. It was hoped to reduce the women's sense of isolation and to help in developing ideas for managing the inherent debris of the abuse, both external and internal. The general focus of each group was to support and sustain the women, not only as parents but also as individuals in relation to their partners, their family of origin, their friends and themselves.

The women who chose to join brought with them a variety of circumstances and both groups reflected this. They both included women who were themselves survivors of abuse and those who were not; and women whose children had suffered abuse through an incident of inappropriate touching as well as those whose children had been terrorised and traumatised over a long period of time. One group covered a wide age range. In the other everyone was on benefit except one person who was very comfortably off. The most potentially difficult situation seemed to lie in the group where one woman was still living with the abusive partner, but she solved this by leaving him during the life of the group. In the event none of these issues became as divisive as might have been expected. Hierarchies did not seem to develop along any of these dimensions.

Following the pattern established in previous groups for young women, the first mothers group met weekly for six months. It quickly became clear, however, that this was too short a time and the second group met weekly for almost a year. Meetings were held for two hours, in the morning, and transport and creche facilities were provided. The first group met in a youth and community centre; the second, much more successfully, in a family centre on a morning on which the centre was otherwise closed. (It was fortunate that the centre was only open four days a week. It would have been very hard to maintain full confidentiality and protect the women from feelings of exposure and intrusion had it been open while the group was meeting).

The timing of the group made it difficult for women who were working to join. There were women working night shifts who would stay up for the group meetings, but women with daytime jobs found it impossible to come. Some other women, who were referred, chose not to join, saying they were worried about confidentiality, or they wanted to think less, rather than more, about what had happened. At least one woman who had originally been interested decided not to join the group in the end: while waiting for it to begin she had moved from belief in her child to a stance of disbelief in order to retain the relationship with her partner - an indication, perhaps of how isolated and unsupported she felt. Another woman came to two meetings but had to leave because the idea of the group was too upsetting to her adolescent daughter: she felt too exposed.

It was intended to start each group with about eight members, expecting that the group would eventually number six or so. The first group fulfilled this but the second, for various reasons, was smaller. (The numbers were supplemented, however, by one member's baby who came at 3 days old and then was present at every session until the group ended when she was six months. She was used by all as comfort and reward as well as distraction and, occasionally, shield). There were three group leaders, all also women - a strongly-held policy. All three were present for important events in the life of the group but other meetings were generally attended by only two (rotating). While recognising that this was not ideal in term of group identity, it made the group both possible in terms of personal commitment over a long period of time, and invincible against the demands of a busy social services department on its staff. The three leaders talked with each other after each session, meeting frequently for planning and regularly for supervision. It was hard to establish precisely how the rotation affected the process. The members of both groups appeared to make very little differentiation between the three workers and there were no discernible attempts to divide them.

Preparation was taken very seriously. One of the group leaders visited all the women who had been referred. This was a deliberate policy to make sure that each one received the same information and impression of how the group was likely to run. She talked with them about the purpose of the group, practical arrangements and issues such as confidentiality. She hoped that the women she visited would talk to her about what had happened and what particular needs they would hope the group would meet. Once all the visits had been completed and definite arrangements could be made, she wrote to all the women confirming the plans and giving details of the first meeting in particular. Anticipating that that meeting would be an ordeal, the letters were intended to be as clear, informative and reassuring as possible.

Group meetings were structured. They began with coffee, biscuits and fruit, and - always - cigarettes. On a birthday there would be cake with cards and singing. Once everyone was settled, there would be a collective effort to remember the last session in some detail and to write it in the diary. Then women would take it in turns to tell the rest of the group how their week had been. This became an important ritual, particularly for the women who felt most isolated and lonely. The belief that their partner was a perpetrator had an especially isolating effect on some of the women: it meant not only the loss of their partner and his extended family, but also the loss of some of their own extended family with 'knock on' effects on friendship networks. Some of the women had no one outside the group to tell about the details of their lives. Yet, given their circumstances, it was not unusual for them to face dramatic and far reaching events on a day to day basis: a situation which would be rendered much more difficult with no opportunity for recounting events or getting support and feedback.

In addition, some of the women were dealing with life effectively on their own for the first time. They often reported problems in their dealings with schools, or solicitors and the court process, or housing departments, or the Department of Social Security. The collective experience of the group in these matters was often extensive and provided considerable help and support.

The telling of the tales also provided an opportunity for women to grasp and involve themselves in one another's lives. They would question each other, remember situations from week to week, and offer advice, experience, solutions, thoughts and ideas. Some members of each group found it hard to end their turn and either simply continued talking or began to involve themselves intrusively in other people's turns. This was an issue which both groups had to address as well as the more general one of this exercise spilling over beyond its allotted time. Group leaders found it hard to cut off individual women whom they perceived as desperately needing the time. Other women became irritated by their talkative neighbours and angry with group leaders for allowing the boundaries to slip. At the same time the collective mood in each group was generally reluctant to bring the exercise to a close because it was often less painful than other issues on which the group might be working.

The end of 'How-was-your-week?' was marked by more coffee,

followed by some work on a particular issue. While the workers had some ideas in mind at the beginning, most of the issues, or at least the timetabling of them, were generated through the group's own material. It was intended from the beginning however that the first six weeks or so would be primarily focused on women introducing themselves to each other and getting experience of a group setting. It was anticipated that there might be a certain amount of coming and going during that period. Once it was over, the groups became closed as they began to address the question of women telling their own stories about what had happened in their family. Each group developed its own process for this, with the group leaders attending to the women who found it hard to wait until collectively the time seemed right.

Once this was completed each group moved into the main phase of work. The after coffee session was used to explore different issues using group members experience. Occasionally some external material was added by the group leaders but their main task for these discussions was commenting on the process and trying to reflect back the experience of the group as a whole.

Given the nature of the group the content of these sessions was predictable. They included:

1. Guilt and responsibility. Most women initially felt globally guilty. The group spent several weeks looking at the issue of responsibility for the abuse in each case, within the frame of expectations of parenthood in general, motherhood in particular.
2. Issues around the process of disclosure and investigation; how the women felt about it; the significance of whom the child initially told; and the meaning and impact of what may have been years of silence.
3. Ideas about parenting; experience of being parented; memories of childhood; threads of experience from mother to self to daughter.
4. Couple relationships; why they chose their partners; what hopes they had of the relationship; how did the system work; where was the power located and what held it there; what did the loss mean; what might be the impact on current or future relationships.
5. Children; the effect not only on the specifically abused child or children but on their siblings; ideas both about surviving and managing their behaviour, and about helping them to recover.

6. Each woman's personal self protective strategies and ways of filtering the impact of the external world.

Material added by the workers included information about the effects of stress; thoughts on assertiveness as a helpful strategy; current ideas about abusive behaviour; and some research findings about sexual abuse. Some of this seemed more helpful to the groups than others. Ideas about assertiveness, for example, were never accepted in either group: women preferred to think of ways of being more successfully aggressive! On the other hand ideas about why and how abusing men do it were seen as extremely interesting. The 'Gracewell Model' of the cycle of abusive behaviour, for example, seemed to help group members to redefine their own responsibility for what had happened in a less global and more selective way. Similarly, research data on the importance of belief and support by mothers in terms of recovery and healing of children served to underline their positive significance as carers and healers, hopefully denting the pervasive notion of failure.

The final phase of each group was obviously about ending. Women talked about their previous experience of endings: what the group had meant to them and what its loss might mean; how they would remember the group; and what support networks could be put in place for them in the future. Ending seemed to be very difficult for everybody.

During the life of the group women talked about themselves as daughters, partners, mothers, sisters, friends. They described guilt, anger, loss and betrayal - all of those were acted out in the group context at some time. Many of them cried many times; all of them laughed and laughed, sometimes until they cried. The humour was rich, raucous and sometimes very very funny.

There were a number of threads which served to bond group members and workers together. One was undoubtedly humour. Another was the common experience of being a woman as mentioned earlier. A third, in the one group in which she appeared, was the baby. Fourthly were the stories: about childbirth, about Mothers Days and Christmases, about celebrations and successes. Interestingly, the important stories for this purpose were the ones about the richness of women's experience, not about victimisation. It was as if a group established through trauma and feelings of isolation and powerlessness was able to find within itself the resourcefulness and strength with which to make a positive bond, not an excluding and hostile one.

Another crucial factor in this was the amount of time the group spent together and the regularity of meetings which became a part of everyone's weekly routine. Relationships could develop out of the details of lives: things could be remembered, checked in a way that helped the women feel held in mind. If someone mentioned a dental appointment, for example, at one session, they were likely to be asked the next week how it had gone. That knowledge would be applied to future appointments with the dentist or someone similar. It is a style more characteristic of neighbours and friends than can usually occur between workers and their clients. Yet it did not involve any blurring or denial of professional boundaries but simply allowed the workers to use another aspect of themselves. It was important in this that they remained focused on the task in hand and resisted any attempt on the part of the group to achieve equality or unification against the outside world. Similarly, it was crucial that the workers' experiences were used as a commentary on the group members' experiences, not used in their own right. Time became a very precious commodity and much of the group process was acted out around the issue of equal time (and attention).

The workers were constantly reminded of the isolation of some of the women, their lack of self esteem, and the importance of the group in providing positive experiences. It had originally been intended to end every session with a ritual exercise asking each woman to make a positive statement about some aspects of themselves or their functioning. This proved impossible: the women could not do it. Unlike their adolescent daughters in previous groups who had managed it very well. But as it became clear, while the girls had all had someone to take care of them, many of the women had no one. Hence attendance at the group was very high, and workers driving to pick up women and their children found them waiting at the garden gate.

One of the difficulties inherent in providing something which goes even a little way towards acknowledging and meeting such a need lies in its ending. These groups were not structured in such a way as to prepare for a self help element at the end. Both groups considered continuing on an informal basis but neither was able to sustain this. It seemed that the women who were the most interested were the ones who were the most needy: the others were perhaps frightened of being overwhelmed.

It was clear from the group members' attitudes at the end and from their considered opinions which were sought later, that they had enjoyed and valued the groups and found them helpful. Among those women with whom workers are still in contact, references to group discussions are frequent and surprising connections are sometimes made. The workers, too, regretted the endings and find themselves also using the groups as a reference point. As well as working in what felt like a genuine partnership with women who were clients, the groups also offered a rare opportunity for joint work with colleagues, and both permitted and demanded measured time for planning and reflection.

A number of the women had rather global hopes for what the group might be able to do for them: 'I want to feel better' was a commonly expressed aim. Similarly it was hard for the workers not to have global wishes about helping women to achieve more control over their lives, and feel less powerless and hopeless in general. Clearly the group could not change circumstances or hope to effect very much in terms of women's ongoing relationships in the external world. But it could offer women the opportunity to be less alone for a brief period of time and maybe to progress from that.

Given the feelings of emptiness and deadness described in the group, an experience of shared understanding may have been extremely helpful. It may even be that being with people who could be warm and attentive to each other and who could also laugh and cry together helped women in very difficult times to sustain the capacity to feel and be alive.

A TIME FOR WOMEN:

AN ACCOUNT OF A GROUP FOR WOMEN ON AN OUT OF CITY HOUSING DEVELOPMENT IN LEICESTER

CLAIRE WINTRAM, KERRY CHAMBERLAIN, MARLENE KUHN AND JO SMITH

This article is an account by three participants and the facilitator of a support group for women. The group was initially established as an adult education class. The article demonstrates how feminist principles provided the framework for mutual respect and liking to flourish. There was considerable time given to establishing ground rules and to recognising and valuing difference. These differences between participants, of physical ability, marital status, age, educational background, parenthood, experience, became the clear beginnings of voyages of both self discovery and greater knowledge and understanding of each other.

In January 1993, I received a call from a local community worker. She asked if I could facilitate a group for women on a Wednesday morning for eight weeks, starting the following week. There was some money left for creche expenses, to be spent before the end of the financial year. I agreed to six sessions, partly because of other commitments, but also because of concern about adequate time for advertising. My participation as facilitator was to be funded by one of the local WEA (Workers' Educational Association) branches, with whom I had been working mainly in the area of women's issues. The community worker had seen publicity advertising other courses I had taught on women and health, and had thought that something similar would be worth doing in this part of town.

From such rushed beginnings, and certainly from a position where I felt less in control of the planning and organisation than is usually the case, a group of tremendous strength and solidarity has grown up. It is the only group in that particular housing development for women that is not in some way connected with being a mother. It has attracted one woman who does not have childcare responsibilities and another who is a step-parent, and both are women with physical disabilities.

Groupwork Vol. 7(2), 1994, pp.125-135

There was very little time for advertising and no time or money to translate the publicity into any of the main Asian languages spoken in Leicester. The class, as it was initially designated (before its official recognition as a support group), is held in the community wing of a local primary school. Every child was given a leaflet to take home for their mother and/or other adult women in the household. This did not prove a very effective means of attracting members - posters put up in the places where women go served the purpose better.

That first term, the class/group met for six one and a half hour sessions. At the end of this time it was obvious that all the women wanted to continue meeting. Subsequently, there have been terms of eight, ten, and eight sessions, each session now lasting two hours. Participants in the group have come and gone. However, three women have been there from the start, and the strength of their views and feelings form a major part of this article. Every woman who has participated has spoken with commitment and conviction of the solidarity she has felt and the learning she has experienced.

The group has been fortunate in having the support and financial backing from the WEA tutor/organiser who has appreciated the need for such a group to continue functioning, and who has seen it as a means of engaging in outreach work with other women living on this housing development. We agreed with the tutor/organiser that after the first few sessions, there wasn't a syllabus as such, as each term and indeed, each week, women themselves would raise the most pressing issues for discussion. There has been money to fund creche workers (although this has had to be renegotiated every term), money to pay transport costs for women needing a lift, and money to subsidise attendance for those women on low income or state benefit.

The housing development is a mixture of council owned, owner occupied and housing association properties. There are some purpose built bungalows and flats for people with disabilities. One of the main characteristics of the place is its isolation. Bus services to town are infrequent. There is a shopping centre now, but for years there was nothing but a mobile shop. Planning, as the development was being built from about 18 years ago, seems to have conspired to make women's lives as difficult as possible. Although there is no doubt that things have improved, dependence on the private car is heavy, with the need for money that this involves as well as being able to drive. The development is marked also by having the highest incidence of racist assaults in the whole of Leicestershire.

The existence of this women's group and the emergence of it as a vital support system has brought about change on many levels. There is change evident in women's attitudes towards themselves, as increasing self awareness and self esteem become apparent; there is change in women's attitudes towards each other as the differences between women with varying physical abilities, from different races, from different cultures, different religions, are openly expressed, examined and valued; there has been change in the role of the facilitator, taking a much lower profile and not feeling the need to be 'running a class'; there has been change too in the way the employing organisation (the WEA) has seen the role and nature of the group, recognising from district secretary downwards that it is serving a vital purpose and offering a unique service to women. In this way, education indeed does become self-discovery.

At the first meeting, twelve women turned up. Two knew each other slightly already and some were able to identify each other by working out who knew whose children. I had been more apprehensive than usual at the outset of this group because of the lack of time for planning and because I had not had much involvement in the publicity. I was concerned that more was being offered than could possibly happen. My apprehensions were totally unfounded and the class has established itself formally as a group, going from strength to strength, with a visit from the tutor/organiser to confirm this. This is not necessarily reflected in numbers - this most recent term, there were five regular participants in the group. However, most of those who have left have done so for positive reasons. One African Caribbean woman left because she wanted to spend more time exploring her own cultural roots. Her ambition was to work eventually with other young Black women on their identity and she felt that the group had given her the space to think about doing this; another woman left because she wanted to put more energy into her church activities; another woman left because participation in the group had enabled her to see that she and her husband needed specialist counselling if their marriage was to survive.

The community wing we used was *almost* private. Almost because occasionally, children would walk through on their way to the language support worker. Sometimes there was a brief distraction from a child of one of the women waving through the doorway 'There's my mum!', usually hastily despatched. We had comfortable chairs, plenty of space, a kitchenette, a creche building two minutes walk away and a completely accessible room. As two of the women use wheelchairs as mobility aids, this and the proximity of the disabled person's toilet were essential. The women made their own way to the meetings, either on foot, by car, or in the case of one of them, with a lift from me.

We drew up groundrules at the beginning of the meetings, and these were re-examined and amended as necessary at the beginning of every term. These included confidentiality - essential in a part of town where even if women didn't know each other at the outset, there would almost inevitably be some mutual acquaintance discovered; not making assumptions about each other - this was crucial because although the group was all women, there were many differences within it and it was stressed repeatedly that assumptions can never be made, our reaction to experiences may well differ greatly and we can only speak for ourselves; we agreed to respect these differences between us even if we did not agree with what another woman was saying or with things she said she had done; we agreed that every woman had the right to participate in discussion in her own way - if she chose to remain silent that would not be seen as opting out, that we would ensure that each woman had the chance to speak each week and particularly if there was something pressing that she needed support in sorting out; we agreed to challenge each other (including the facilitator) on issues of oppression, to challenge language and ideas that are racist, sexist, homophobic, ageist, disablist and that oppress people with mental distress. These groundrules served their purpose time and time again, in times of conflict and disagreement, in times of distress, at times when an individual woman might feel that she didn't have the right to take up group time, or that she might be going to shock others with what she needed to say.

The initial plan (based on the work I had done for the WEA elsewhere in the city), was to include: looking at the expectations there are on us as women and what our wants for ourselves are, a look at the discrepancies between these, where these come from and who benefits from the discrepancies; a look at family relationships and what is good and what is problematic; a look at what gets in the way of women promoting positive health for ourselves and the connections between physical and spiritual well-being.

We did do the first exercise, but from there, things took off in their own direction. Over the fifteen months that the group has been meeting with me as facilitator (the women are continuing to meet this term - Summer 1994 - taking it in turns to facilitate), issues discussed have included: death and dying and the fears surrounding this; breast cancer and promoting positive breast health; smoking and its health implications for women; racism and the way it affects Black women's lives; the ways in which white women have learned racism and how to challenge this; anti-semitism and its impact; dealing with stepchildren and the joys and problems of 'reconstituted' families; sexual behaviour and women's relationships with men; sexual preference; attitudes to women with disabilities and sex; thrush; pre-menstrual syndrome; HRT; diet and nutrition and the part they play in women's health; relaxation; assertiveness; our own upbringing and the differences between us; bringing up our sons and daughters to lead better, less oppressed and oppressive lives than we have done; challenging violent and dismissive partners; the aspirations we might have had for ourselves, the ways these have or have not been met and what power we still have to change any of this; engaging in paid work or further education or not - the possibilities for women - and the impact on family life of doing so; finding ways of saying what we want so that if we do enter new relationships, we don't make the same mistakes as last time; comedy and humour and how we'd die without laughing (but not die laughing!); language and the way it's used to put women down - we looked at this particularly in relation to body image, racism and issues around disability, - this gave us ample scope to think about the ways in which the language we use affects our thought processes and vice versa and what can we do to break out of entrenched patterns; the things that women have given up because of developing heterosexual relationships and having children; relationships outside marriage; violence within the home and ways of surviving and if possible, confronting this; women's own violence, recognising this and where it might come from; sexual violence and finding safe ways of confronting this; finding out about local resources to provide women some support; a visit from a politics student to find out about women's attitudes to women in politics; living as a woman with disability - an enormous amount of discussion has taken place around this issue with much learning happening on all sides.

The most moving aspects of the group have been women's willingness to share very personal and painful information with each other, to listen, to offer support and where appropriate, advice. Women have helped each other through times of sustained violence in their relationships, or in dealing with a single and completely unprecedented violent event. They have kept in touch with each other between weekly sessions to check on safety, and contact has been maintained throughout the school holidays. Women have never trivialised each other's experiences but have always listened with respect and concentration, drawing out what each woman is trying to say. There has been constant co-facilitation, although it was never set up in that way. Women have acknowledged differences between them and have been honest about fears at the outset that these differences might be barriers - e.g. one woman was worried that the two participants with disabilities might be angry at her ability to walk and resent her presence - we looked at this in terms of her own fear and what this stemmed from.

Women have sought to use their own experience to give each other ideas about what to do next, for example, when suffering violence from a partner, or when a child has been shoplifting - but without ever dictating, rather suggesting, and giving the other woman the chance to try things out in her own way. There has always been concern the following week to check up on whether this advice was of any value and if so, in what way.

No-one was ever judged for her actions. There was certainly conflict, particularly in the areas of whether it's OK to smoke or not, whether women should be physically violent, whether women should show anger or is this against biblical principles?. This was acknowledged and confronted with an acceptance that the different standpoints would remain.

Women also showed each other tremendous respect in not being shocked or horrified at events that were described. This does not mean that they were not shocked by things that had happened to their co-participants, but that they did not make it difficult for each other to carry on with descriptions of medical intervention, sexual assault, physical brutality, by expressing disgust or unwillingness to listen. Over time, women tested out what it was safe or not safe to say, and with one woman, it took a year to start talking about events that were happening between her and her husband and which were clearly causing her immense distress. Every time she had tried to talk about them previously, she felt that others would be shocked and not want to hear, but she was given constant reassurance that she had the right to say what was on her mind. As a consequence, she was able to confront her husband about certain things with results far better than she had expected. This capacity to listen to and respect other women's pain and distress and give it value is one of the major strengths of the group.

What follow are statements from the three members of the group who have participated since the beginning. These statements demonstrate the value of the group with the greatest clarity and immediacy.

J's statement

I first heard about the 'women's group' in our area from a disabled friend of mine. But why did I join, when as a disabled woman most of my friends, social life and interests are linked with the disability movement and to spreading the philosophy of that movement? What could I gain or indeed contribute that would be of value to a group of non-disabled women?

The answer to the first question, why did I join (particularly as it is so far removed from my usual sphere of interests), has two parts - firstly, my friend said how interesting and enjoyable she found it and thought I would too. She was right, I really look forward to our Wednesday morning meeting.

Secondly, in spite of my involvement with the philosophy of full integration and equal citizenship for disabled people, it just had not occurred to me to join a non-disabled group/activity! I was quite shocked by the admittance of self-inflicted segregation (even though it was not consciously done) and was forced to ask myself why this was so. Was it simply that I had been so involved with disability issues that there had not been time, or was it something deeper? Could it be that after all the years I've been disabled, I still feel only equal amongst other disabled people? The thought that this might be true was quite disturbing as I thought I had laid that particular ghost to rest years ago.

In answer to the second question, what could I gain or contribute to the group? Well, since joining the 'women's group' I have gained a great deal of insight into many facets of the lives of non-disabled women as well as into my own life, but perhaps more importantly, insights into the many forms of oppression that women face.

As a disabled woman I am well aware of every type of discrimination and oppression that disabled people face every day of their lives. Earlier I spoke of the doubts which arose about my feelings of equality among non-disabled women. Well the answer is yes, I do feel equal, because I have learned from the 'women's group' that the lives of many non-disabled women are paralysed by various forms of blatant and subtle discrimination and oppression. It's a paralysis that prevents them from developing or discovering their talents or achieving their full potential, in much the same way that some disabled people are prevented.

I now know that my disability liberated me from some of the discrimination, oppression or pressure of the social conventions which some women had to face in their youth. For example, to leave school, get a job, wear the right fashion, be seen in the right clubs/discos, have a boyfriend, peer pressure about sex, getting married, children etc. Because society did/does not expect me as a disabled woman to desire or need these things, particularly sex, marriage or children, I was free to stretch myself intellectually. This meant further education, and pursuing whatever interested me, travelling and gathering a wide circle of friends, opportunities I don't think I would have had if I had not been disabled, opportunities some women in the group certainly did not have.

The other important insight I have gained from the group is about the sheer tenacity of women, their courage, their deep loyalty (often given to undeserving partners), their sense of humour and ability to make the best of bad situations, their enthusiasm, but most of all their hope for a better future whether it be for the short term or the long. Lastly but by no means least, I have gained a great sense of pride and belonging to the sisterhood of women, something I'd never felt before I joined the 'women's group'.

But what do I contribute to the group? I have to say in all honesty that I feel I gain very much more than I give, but I hope (along with my disabled friend) I have given the group a better understanding of what it is like to be disabled, and have shown them our lives have just as many similarities as differences. But most of all I hope that I give to them the same respect, support, encouragement, friendship and pleasure in belonging to the 'women's group' as they give to me.

M's statement

Why do I enjoy my two hours in the women's group? It means two hours away from any commitment, be that inside or outside my home, two hours away from interruptions, telephones and doorbells.

I feel comfortable in the surroundings. Parking and access are fairly easy, the toilet facilities are good and on ground level. These points are very important for someone with a disability.

We are always welcomed with a cup of tea which is much needed after the morning rush.

When we start our talk session it's good to express how you feel, whether the topic concerns you personally or is something you feel a strong commitment or empathy about.

A friendship and bond grows with the members and the co-ordinator of the group and not only can you express your own feelings and ideas, it's good to listen to everyone else, remembering that not everyone's opinions are the same.

One last and most important point is the code of confidentiality, that is everything said inside the four walls is not repeated out of them.

K's statement

Having been at home tending to my children, pets, husband, garden and household chores for the past ten years, I thought it was time to do something for me. I saw the Women's Group advertised at our local school and decided that although I wasn't quite sure what it was all about, I'd take the plunge!

I must admit I was rather nervous the first time I attended as I had been suffering from anxiety and depression for quite some time and had lost most of my confidence in the process. I had become agoraphobic - to be quite honest, had the group required me to travel any further than the local school, I don't think I would ever have made it. But am I glad I did! I have met some of the most interesting people and all of them so genuine. We have all shared our innermost thoughts with each other and supported each other through numerous difficulties along the way.

I myself have had some major difficulties to overcome which although not yet solved, are definitely becoming a lot easier to work though. I have found that at a time when I have had a very poor image of myself and very low self-esteem, and could quite easily become addicted to medication, I have instead become addicted to my weekly intake of friendship, sharing, loyalty and guidance. I now know that if I have a problem there is always a kind face, a listening ear and a shoulder to cry on should it be needed.

These women I trust implicitly. We all come from different backgrounds and have different problems but I now feel I can relate in some way to them all. I have also found the group mentally stimulating, it has opened up lines of thought that would never have entered my head, for example, two of the women at the group are disabled and I have found it invaluable being able to discuss various issues concerning disabled people. We've also talked about women in politics, racism, sexism, health issues, legal matters, child abuse, women subject to violence, religion - the list is endless!

> If all this sounds a bit heavy - well it's not at all. We've also had some of the most amusing moments at the group, for every sad tale that comes to light there's always a funny one to take its place. We've had some real good laughs.
>
> I have a lot of friends outside of this group but it's really strange that these women that I have now formed a great friendship with I value the most, maybe it's because we have groundrules - something that you just assume would apply with other friends - but it's all too often the case that friends let you down. Not these women. I really trust them.
>
> My husband calls it my 'gossip group'! What an absolutely typical comment to come from a man! If only he knew that whilst he thinks we sit gossiping over a cup of tea, I'm actually feeding the intellectual part of my brain - the bit I thought I hadn't got, probably due to the lack of intelligent conversation from himself!
>
> How absolutely brilliant to be with interesting intelligent women that understand you! My only fear is that one day somebody might take all of this away again - not likely - I won't let them!
>
> Women can become so hammered down by the role they feel has been almost enforced upon them. It's true, you don't have to be a wife, mother etc. if you don't want to be. Unfortunately, so many of us have been brought up to believe that this is our role in society, but it needs a group like this to make women realise that they have wants and needs too. They need to feel valued, appreciated, loved, they need to feel part of life. Life can if you let it, become so 'humdrum'. Women do have choices, we need to know how to assert ourselves to make them.
>
> This group is so special to me; it's something I want, I need and I'm going to keep it!

These statements show how three women have found the group a life-saving haven, how huge a relief it has been to realise that experiences she has are not hers alone, how uplifting and empowering it is to make friends, to meet women who respect and accept you whoever you are and who believe you have something worthwhile to say. So many women have had so many damaging experiences, whether in their childhoods, at school, from the hands and/or tongues of partners, from the medical profession, that for many, it was the first time for years where they felt a real person and not solely identified by their status as wife, partner, mother, stepmother, aunt.

The two women with disabilities - whose experiences are very different from other women's in the group, but also from each others', have given very moving accounts of their lives and have shared their anguish and joy.

Non-disabled women in the group have measured the distressing aspects of their own experiences against the lives led by their disabled co-participants and have seen things from a different perspective. The two women with disabilities, in very different ways, provided an alternative view of the world, imbued with massive amounts of humour, wisdom, patience, staying-power and courage. The acceptance and support that grew up between women was tangible.

The group has become a place of safety against the outside world, of growing in understanding and awareness, of laughter for the sake of it and in the face of adversity, of homemade fruitcakes, of sharing of information and ideas, of strength of liking and support, of breaking down of myths and barriers.

There is clear validation of the need for this work to continue and for women's groups to be established as a form of resistance to and a buffer against the outside world. They are also a means of finding out how to survive in it more creatively.

A group of this nature, working on feminist principles that recognise each woman's uniqueness and strength, and value her experience and her wisdom, and enable her to explore and share those in a safe setting, can bring about fundamental changes in the life of each woman and in the life of the group. As is so often the case, funding for such work is under threat, because the group is not seen to fulfil any readily identifiable educational purpose. The testimony of the co-writers of this article and other participants' statements prove otherwise.

As one of the participants put it after the first few meetings:

> If there were more groups like this, psychiatrists would go out of business.

Groupwork for Mental Health Providers

Utilising the Enchanted Self Concept

Barbara Becker Holstein and Doreen Laperdon-Addison

This paper is about their joint collaboration. Based on Dr Holstein's discovery of an enhanced capacity for Wellness in women. This collaboration has led to mind body workshops to help people retrieve, reclaim and reintegrate positive aspects of themselves. This article focuses on a four hour workshop given to mental health professionals at the Annual Association for Women in Psychology Conference in Oakland California in March, 1994. The major conclusions from this workshop were, first, that mental health providers are hungrier for self replenishment than the collaborators realised; second that the methodology of alternating movement exercises with cognitive exercises facilitates a more integrated mind / body experience resulting in a fuller retrieval of earlier positive ego states; and third that combining personal replenishment with clinical methodology was diluting. Future workshops would be more clearly divided.

Six years ago, Barbara began interviewing women to learn about the messages they received in girlhood - 'open messages', such as 'You're dumb but beautiful', as well as disguised or unspoken 'secret messages', such as, 'there are more opportunities for boys out there than girls, so get married early!' She was interested in how negative, destructive, and at times, violating messages from girlhood impacted on the adult woman. As Barbara began to analyse the data from the eighteen women interviewed, ages thirty five to early eighties, she was struck by the women's true capacities for joy, and their ability to self replenish, discarding early dysfunction along the way. All could reclaim, reintegrate and/or adapt positive ego states from their childhood into workable, pleasurable, and often joyful adult ego states.

These enhanced adult ego states were not repetitions of clearly identifiable ego states from childhood or adolescence. Rather they were new integrations of elements of earlier positive states, a rebirth of a sense of well being in adult form. This enhanced sense of well being was labelled by Barbara 'The Enchanted Self'. Barbara then tried to determine how these states of well being evolved from the childhoods these women talked about. Many other connections were not clear. Often it seemed as if a magic wand had been tapped on the woman's head in her adult life. For example, when Barbara interviewed Edith, age 55, Edith talked about many of the dysfunctional aspects of her childhood. She remembered fighting, efforts to dominate between her parents, and the constant criticality. Edith had become an overly functional, meticulous child. When encouraged by Barbara to examine her childhood further, she began to separate the positive memories of herself from the dysfunctional family experiences. She remembered some wonderful times; delightful family picnics, fishing with her grandfather, shelling peas with her grandmother on the porch. Edith's compulsive traits created by her negative childhood experiences became talents for her in adulthood. Edith became a highly successful, professional business woman who had gained self esteem and gratification from her competencies. Now she was able to develop other sides of her that were kindled in childhood but not fully developed, such as when she went on picnics or fished with her grandfather or sat with her grandmother, i.e., softer sides.

As a child, Edith had wanted to take dance lessons but was not encouraged to do so. In her adult life chronic knee problems led Edith to study ballet. Her aggressiveness and drive gave her the courage and determination to do so. Through dance Edith was able to recognise and strengthen her mind/body connection which has empowered her both personally and professionally. Thus Edith's Enchanted Self in adulthood seems to be the successful integration of compulsive traits created by negative childhood experiences combined with new talents which also had their origin in her childhood.

The impact of the women's responses led Barbara to realise that clinicians often do not tap into wellness capacities in their clients. She hypothesised that this might be due to the lack of professional training in learning how to help clients retrieve and reincorporate positive ego states from childhood, coupled with professional stress leading to burnout.

Barbara began to work on an outline for a book on The Enchanted Self. She had written several sample chapters. It was around this time that she met Doreen while taking a ballet class. A friendship developed. Barbara asked Doreen to give her some private movement lessons. Barbara, like many women in their forties, was experiencing minor injuries and some stiffness in her body. Sitting in the dressing room at the dance studio Barbara and Doreen talked about Barbara's longings to free her movements beyond the dance technique. Doreen assured her that this could be accomplished. A few movement lessons took place at Barbara's home, centred on movement exploration and body alignment.

The goal was to improve alignment and ease of movement while exploring personal expressivity. Fate intervened. Barbara needed an emergency hysterectomy with only one week's notice. Upon her return home Doreen came over to visit. Barbara sat on a chair with pillows bracing her for support and comfort. Doreen led Barbara in a series of movement exercises. The objective purpose of the exercises was to allow the body to seek out what it needed for recovery. The primary instructions were to allow the fingers and hands to guide Barbara's movements. With her eyes closed Barbara moved her arms. One arm moved slowly and gracefully in a gathering motion while the other arm pushed away aggressively. The more aggressive actions took place in high level, side and back space. The softer motions occurred nearer the body towards the front and side in mid space level. Barbara felt this movement exercise to be extremely replenishing and self nourishing. Doreen was moved by the beauty and integrity of Barbara's movements.

Upon Barbara's physical recovery, their friendship deepened on many levels. The Enchanted Self interviews and rough draft chapters for Barbara's book were shared. They made the decision to start the long journey of being collaborators.

The past year and a half have been full of discovery for both of us. Initially we met two to four hours once a week. The first four or five months that we met permitted us to exchange information and philosophies around our disciplines. Through that exchange of information we became convinced of the importance of retrieving positive ego states through the body/mind connection. We wanted to develop a variety of powerful ways to help people retrieve their own positive states of mind and body. We further defined The Enchanted Self as involving several different positive states. Positive fingerprints of the mind are positive cognitive memories and the feelings associated with them. Positive fingerprints of the body are enhanced memories retrieved through the body. Shadow prints are extremely subtle memories that may emerge in the retrieval process that are not associated with language. We felt that an awareness of the different types of positive states of being was extremely important both to the facilitator and the participant as people so often diminish, devalue and/or disregard positive memories.

Working together for a year has resulted in the following: The Enchanted Self workshop which can be modified to meet the needs of different groups of people; a 23 minute dance choreographed by Doreen, entitled The Enchanted Self, a multi-sensory experience designed to elicit positive memories and feelings within the audience; and a monologue by Barbara based on interview material. The monologue has expanded into a performance piece where Barbara portrays a composite character named Mrs Brown who tells her story while Doreen dances as the younger part of that character.

The workshop we would like to discuss took place in Oakland, California. It was a half day workshop presented by the Association of Women in Psychology in March of 1994. It was designed for professionals in the mental health field. The focus of the workshop was twofold: first personal replenishment for the professionals who attended, second, to share with them clinical techniques that they could bring back to the treatment room to encourage positive states of well being in their clients.

Theoretically and professionally we were both concerned that the clinical treatment hour does not gear itself enough to encouraging the client to recognise her own positive earlier memories. Often the work of the therapy hour is geared to the diagnosis and correction of dysfunction, i.e. bad news. Clients are often put in a position where they are not encouraged to think about positive memories of girlhood, younger days, or to look for earlier signs of talents. Barbara and Doreen had shared research including that by Carol Gilligan (1982) and Emily Hancock's book (1989, *The Girl Within*, documenting that girls often have powerful moments growing up that they then disregard and/or forget about as they go into adolescence. The sense of power and the sense of feeling vital and alive are not clear capacities that women know automatically how to tap into.

We also discussed the role of Laban Movement analysis (a way of describing and analysing human movement that enables one to understand and improve one's own expressivity) and Bartenieff fundamentals (a form of body re-education) as a means of discovering one's Enchanted Self by remembering physically how one moved, the quality and range of movement and the feelings associated with the movement. We discussed the importance of non-verbal communication as a powerful tool in accessing positive images and memories. Also we shared some of the research findings that clinicians themselves are often burned out and/or suffer deplenishment of joy.

The actual workshop had seven participants. We gave background about ourselves as collaborators and about the theory of The Enchanted Self. We asked the women to share why they were at the workshop. It was immediately apparent that each was there for personal replenishment. Several of the women talked about exhausting clinical jobs dealing with difficult situations, survivors of rape and physical violence, and long hours and difficult case loads.Concepts were shared and then we performed "Mrs Brown". Afterwards people seemed eager to move.

The first movement activity was a general warm up and movement exploration. Doreen asked participants to take scarves and move with them in any fashion they desired. Some guidelines included moving in high, low, back and front spaces, gradually moving the arms in more three dimensional pathways, such as figure eight patterns.

Participants eagerly took to the idea and moved very freely. The second exercise involved more intimate moving. Participants were instructed to explore movement using their elbows to guide them. The women became more aggressive. They then chose the lower back and ankles. These choices demonstrated the participants' need for exercise to relieve aches and pains. Doreen concluded this exercise with instructions for the women to use their fingers to guide their movements. This refocused the group on the images and memories that can be triggered through movement, and of the knowledge and wisdom gained by listening to one's body. The women were amazed at how enlivened their body parts felt. We discussed how the body instinctively knows what it needs. One of the women talked about the confinement she felt at her job as a therapist and at meetings, feeling a need to move around but often unable to do so.

After these two movement exercises, Barbara led the group in a cognitive memory exercise. She asked the women to sit comfortably, close their eyes if they liked, and to retrieve positive memories from a particular age range, intuitively going to an age range where they felt there were some positive memories. She encouraged them to let go of the negative if they found themselves experiencing negative memories, and continue to search for the positive. All the women were either sitting or lying on the floor. Doreen put on some soft, lively music. One of the women tied scarves around her ankles, laid down on her back and put her feet up on a chair. She looked so childlike, yet feminine as she lay there in deep reverie. What amazed both of us was how totally relaxed the women appeared to be during the exercise. The women worked silently for ten to twelve minutes. When they were done with their reveries we asked them to sit up, and those who cared to do so to write or draw what they had remembered. When everyone had finished we discussed memories that the women were willing to share.

One of the women remembered how strong and good she had felt around the age of five or six. She lived in Michigan where she and her friends would go to a lake and rent inner tubes. They swam in the lake with these giant tubes that they barely could see over. Afterwards, she and her friends would clean off the tubes, wash off all the sand and then swing the tubes over their little shoulders and struggle up the hill to return them. The rental man was always delighted and complimented the little girls on returning clean tubes. He would say to them: 'I always know who the girls are who live here because they bring back clean tubes, just how I like it'. Her capacities to describe this scene were incredible. We felt part of this memory, sensing the strength, fatigue, and pride that these young girls must have felt.

Another woman reminisced about a day at the beach when she was a young child. She would squat down and pick sand up with her hands spending a long time feeling the sand. She remarked how centered she felt and how little children seemed to really embody that type of feeling. We asked her if she felt centered as an adult. She said, at times, as a therapist. She feels particularly centred when she is doing dream work analysis. Barbara reflected that one of the beautiful things we're able to do as adults is transfer feelings such as being centered sitting in the sand from a physical sensation in childhood to a mental sensation involving cognitive processes. Barbara commented that it was interesting to see this woman's magical child come through in a metamorphosised form in her adult clinical skills.

The oldest woman in the group, who appeared to be in her late fifties, had taken paper and coloured it brightly on one side with much darker colours on the other side. She commented that the bright colours were associated with powerful strong feelings she had as a youngster. However, when she became a teenager she no longer felt that strength. She didn't feel that special way about her body, nor had she been able to find it as an adult. She yearned to get back in touch with these feelings. Another woman talked about roller skating and how strong and competent she felt. However, as an adult she could not equate comparable feelings of strength and competency. Another woman discussed how adolescence had taken her away from a sense of strength, freedom and joy. Adolescence became associated with breasts, periods and 'all that stuff'.

The cognitive memories of these women were powerful. They evoked both the physicality of how the women's bodies felt when they were younger with images of what they did. We felt that having two movement exercises precede the cognitive exercise was good pacing. The women went into a type of reverie for the cognitive exercise because they were physically loosened up. Thus the mental technique was augmented by comfort and relaxation within their bodies as well as the beginnings of body memories that had been elicited by the movement exercises.

In the final exercise we presented the women with a large closed zippered flower satchel. The directions were for them to play and or work with the satchel in pantomime. We were mesmerised watching the women interact with the bag. They turned it into many things, from a baby that they held tenderly, to what resembled a poisonous object. As a poisonous object the women looked frightened as they quickly tossed it to others. As other times it appeared to be a treasure. Some times the women moved quickly with the bag, literally as if on a fast assembly line. At other times they moved more luxuriously, as if in a languid dance. On occasion the bag was hidden from one another. Sometimes the women were possessive, refusing to give the bag up. One woman sat on the bag as if she were a chicken, hatching an egg. We saw looks of relief and abandonment on peoples faces when the bag was taken away by someone else.

There was a constant sense of connectiveness and playfulness amongst the women. Everyone was included, no one was forgotten. The highlight of the bag exercise was when one of the women started to unzip the bag. This was done with great ceremony. All clustered around eagerly waiting to see what would emerge. When the bag was opened all the women reached in and began to fling things out of it. There were scarves and written material in the bag. The women started playing and dancing with the scarves and hiding the written material. There was a sense of surprise as if they had found some secret things. This built into a crescendo when suddenly there was a joint resolution to put everything back in the bag. As the scarves were returned to the bag, one woman discovered a program entitled The Enchanted Self. They all viewed it with surprise and glee. After everything was placed inside the bag this woman proceeded to stick the program into a side pocket so that the words, The Enchanted Self stuck out.

Barbara and Doreen were emotionally moved by the artistic dance these women had created. After the bag exercise we moved toward closure for the workshop. Barbara had been eager to present a clinical vignette from her practice. She shared with the participants how she had brought The Enchanted Self concept into her treatment room. The participants seemed somewhat emotionally flattened by this return to clinical issues. Although the case struck some interest, both Doreen and Barbara felt that they had made a mistake in concluding the workshop via a clinical vignette.

Discussion of methodology after the exuberance and playfulness that the bag exercise had elicited was probably not appropriate. In the future, workshops for professionals would be more clearly divided, one for self rejuvenation and one for clinical training in The Enchanted Self methodology.

Our participants wanted to experience a more enhanced sense of well being. Theoretically and professionally there is a lack of integration of the most positive moments of childhood into adulthood. This was confirmed by several of the participants. We would suggest that clinicians begin earlier in their development to learn to recognise the schism between their positive childhood self and their adult self which may not adequately incorporate these positive childhood ego states.

We are strongly convinced that using a mind/body approach in retrieving positive memories rather than utilising just one method or the other is a more facilitating way to help clinicians recover positive fingerprints and shadow prints of the mind and body. It is our observation that the initial movement exercises freed the women and they were able quickly to tap into rich cognitive imagery. The cognitive exercise prepared the women for a return to childhood playfulness and connectiveness, which was an integration of mind and body as seen and experienced in the bag exercise.

Our conclusions are:

1. Mental health providers are in need of opportunities for self replenishment.
2. Therapists should not be asked to switch gears too quickly between self replenishment and putting on their clinical hats.
3. The methodology of alternating movement exercises with cognitive retrieval exercises seems to be an excellent way to elicit a positive sense of wellbeing in workshop participants. Retrieval of positive early memories are documented through their verbal sharing as well as through their behaviours in terms of playfulness, humour, and connectiveness with each other.

References

Bartenieff, I. and Lewis, D. (1980) *Body Movement, Coping With The Environment*. New York: Gordon and Breach Science Publishers.

Gilligan, C. (1982) *In A Different Voice*. Cambridge, Mass: Howard University Press.

Hancock, E. (1989) *The Girl Within*. New York: Fawcett Columbine.

Laban, R. *The Language of Movement*. Boston: Plays, Inc.

Laban, R. and Ulolman, L. *The Mastery of Movement*. Boston: Plays inc.

McWilliams, N. (1993) *Psychodynamic Character Diagnosis As Differentiated From DSM III-R Diagnosis. Individuality in Depth.* Paper given at The New Jersey Psychological Association Meetings, Fall.

Moore, C. and Yamanoto, K. (1988) *Beyond Words*. New York: Gordon Breach Science Publishers.

PROMOTING POSITIVE IMAGES:

THE ROLE OF GROUPWORK IN PROMOTING WOMEN MANAGERS WITHIN ORGANISATIONS

JUDY FAWCETT

This article uses the notions of oppression and discrimination which underlie the organisational factors which prevent women managers from realising their full potential. It looks at the role of women as carers in society, women within Social Services Departments and the perceived role of women managers. It goes on to argue that such discrimination is harmful to both the individual and the organisation and means that the organisation itself is failing to utilise its staff to their maximum. Organisational cultures need to change to work to the strengths of both men and women and this entails overcoming the obstacles presently in place and problem-solving. One way of addressing these issues is by the positive and powerful use of the group by women managers as a means of support to combat sexism and racism within the organisation and as a way of preserving integrity without missing opportunities for advancement.

My starting point is that we live in a patriarchal society and that, briefly, this means that male systems and male thought processes still dominate society as a whole and, in particular, still predominate within the personal social services in both the statutory and voluntary sectors. The dilemma, therefore, both for women within the profession and for women as consumers of the service, is whether to collude with the patriarchal system or whether to take issue with it, challenging it and putting forward an alternative female-based system which will be more meaningful and more productive in equalising the balance of power between the sexes. My thesis is that this is precisely what we need to do if we are to offer equal opportunity to both men and women, firstly within the profession as a whole and, secondly, to the consumers. As long as we persevere with the present model we are operating a discriminatory model of service provision which puts women at a disadvantage and extols the virtue of predominantly male values.

Groupwork Vol. 7(2), 1994, pp.145-152

Let us start by looking at women as carers within our society. Women constitute three-quarters of the five and a half million carers in Britain today and this reflects the traditional role which women are expected to carry out without complaint. Within both extended and nuclear family systems the traditional model embraces the concept of the male as breadwinner and head of the household providing task centred and career focused models of action. Women have always been perceived as nurturing, compassionate, caring and dependent upon their male partners. If one accepts this model, it is therefore self-evident that both men and women accept this premise not only with regard to children but also regarding other relatives. It is the female role to care and provide services for members of our society – thus releasing the male to move upwards in his chosen career without let or hindrance.

Women make up 70 per cent of consumers of the personal social services, both in their own right as, for example, elderly frail residents receiving care provision, and as the mothers involved with social workers and other professionals on behalf of their families. Over one million homes are headed up by a single parent, usually female, and most rely on state benefits. These parents, therefore, struggle not only with the emotional stresses of bringing up a family but are also faced with the structural aspects of class, poverty and gender (Becker and Macpherson, 1986).

The gendered world of social services departments adopts a traditional approach to these service users. As consumers in their own right they are allotted female carers who act as substitute daughters, reinforcing the stereotype (Jones, 1989). As mothers they, rather than other family members, are targeted as the problem and expected to change their behaviour or, more importantly, the environmental factors which impact on their lives (Comley, 1989).

Women take the centre stage in family life and juggle home, work and the liaison activities on behalf of the family (Balbo, 1987). Balbo calls this 'patchworking' and this time-consuming task brings them into contact with not only schools and clinics but the social services.

The response to survivors of child sexual abuse and their mothers illustrates this. Women social workers have to fight with male managers for the space and resources to treat traumatised victims, while mothers are labelled the villains of the piece, either because they are perceived as failing to protect their children or, more recently, accused of making false allegations against male partners in custody disputes.

One would expect that the composition of social services

departments would reflect that of service users. Married women account for 60 per cent of the national work force and 56 per cent of these are employed by the welfare state, reflecting the traditional role of women as carers (SSI, 1991). Daphne Statham (1990) refers to the expectation that, in western Europe, the attributes needed in caring for dependent adults and children are those routinely expected of women: availability at short notice, flexibility, the ability to assess and anticipate future needs and the stamina to engage in routine and unpleasant tasks with little measurable success. She refers us to the work of Clare Ungerson, whose thesis is that women perform the intimate and messy tasks in life because there is a taboo against men becoming involved since this would threaten their need for a sense of order (Ungerson, 1983). This fear of messiness and untidiness extends to the area of emotions, where, again, men are reluctant to become involved, although it is a core element of the social work task.

The preponderance of women within social services departments, as in other services like nursing or teaching, leads to low pay and status for these positions, unlike the more established and male dominated professions such as medicine or the law. Statistics show that most men escape into management roles after two years, to avoid the pain and the messiness of the job (SSI, 1991).

Local government is also the largest employer of new graduates in Britain and women account for over 40 per cent of its graduate intake. Over a third of the women graduating in any one year enter local government, and organisations traditionally recruit graduates as actual or potential managers. In spite of this in 1980 there were only 58 women in chief officer positions in local government departments (Popplestone, 1980).

One has only to look at the distribution of the sexes in Diploma of Social Work graduate and non-graduate courses to see that there is a preponderance of women. Additionally, in non-graduate courses there are more likely to be more mature entrants, the majority of them women returners. The numbers are even higher if we also include home helps and other domiciliary services in the overall staffing.

Research into the motivation, attitudes and skills of women managers reveals a negative view of the expectations of organisations and of women themselves (Popplestone 1980; Eley 1991; SSI 1991). Male managers are the reference points and women are expected to conform to the stereotypes. There is emphasis on systems, budgets, tasks, crisis intervention and long working hours. A recent European survey showed that Britain places emphasis on long hours as a criterion for competence, unlike Germany which sensibly sees a forty hour week as the norm (Hanna, 1991). Eley (1989) conducted a survey which showed that women placed greater emphasis on staff support, supervision, a facilitating and consultative approach and on setting high standards for themselves and others. Foster (1987) found that women, for geographical and personal reasons, went for internal management promotion and specialist, diversified roles such as lecturing, rather than regular promotion at regular intervals. It would seem that women are motivated by notions of self fulfilment rather than career planning.

This analysis is incomplete without reference to society's socialisation processes. The dominant ideology dictates that men are brought up to be leaders, aggressive in outlook, task centred and in control of their emotions. Women, on the other hand are socialised into caring, nurturing and supportive roles within the family. Men are self-directed, women are other-directed and, as Arieti and Bemporard (1980) say, men gain self-esteem and self confidence from within, while women are socialised into seeking reassurance and recognition from others. The result of this is that women do not see themselves as having the skills to do the management task and are less comfortable in competitive environments, such as job interviews and negotiation situations. Their acknowledged skills can also be used against them. They can be used by male colleagues to sympathise with and support them, coping with the messy situation such as the aftermath of decisions about staff redundancies, or else they are labelled 'process people' and not seen as competent in other areas. A commitment to high standards can also lead women to concentrate on internal maintenance and not to seek opportunities to shine in public.

The biggest obstacle, however, is still the male macho management style and ethos, where men feel comfortable with a common code and women are seen as a threat to the established mores.

This then is the stark reality facing women who are actual or potential managers in a male dominated world.

If we also consider the position of black women in management, this picture is even more depressing. Most black women are in Section 11 posts rather than mainstream management jobs. It is therefore no surprise that black women take the view that combating racism in institutions must have a higher priority than combating sexism, since they are doubly oppressed in terms of their skin colour and their gender. Black women managers are few and far between, and, like their practitioner counterparts, feel that their appointments are tokenistic. Alternatively, they are set up to fail, by being expected to represent black communities and to achieve unrealistic objectives set by the white male organisation. The failure of an individual white male manager does not lead to condemnation of the whole group, as happens with women, whatever their skin colour (Watt and Cooke 1989; Rooney 1982).

My experiences of talking to women managers and of belonging to a support group for women confirm that women feel alienated and distanced from the organisational culture within which they work. One woman talked of how she came into her new job filled with enthusiasm and determination to do a good job and to keep her integrity and value base. Within one year she felt devalued and deskilled. Her priorities were to create a quality service over time and to adopt a participative and collaborative style of working with her staff. She found that male peers adopted a different set of priorities and that she was labelled as the 'process person' and her views on other management areas were ignored. She discovered for the first time that she was suddenly invisible and her opinions were only validated when a male colleague took them up as his. The male culture of the club and talk of sport and cars was alien to her and the competitive and aggressive form of debate distasteful. She began to question her own value base and feel tension between these principles and the demands of the organisation. She felt that she was being judged nor only for herself but as the representative of women, almost an experiment.

On talking to other women managers she discovered that they felt the same and they decided to set up an informal support group. These women met on a monthly basis and found the group helped them survive and develop strategies for addressing the problems. As part of the same management team they planned a common response to policy issues and were able to argue successfully for changes, particularly in the area of equal opportunities. They gained a strong voice within the team and it was noticeable that, gradually, the style of leadership began to alter. They were also able to challenge conscious and unconscious sexist remarks and behaviours and check out with each other if they felt that they were being sucked into male attitudes and priorities inappropriately. Gaining in confidence, they each made decisions about their careers. One remained a team manager, one sought and gained promotion, one made a positive decision to move to a prestigious training post and two came to positive decisions to move into different settings. Whilst all these were beneficial to the individuals concerned, it was surely a loss to the organisation and its development that only two remained in the management system.

Daphne Statham (1990) says that all organisations need both male and female managers, especially black men and women, to be effective and to have a gender perspective reflecting the users of the service. Both bring different strengths and weaknesses to the role and these can complement each other and move the organisation on to improve and develop the service.

My contention is that a peer group for women, recognised and encouraged by the organisation is crucial if this is to happen. The process that needs to happen is that the obstacles to the advancement of women need to be identified and strategies for problem-solving and changing the culture must be devised.

Butler and Wintram (1991) state that, for women, groupwork is one way of carving out space for themselves in a hostile environment and we have already seen that this is true for women managers. They go on to say that feminist group work validates women's rights to seek power and control over their own lives, gives them the security to challenge the stereotypes of themselves and offers scope to re-evaluate themselves and their strengths. Whether or not all women managers support the feminist analysis of society, all can identify with these aims.

The group can be used to validate personal attitudes and beliefs in the face of male hostility or disbelief. It can offer the opportunity to plan and practise assertive and alternative approaches to problems and increase the likelihood of success, which in turn will increase self-confidence and self belief. It will also be instrumental in identifying the need for women to have career plans and to identify supporters within the organisation.

This model stresses the importance of both task and process, the self validation but also the need for looking beyond self to ways of changing the organisational culture. This is a process which takes time and needs consideration in a positive and caring environment. The collaborative style of women will facilitate this but will not fudge the need to confront in a positive manner. The specific areas that any group needs to cover are well expressed by Daphne Statham and Grimwood and Popplestone (1993). Statham reminds us that the work of Dale Spender (1980) reveals that, in meetings men speak more often than women. The learning of skills for positive interventions in meetings can be on the agenda. Women are often accused by male colleagues of being emotional rather than rational in the presentation of their arguments. Seeing that there is a place for both logic and emotion the group can legitimise emotion as a positive attribute. In order to survive in the work place women need to be kind to themselves, celebrate their achievements and learn from their mistakes (Phillipson 1990).

The learning about self and the organisation will also enable women to take those strategies beyond the group and into the work setting. With support and encouragement from other women, they can put gender on the agenda, and demonstrate that gender sensitive practice is effective.

These are the positive skills that women bring to management. Earlier on we looked at the diffidence which can hinder their advancement. There are skills that we can learn from men which will complement and enhance them. We need to learn to network with other women and men, forging alliances and making contacts which we can use to further our views and ideas. We can influence policies on equal opportunities, particularly the use of legislation on employment and sexual harassment and ensure that they are taken seriously and not just paper policies. We need to be clear about our career planning and how and where to get support for it. We also need to be forceful in demanding women-only training courses and validating them as legitimate enterprises.

Finally, as women, we bring the ability to juggle many balls in the air skilfully and purposefully. We need to acknowledge that there are parallels between the workplace and home and that women are managing in their private lives what they have to manage in public services. The changes in public services, both in structure and purpose will require managers to adopt the skills of listening, negotiating, compromising and process, if users are not to be overwhelmed by the move to market forces. We as women have all these in abundance. We need to believe in ourselves and use them.

References

Arieti, S. and Bemporad, J. (1980) *Severe and Mild Depression*. London: Tavistock.

Balbo, L. (1987) 'Crazy quilts' in Showstack, S. (ed.) *Women and The State*. Hutchinson.

Becker, S. and Macpherson, S. (1986) *Poor Clients: The Extent and Nature of Financial Poverty Among Consumers of Social Work Services*. Nottingham: Nottingham University.

Butler, S. and Wintram, C. (1991) *Feminist Groupwork*. Sage.

Comley, T. (1989) 'State social work: a socialist-feminist contribution' in

Hallett, C. (ed.) *Women and Social Services Departments*. Harvester.

Eley, R. (1989) 'Women in management in social services departments' in Hallett, C. *Women and Social Services Departments*. Harvester.

Fawcett, J. (1988) 'Setting the scene for a long term project', *Social Work Today*, 19(30).

Foster, J. (1987) 'Women on the wane', *Insight*, 2(50).

Grimwood, C. and Popplestone, R. (1993) *Women, Management and Care*. Birmingham: BASW/Macmillan.

Hallett, C. (ed.) (1989) *Women and Social Services Departments*. Harvester.

Hanna, L. (1991) *Guardian*, 29 October.

Jones (1989) 'Women in social care' in Hallett, C. (ed.) *Women and Social Services Departments*. Harvester.

Phillipson, J. (1990) 'Management is her story', *Social Work Today*, 5 April.

Popplestone, R. (1980) 'Top jobs for women: are the odds stacked against them?', *Social Work Today*, 12(4).

Rooney, B. (1982) 'Black social workers in white departments' in Cheetham J. (ed.) *Social Work and Ethnicity*. London: NISW.

Spender, D. (1980) *Man Made Language*. London: Routledge Kegan Paul.

SSI (1991) *Women in Social Services Department: A Neglected Resource*. London: HMSO.

Statham, D. (1990) *Women, Promotion and Prejudice*. Unpublished.

Ungerson, C. (1983) 'Women and caring: skills, tasks and taboos' in Gaimanikou et al. (eds.) *The Public and the Private*. London: Heinemann.

Watt and Cooke (1989) 'Another expectation unfulfilled: black women and social services departments' in Hallett, C. (ed.) *Women and Social Services Departments*. Harvester.

Using a facilitated self help group for women whose children have been sexually abused

Olive Otway and Anne Peake

This paper explores the experiences of women whose children have been sexually abused by someone they knew and trusted. The authors look at how self-help groups may be one way of responding to the needs of mothers. A pilot group is looked at in detail to illustrate the usefulness of such an approach.

The experiences of women whose children have been sexually abused

When a woman is told or realises that her child has been sexually assaulted by her partner or someone she knew and trusted, one of the worst things that could ever happen, has happened. Nothing will ever be the same again; not her child, her life, her family, her faith in people or her hopes for the future.

The investigation of the abuse may lead, suddenly, to her own indictment on a number of levels; e.g. for being a failure as a wife or partner, for failing to protect her child, for working nights, for being ill, or for not knowing about the abuse. Each time this happens the blame for the abuse is diffused and becomes less clearly the responsibility of the person who committed the offence.

Also, the professionals investigating the abuse and assessing the family may not understand that believing your child is a process and may not be an immediate event. A woman's reaction to the abuse should therefore be viewed in a way that takes account of her personal situation and the wider social context in which she lives (Dempster, 1992). This explanation likens the woman's evolving reaction to the grieving process and experiencing a sense of loss. It also supports the finding that the mother's initial reaction is not always indicative of her ability to protect her child and that if a woman expresses disbelief, this may well change during the investigation and assessment period. Indeed parallels may well be found between the feelings and experiences of mothers and their victimized children.

Hooper (1992), found that the experiences of women non-abusing parents who were faced with child protection procedures were mixed. She discovered that women were often ill-informed and confused, were unfamiliar with procedures, uncomfortable in the interviewing process and case conference settings, and unsure as to what was expected of them. In some instances what the women experienced felt like another form of abuse by the statutory agency.

Women may under these circumstances offer inappropriate answers which could have a significant effect on the assessment and response of the agencies. Hooper's study offers an alternative theory to earlier works which had criticised women as inadequate mothers in responding poorly to the disclosure of their child's abuse. Mothers were often viewed as colluding and failing to protect children, and their potential for involvement in their children's survival was ignored (Dietz and Craft, 1980).

Whilst feminist critiques of both the position of women and children within families, and also the way they are 'processed' by the 'Child Sexual Abuse Industry' (Hudson, 1992), have gone some way towards shifting the balance away from the 'dysfunctional family' approaches to child sexual abuse, with the mother's role as pivotal within them, there is still considerable confusion in the social work profession about what constitutes anti-oppressive practice in this area. It is therefore surprising that professionals may expect a perfect response from mothers when our own responses, informed by knowledge, training and experience in the area of child abuse, can be so varied.

Working towards the empowerment of women, whose children have been sexually abused, through the use of a self-help group

Responding to the pain and trauma of sexual violence through the medium of self help has now become an established and valued response for survivors (Bass and Davis, 1988). However, self help or therapeutic groups for non-abusing carers are less common even though the efficacy of self help support is well chronicled by those who have been involved in such groups (Hall and Lloyd, 1990).

As feminists, we agreed with the view that the sexual abuse of children by men is an abuse of power and trust (MacLeod and Saraga, 1988), so for us a logical response involved the empowerment of those who are viewed as being less powerful.

We also believed that the processes and procedures that women and children, and to some extent workers, have to complete have a distancing effect on all concerned. It is difficult to confront the deep seated trauma that sexual abuse presents to a non abusing parent, if her child is dependent on her to remain in control of the very difficult process that she may be experiencing, as well as to co-operate with all of the agencies involved. Some women therefore will have different needs at different times following the discovery of the abuse of their children.

As professionals we were already involved in a variety of services for those affected by sexual abuse. These services included; running groups for children who had been abused, support groups for social workers, training sessions and a consultation service for professionals. We became aware that mothers as non-abusing parents were expected by agencies to manage on their own with little involvement from others in how to cope and respond to the violation of their children.

Following the Cleveland crisis, Sue Richardson pointed out that one lesson that was learnt was that no one worked to empower the mothers of the children involved in the investigation by police and social workers concerning the allegations of child sexual abuse (Campbell, 1988).

Some authorities have indeed tried to respond sensitively to non-abusing parents in their policies; particularly those who pride themselves on having a set of child protection procedures which follow a feminist perspective, for example, by allocating two social workers to distinguish between the important but differing needs of both mother and child (Boushel and Noakes, 1988). But such policies, despite their good intentions, can be hampered by lack of resources and also the obsession with procedures that have been established as a form of defence to distance workers and agencies from the pain and meaning to society of child sexual abuse (Hudson, 1992). Measures that have initially begun to offer both practical and emotional support are often reduced to the employment of techniques which can best be described as little more than surveillance.

We have also found that women's needs can change over time. It has become apparent, especially post investigation when social workers may no longer be involved, that a need for advice, information, support or therapy may re-surface in the same or a differing form than at the point of disclosure/discovery of the abuse.

A woman's own needs may well remain submerged during an investigation as the focus is on her child/ren and the huge number of factors that she, as a parent has to negotiate. These may include practical issues such as housing, finances, legal proceedings and the emotional impact of the abuse and its aftermath. It may only be post investigation that a woman's own needs and her ability to articulate these may emerge.

Establishing a group

In an attempt to respond to the varied and complex needs of mothers we planned a self-help group taking into account the features pointed out by Moeller (1983) when working with non-abusing parents, namely:

1. members are equal in status;
2. members make decisions for themselves;
3. decisions are the responsibility of the group;
4. members join the group because of problems they are experiencing;
5. content of the sessions are confidential;
6. involvement in the group does not accrue a financial cost to the members.

As we wanted to help empower the women who came to the group, we assumed that the women would know best what they needed if they had the time and support to think; and that if they didn't know, telling them would not be the answer. We believed in the capacity of the mothers to protect their children and to do what was best for them. Like McNay (1992), we wanted to move away from a social work intervention that is drawn from an analysis of dysfunction towards one of empowerment. As such we wanted our intervention to be needs led so that rather than assessing how best to solve problems we wanted to be able to identify the material and emotional resources and skills that the members of the group required (and possessed) in order to meet their needs.

We believed that an open self-help group could offer this facility and would run for as long as it was valued by its members.

We also felt that for women whose children have been abused and are involved with statutory agencies, being part of a self-help group can take place alongside other services such as individual counselling (Pancoast et al., 1983).

The local authority assisted in setting up the pilot group by supplying a room, transport, refreshments and a small grant for child care.

The group had three main features:

1. Open group.

The group was open. There was no waiting list and no interview/assessment procedure. This ensured that we could respond quickly to meeting with the woman and offering contact with others who were or had been in similar circumstances. A rapid response could therefore be guaranteed when she may be in crisis, feeling vulnerable and isolated.

The only criteria were that the mothers were not presently living with the abusers, that their children had been abused by adults known to them (as opposed to strangers), and that they were the mothers/caretakers at the time of the abuse (as opposed to foster carers whose needs were likely to be different and at times may conflict with those of birth parents).

2. Open-ended group.

The group was designed to offer help for as long as it was needed. The aim was, once started it would run every week for whoever needed it. For the reasons we outlined earlier we felt it was important that women could come and go as they wanted. In fact most women attended weekly, but there were some women who came periodically, for example just before court proceedings. The group was a resource for women, whereby they became resources for each other. For instance, one woman sought support from the others in the group while she coped with court prosecution of the abuser named by her children.

The group was also a resource for the local authority. This was illustrated by a group member writing an open letter to women who had learnt of the abuse of their child/ren. This letter became a feature of initial child protection case conferences and was given to the mother present as a source of help and support.

3. The content of the weekly sessions.

We had no pre-set programme prior to the start of the group, only a general idea of some of the issues that may be raised. As this was an open group with members with different needs and backgrounds, cultures etc. we let the members set the 'agenda' for the week. We therefore began each week with the question to each woman in turn 'how did your week go?'. With time and confidence women would raise the issues most pertinent for them at the time of the session. Sometimes it helped just to be listened to in sympathetic silence, sometimes advice would be sought, at other times some women felt it was enough 'just to be there'. The mothers were encouraged to share the ideas and solutions they had tried by way of providing advice to those experiencing familiar difficulties. The group workers might prompt the discussion but were always mindful not to provide solutions and foster inappropriate dependence. The individual issues women raised covered: their own childhood and histories, current feelings and problems such as who would be a good solicitor to fight custody for a mother, questions and views about the nature of child sexual abuse, and day to day problems such as managing the behaviour of abused children, coping with debt, agencies, etc.

The women themselves told us what they needed, which they have now produced as a leaflet to use in training sessions (Peake, forthcoming). A summary of their needs is as follows:

What mothers would benefit from when it becomes known that their children have been sexually assaulted

- A legal system that helps to protect children who have been sexually assaulted.
- Presently the law can be quite confusing and complex, it would be beneficial for those concerned if the law was easier to understand.
- Sometimes it is the mother and children or the children who have to leave the family home, rather than the abuser. This can cause more distress and could be avoided if the abuser left.
- If the women and children decide to leave the family home for safety reasons there should be 'safe houses' for them to go to.
- Women need a lot of advice when sexual assault has taken place, for example, welfare rights, legal, housing and financial advice. Advice needs to be given in a calm, clear manner.
- There needs to be a choice of separate and/or together counselling for children and their mothers.
- Meeting other women who have had similar experiences can be beneficial and helpful.
- It is necessary to be believed and not to feel blamed and responsible over and over again.
- If children are to be a witness in criminal proceedings they need to have preparation and support from an experienced worker. For mothers to help their children they too need to know and understand the court system.
- There should be available on going support and assistance to help mothers over a long period of time, not only at the point of disclosure of sexual abuse.
- Mothers need support and advice when dealing with the consequences of abuse in their children's behaviour.
- Medicals for children should be sympathetic and 'child centred' with a choice of gender and ethnic group for the professionals.

The surroundings the medical takes place in should also be pleasant.

- Resources for women and children who have experienced sexual violence should be well publicised.
- There should be facilities for children and babies in service agencies and public places.
- A free 24 hour telephone advice line for non-abusing parents and children would be useful in times of stress and difficulty.
- Police protection, if needed, should be readily available and accessible.
- Specialist police teams in every locality should be available: for example, police child protection teams and domestic violence teams.
- For mothers to be able to support and help their children after experiencing sexual assault they need to have information, resources and facilities such as those mentioned above'.

By Pamela, Caroline, Anne and Susan.

What these collective views (which took a considerable amount of time and courage from the group members concerned) show, are the wide range of needs of both the mother and child and whilst it is clear that many of the points raised are concerned with wider structural and procedural matters such as legislation and housing policies, there is also a need for some form of co-ordinated service that gives non-abusing mothers and their children flexible choices of help and support over a sustained period of time.

Outcome

The group ran for over eighteen months with 15 mothers attending regularly. Between them they had 36 children. The women came from a range of backgrounds, cultures and ages.

There were also women who were initially referred to the group but who did not attend regularly. This was for a variety of reasons, for example, they were working on that day or because the group did not appeal to them but the social worker involved thought they might like to come along to the meetings. These women had the opportunity of knowing that the group existed, that there were women who had children who had been sexually abused and that they were not on their own.

Some of the women who did not attend the group also benefited from its existence. There was one woman in the area who felt unsure of how to react to her child's abuse and the affect it would have on her standing in the African community to which she belonged. She also had concerns about contact with the 'authorities' and how they would react to her as a black woman (Mama, 1984). We were able to offer her telephone contact with one of the members of the group from the same background who was able to share her own experience of going through the child protection procedures and the reaction of her community.

One woman who ran her own hair dressing business never came to the group meetings but regularly met up with some of the women during 'social get-togethers' at the women's houses or in the park or other outings during school holidays: contact both she and her daughter enjoyed.

Evaluating the efficacy or outcome of a self help group such as this one is not an easy task. However, Winton (1990), evaluated a non-abusing parents' group using three outcome criteria: a decrease in children's difficult behaviour, a decrease in parental stress levels and a positive assessment of the group by members.

Feedback on the group described came from the group members, the changes that we were able to see in the women and their circumstances over a substantial period of time, and views of professionals also known to the women.

We did not have a report of children's behaviour significantly improving during the life of the group, but the women felt that they were able to understand and respond in a more positive way then they had previously.

Several of the women demonstrated an increase in confidence and self worth through gaining employment, learning to read, making friends, going to college, managing difficult behaviour from their children, challenging views held by others, and generally surviving the trauma of sexual violence.

When listening to the women themselves one heard that it was important to know that the group was there for them, knowing others had experienced similar crimes against their children, learning that the abuse was not their fault and that responsibility lay not with them or their children but firmly with the abuser. They learnt from each other's mistakes, they cried together but also laughed together and had fun.

Contacts outside the weekly meetings were valued, such as outings during the school holidays, visits to each other's houses and telephone calls to each other during stressful situations. Talking about their children's (at times), demanding and difficult behaviour was appreciated by some group members, who felt that they were not stigmatised but understood and empathised with.

Some women expressed that continually feeling powerless had decreased especially with the knowledge that they had directly influenced local authority policy through talking with social workers, police, medics, solicitors and the child protection officers about their experiences and by compiling advice for those who face the trauma in the future.

The group was also successful in gaining money from a charity which meant the members had control over how the money should be spent for the benefit of the group.

We received feedback from other professionals who had contact with the women and their children. Many of the professionals saw a growth in confidence but they also reported feeling a sense of relief in that the women had a place to go to which could offer them time and space. Some workers reported not having enough time to give the women, others did not feel qualified or confident enough in the area of sexual abuse.

For us as facilitators we learnt that we should not place all the responsibility for the group with the members. That responsibility had to be shared and that at times we had to step in with suggestions for direction, especially at times when energy and motivation flagged.

Conclusion

This paper has attempted to explore the experiences of women whose children have been sexually abused, and it has looked at one form of intervention that may be of help to social workers and related professionals when considering how best to meet the needs of women who become consumers of a social work service because of their children's abuse.

By focusing on the evolving needs and responses of a non abusing-parent as a process defined by her personal and wider social relations and on a form of intervention that is empowering, we believe that self-help groups which are open and not time limited can offer women flexibility and a space for themselves. The sessions may help members to define their needs and through the interaction with other group members and facilitators to develop a method of empowerment and growth.

For us this group is a testimony to the strength of those women and a thank you for the insights that they gave us.

...Like Juno, you make me humble in your shadow (Rouf, 1992).

References

Bass, E. and Davies, L. (1988) *The Courage to Heal: A Guide for Women Survivors of Child Sexual Abuse*. New York: Harper and Row.

Boushel, M. and Noakes, S. (1988) 'Islington social services: developing a policy on child sexual abuse', Feminist Review, 28, pp.150-57.

Campbell, B. (1988) *Unofficial Secrets*. London: Virago.

Dempster, H. (1992) The Aftermath of Child Sexual Abuse: Women's Perspectives in Waterhouse, L. (ed.) *Child Abuse and Child Abusers*. London: Jessica Kingsley Publishers.

Dietz, C. and Craft, J. (1980) 'Family dynamics of incest, a new perspective', *Social Casework*, December, pp.602-609.

Hall, L. and Lloyd, S. (1990) *Surviving Child Sexual Abuse: A Hope for Healing*. Crowborough: Highland Books.

Hooper, C. (1992) *Mothers Surviving Child Sexual Abuse*. London: Tavistock/ Routledge.

Hudson, A. (1992) 'The child sexual abuse 'industry' and gender relations in social work' in Langan, M. and Day, L. (eds.) *Women, Oppression and Social Work*. London: Routledge.

MacLeod, M. and Saraga, E. (1988) 'Challenging the orthodoxy: towards a feminist theory and practice', Feminist Review, 28, pp.16-15.

Mama, A. (1984) 'Black women, the economic crisis and the British state', *Feminist Review*, 17.

McNay, M. (1992) 'Social work and power relations' in Langan, M. and Day, L. (eds.) *Women, Oppression and Social Work*. London: Routledge.

Moeller, M. (1983) 'Self-help and the medical practitioner', in Hatch, S. and Kirkbush, I. (eds.) *Self-Help and Health in Europe. New Approaches in Health Care*. Copenhagen: World Health Organisation.

Pancoast, D. L., Parker, P. and Froland, C. (1983) *Rediscovering Self-Help: Its Role in Social Care*. Beverley Hills: Sage.

Peake, A. (1990) *Professionals Working with Child Sexual Abuse: Training Pack*. London: Children's Society.

Peake, A. (forthcoming) *Strong Women's Booklet*. London: Children's Society.

Rouf, K. (1992) *Pandora's Box*. London: Children's Society.

Winton, M. (1990) 'An evaluation of a support group for parents who have a sexually abused child'. Child Abuse and Neglect 14(3), 397-405.

'ALL I'VE GOT IN MY PURSE IS MOTHBALLS!'

THE SOCIAL ACTION WOMEN'S GROUP

SANDRA BUTLER

This research-based paper gives an overview of the social action women's group of the Radford Shared Care Project, Nottingham, a resource offering a radical approach to keeping children out of local authority accommodation who are at risk of significant harm from their parents. As a vehicle for women's self-development, the practice relevance and effectiveness of the group's value base is unpacked. The groupworkers' style of facilitation is explored in terms of the necessary conditions for the creation of an atmosphere of equality, namely, attending to women's physical needs; encouraging women to establish their own agenda for the group; making connections between individual and collective experience; utilising listening skills and positive reinforcement; and finally, recognising women's power. By examining key recurring themes within and across group sessions, the article validates the structural dilemmas with which group members were faced. Women's sexuality and relationships with male partners became entangled with the processes of racism and the difficulties of bringing up mixed parentage children. Faced with relentless hardships, women easily identified the politics of poverty and central government's punishment of the poor. This process of naming structural and individual experiences is critical to women's empowerment, building a bridge towards the creation of their own solutions and the necessary action to achieve them.

This article has arisen out of the first year's work of a five year qualitative research study of the NCH Action For Children/ Nottinghamshire Social Services Radford Shared Care Project (Butler, 1994). The project offers intensive, culturally appropriate assistance to families where children and young people are at risk of being removed from home into local authority accommodation. Project workers work with parents in their own homes, addressing issues such as child abuse and neglect, behavioural difficulties and control, and play stimulation. The groupwork programmes complement the family work, focusing on parenting skills and the promotion of women's self-confidence, self-esteem and autonomy.

Groupwork Vol. 7(2), 1994, pp.163-179

The social action women's group draws its membership from current project families and women who have recently finished work with their project worker. Women who use the group have extensive and often debilitating experiences of welfare agencies in that their parenting standards have been scrutinised and labelled as 'inadequate'. My analysis will concentrate on the women's group over an eight month period. The group met on a weekly basis for two hours, 9.30 a.m.-11.30 a.m., with creche facilities provided. Group facilitators were an African-Caribbean woman worker from Nottingham Young Volunteers and a white woman paid on a sessional basis. In a group where one quarter of members were Black and half the white women had mixed parentage children, a 'mixed'-race co-working team was essential.

The major principle of social action research and practice is about users taking action for empowerment (Mullender et al., 1993-94; Mullender and Ward, 1991a, 1991b). The research aims to monitor and evaluate the project's work by exploring the formal and informal dimensions of the shared care process, so that learning, development and change in the project can take place. Starting with the issues, ideas and understandings of all project participants, the research moves into an evaluation of the impact of the project's activities and developmental plans. Emerging data is shared with participants, who are enabled to generate their own solutions and the necessary action to achieve them.

Material for this article originates from written evaluations provided by the two groupworkers, taped interviews with the white woman groupworker, the project leader and women's group members. Interviews were transcribed, with the texts only lightly edited. To be consistent with the user-led strategy, I have let the users' and workers' own voices be heard as much as possible. I will begin by reviewing the value base of the group, moving on to explore the groupworkers' style of facilitation and the content and process of group sessions, where structural forces shaped interpersonal discussion.

Value base of the social action women's group

One of the aims of the project is 'to enable parents, individually or co-operatively, to sustain action likely to lead to the greater development of their abilities and self-awareness.' The Joint Service Level Agreement between Nottinghamshire Social Services and NCH Action For Children (1993) states that 'Parents and carers will be invited to join an ongoing group programme aimed at equipping them to take up issues on their own behalf' (4.12, Pg. 6). Whereas

British child protection systems tend to pathologise parents and children (Parton, 1991; Frost and Stein, 1989), the Shared Care Project sets itself the objective of confronting the personal and institutional mechanisms through which oppression operates, building upon and emphasising families' strengths. The project recognises key facets of inequality and social injustice which operate in this multi-racial area of Nottingham caused by poor housing, high unemployment, low income, limited educational opportunities and the endurance of racism and sexism. These shape the social construction of differing life choices and opportunities, yielding differential access to services and experiences of discrimination for project families. Women who use the project live in dangerous inner-city areas and housing estates, and suffer considerable racial and sexual harassment.

Within the context of a project whose primary function is to enhance the safety and wellbeing of children, the project leader 'worries' that the project is condoning some aspects of sexism by concentrating on women, their role as mothers and their parenting skills. Groupwork therefore plays a pivotal role in creating space for women's self-development, where members can define the issues that are important to them, other than those tied up with being a parent. Previous research (Fleming and Ward, 1992) revealed that women's empowerment had a positive effect on their children's wellbeing, demonstrating the inter-relationship of women's needs and rights with those of their families.

The groupworkers are committed to socialist values of collective responsibility, meeting community needs and preventative work. They described the aims and values of social action groupwork as enabling women:

1. to set their own agenda of issues, by exploring *what* are the women's preoccupations;
2. to gain a different perspective on *why* they are in their current positions, thereby removing the blame and guilt;
3. to recognise that they are caught up in structural events that are historical for them because they have come from families which are disadvantaged;
4. to discover ways of breaking out of these patterns, to find a measure of independence;
5. to discover *how* they are going to achieve change themselves - what steps they are going to take, what support they might need and what the process is for them to move out of their current positions;

6. to be challenging of themselves, of each other and the groupworkers;
7. to develop a sense of self-worth, recognising the contributions they make to society;
8. to develop a partnership with each other and the groupworkers.

There are many elements of the above which demonstrate the project's aim of sustaining action to enhance women's abilities and self-awareness. The *action* referred to in items 1-8 is about not only personal change, but also social and structural change. The potential contribution of groupwork to this wider vision is clearly identified in the following extract:

> The groupwork helps women to question the causes of some of their difficulties and the recognition of the oppression that they're under, that can help their awareness of the world and hopefully even lead to wanting to take some action collectively. This would probably be the biggest thing that the project could achieve (project leader).

As has been recognised in feminist groups (Butler and Wintram, 1991), the project leader sees the role of groupwork as a vehicle for breaking down the barriers of isolation, as a source of validation and friendship, and as a means of developing and recognising aspects of women's selves that have hitherto been hidden, distorted or suppressed:

> I think that women are different in groups than in a one-to-one, where they can help one another and develop their self-image in two ways. Firstly, that it's not all their fault, they're not inadequate because there are enormous pressures on them and they're not alone. Secondly, that they can say something useful to or befriend somebody else and be valued by them. This can lead to the development of the spiritual and ethical aspects of their lives. So much can be done through a group, to find that they have strengths they didn't know they had (project leader).

The expressed commitment to the principles of the social action group needs to be examined in relation to the effectiveness and the relevance of these values in practice. In the following section, I shall analyse the practical implications of social action values by considering key aspects of the group's content and process, and by revealing the structural dilemmas with which group members were faced.

Content and process of the social action women's group

Groups are dynamic and fluctuating, sometimes conflictual and at other times they assume an organic wholeness, with content and process heavily intertwined. In this section, I will unravel strands of this content and process by analysing the groupworkers' style of facilitation. I will then explore the group's personal/political agenda, and how group process was used to confront racism and sexism.

Groupworkers' style of facilitation: creating an atmosphere of equality

> The group has been working at establishing itself and developing an understanding of things through the process of sharing, that is non-stigmatising, that they're not victims (groupworker).

The groupworkers were able to achieve social action aims 1 and 8 because they utilised a style of facilitation which encouraged women to develop the group norms and goals by defining and analysing the problems they faced. Most important, this collaborative style affected the group process:

> I draw out women's contributions, enabling them to put words around things and stay with what is important for them. I encourage women to talk because some of the women find this so difficult. There's always the woman who wants to talk a lot and the hard work for me is getting the quiet ones involved in talking about their concerns (groupworker).

Analysis of the interview transcripts and group members' feedback revealed that there were five necessary conditions to the creation of an atmosphere of equality during the group's life. First, careful attention was paid to women's physical needs (food, drink, venue). Given the depths of women's low self-esteem, members felt hesitant about doing even small tasks such as making the tea/coffee or filling the kettle. The groupworkers were empathic in dealing with women's fears in these areas, so much so that after four months, the women were sharing food. Secondly, in carrying out the first aim of social action, the group did not start with a pre-planned programme but instead women were encouraged to establish their own agenda:

> The group unfolds from where the women start talking. They initiate what it is they want to talk about. The process is about picking up from a very ordinary statement, and turning it into a discussion. What we get into during most weeks is where one member needs a lot of attention, so part of the time is often taken

> up with the group focusing on whatever crisis has happened. A lot of counselling goes on (groupworker).

Thirdly, connections were made between individual and collective experience through the process of 'conscientisation' (Freire, 1972), which intimately links knowledge and power:

> We try to *bring out the issues generally* for the women from small, personal examples. We share a willingness to discuss issues such as sexuality and we're not shocked. We have to be careful to *pull things together* a quarter of an hour before the end; this isn't easy when you're in a good discussion. So it's picking out a topic in what women are saying, keeping your ears flapping. For instance, if someone's talking about 'that f—ing Housing Manager', I'll start off by saying, 'It sounds like you had a really bad time'. I acknowledge the feelings and from there we'd develop it in terms of, 'What do you want to do? How might you do it?' (my emphasis) (groupworker).

Fourthly, listening skills and positive reinforcement were used to undermine the process of stigmatisation and build on women's strengths:

> We *listen really hard* to their views about what's going on and tell them that they are *doing pretty well*. I'm very sincere about this because I don't know sometimes how they get through from one day to the next. I don't think they know that because their expectations are quite low. It's our whole manner of being with them, it's so important and affects whether they feel equal or not. Not being patronising, I don't think I am (my emphasis) (groupworker).

Finally, a recognition of women's power was central in encouraging group members to connect personal preoccupations with social conditions and collective solutions:

> The women do tend to be dependent and expect you to do things and always want permission. That makes it all the more important that they can actually feel they've got some *power*, that they can learn from each other (my emphasis) (groupworker).

The impact of these five conditions is reflected in the perceptions of one group member who talked about the importance of sharing experiences in the group, with trust and safety developing alongside this. She had been enabled to disclose instances of sexual violence in her life:

> We talked about rape and sexual assault in the group. I know I'm not the only person who's gone through it. Everyone is honest and open with everyone else. I don't feel as though I have to keep my mouth shut. I feel safe. Everyone's been through a rough time. It's funny, I've felt as if I've known the women all along. The support has just been there (white woman).

In keeping with social action Aim 8, the style of facilitation enabled the groupworkers to develop a partnership with women because of their belief in women's capabilities and understandings.

Personal / political agenda

The content of the women's group can be untangled through the recurring themes and patterns which emerged within and across sessions. Women's conversation is a broad landscape within which topics meander and flow. However, the explanations and arguments contained within this circularity are the tools with which women construct their social reality. An evaluation of group content against the social action values reveals that aims 1-3 were met in terms of women identifying *what* the issues were for them. This process of recognition, of naming experiences is critical to women's empowerment. It is an affirmative act of self-definition. I cannot review the complexity of all these themes, but I have selected several which demonstrate the emotional and social reasoning which women go through to make sense of their worlds. There is evidence that the group provided a valuable forum for tackling some fundamental political issues, enabling connections to be made between personal experience and structural forces:

> Group members do see themselves as victims but we can stress the fact that they are caught up in structural decisions made by men in a wider sense and men in their personal lives who are constantly letting them down (groupworker).

Within this context, I shall explore the debates women had about their sexuality; their relationships with male partners; racism and bringing up mixed parentage children; and finally, money management, poverty and politics.

Sexuality

In the group, sexuality was treated in terms of whether women had a sexual life and whether this meant having more children. As one woman was pregnant there was much ambivalence in the group about this issue. Women's group members, in keeping with dominant societal beliefs, equated sexuality with penetrative sex, reproduction, sexual behaviour and sexual orientation. They made assumptions about this being exclusively heterosexual:

> One woman talks very openly about her sexual experiences and about men on building sites and what she'd like to do in graphic detail. If you ask her what she wants, she'll say, 'Ah, I wanna really good bloke', and she gets all raunchy. She says things like, 'The woman next door for instance, she can tell straight away if I've had a good night, if I've had it'. They say things like 'They'd better get some fun out of sex, they'd better get on with it, before they're too old', and I remember saying, 'You don't have to worry about that, it might get better'.
> Those who haven't got a sexual life at the moment, and are still young, are asking 'Is this all there is to it for me? I'm in my early twenties and there's nothing going on. What can I do about it?' Then there's all this talk about 'Well, I've got a man but he's a rotten lover anyway, so what are you making a fuss about?' It's treated more light-hearted than other issues, but there's an element of *huge* disappointment for women in terms of their sexuality (groupworker).

This disappointment indicates that women had an impoverished view of their sexual potential. At the same time, being 'sexually attractive' was important to them, with some group members taking harmful slimming tablets purchased from a sex shop as a way of regulating and controlling their weight. Black women in the group were excluded from the standard of the unspoken whiteness of the beauty myth promulgated by the fashion industry and the media. All the women involved in heterosexual relationships were engaged in forms of self-surveillance, complying with the normative narrative scripts which demanded their consent and participation, irrespective of their own sexual or erotic feelings. Whilst women found men disgusting, they also desired them. All of this was compounded by homophobia. For instance, the group discussed one woman's fears about an imminent short prison sentence. She had been told many stories about prison violence, especially incidents perpetrated by lesbians. The group examined the heterosexist assumptions underpinning the 'advice' about lesbian behaviour and how she would survive the experience of prison.

In contrast to the ways in which other topics were handled, women explored their sexuality through humour mingled with sadness.

Relationships with male partners

A great deal of group time was spent in talking and laughing about men. Discussions revolved around women's sense of responsibility towards their male partners, both live-in and non-live-in, and how the pernicious influences of heteropatriarchy shaped male assumptions about their non-participation in child care. Heterosexual women are at greater risk of having inequitable personal relationships due to asymmetrical power distribution (Jacklin, 1993). The contradictions involved in male supremacy were pulled apart in the course of group discussion:

> There's a lot of men-hating and laughing at men goes on. They've got little boys as well and I'd like to see them discover the positives in men because of their sons' lives. But they do have a bad time with men. One of them has a live-in partner, who has let her go to prison for a few days rather than he himself pay the TV licence. Another woman has two children by a non-live-in partner who's quite possessive and watches over what she does with the children, but he's never there to let her have a night out, *ever*. She's not had a night out for six years. Another one has a grown-up son and she gets involved with men who let her down - she gets into abusive relationships. Another two women don't have physically abusive relationships, but their men don't take any responsibility for the children, or for them. They're certainly not *nurtured* as women in these relationships at all, definitely not (groupworker).

> He never helps, *never*. Bringing up kids is such a tremendous responsibility, but men, they don't see it that way. He might turn up one day. But I wouldn't like that really because he'd upset the kids all over again and I'd have to pick up the pieces. I'd prefer him to keep away all together (white woman).

The group looked at the effect of poverty and 'race' on the quality and consistency of their relationships with male partners. Pressures of lack of money undermined any notion of 'free choice' in relationships. As a result, many group members were exposed to complex feelings of love, lack of respect, anger and sensuality which spilled over, affecting their parenting skills and their determination to carry on in these damaging relationships, despite their utter exhaustion. At the same time, white group members needed to grapple with simultaneous positions of disadvantage and privilege, in that the limited rewards of associating with white men penalised Black women.

One Black woman recognised the effects of this internalised sexism/heterosexism on women's topics of conversation. Her criticism of the group's preoccupation with men's oppressive treatment of women was that she wanted to talk about *being a woman* and the effects of poverty, poor housing and social welfare services on her psychological wellbeing:

> The women only want to talk about what men should do, what men don't do, what's wrong with men, it gets boring. They talk about the same things all the time. Maybe it's because they're all the same kind of women. They've mostly had experiences of violence, so maybe they want to get their own back, I don't know. I just sit there and listen. I'd like us to talk about different things, what you can expect from Social Services, social workers, benefits, everything. But we don't talk about things like that. I'd like to say, 'How would you like to be stuck in a flat with no furniture for four months?' That's how I've had to live. But I don't feel able to say these things. Every week it gets back to the same topic, men, why men can't be left with the kids, let's see if they'd like to do the housework all the while. I know they've got pressures, but I have too. *I'd like us to talk about us, women* and our ordinary problems (my emphasis) (African-Caribbean woman).

Within the web of women's complex and varied social realities, she saw herself as positioned differently from other Black and white women in the group by virtue of her life-style and status as a lone mother with no current male partner. Her 'difference' was part of a thread of racist discourse and exclusion within the group which was highlighted and confronted through group process and the style of facilitation.

The interplay of racism with heterosexism was addressed through the issue of dual heritage relationships. An instance of racist conflict and discord in the group enabled the dynamics of oppression to be confronted. Group interactions became intense when one white woman walked out of a session because other group members said they did not like white women having Black partners. Other women knew that she had children of mixed parentage, but they had used their own prejudices based on partial, situated knowledge to be 'insensitive, very judgemental and very coarse' (white groupworker). Stereotypes about African-Caribbean men's sexual prowess abounded. When the woman returned to the group, the workers recognised her pain and distress, enabling members to see how offensive their behaviour had been. Both groupworkers stressed the importance of understanding rather than ridiculing these relationships, given the diversity of ethnic identities in Britain.

The group decided to devote one session to increasing awareness about dual heritage relationships. A thirty minute video was shown, charting the history of reactions to these partnerships, followed by a discussion. The group examined its *collective heritage* in terms of African, European, Asian, Welsh, Irish, American/Italian, Scottish, Irish/Welsh descent. By acknowledging the extent of ethnic diversity in the group, women's different positions could be aired without fear of reprisals. The group realised that opinion about dual heritage relationships was affected by distrust, hatred and even repulsion, with these prejudices determined by not only racism, but also working class dynamics. Whilst poor white women in the group had limited choice and advantages in their intimate relationships with poor white men, they had rendered Black/white heterosexual relationships invisible.

This session was a springboard for the identification of other resources and support systems which could increase group members' knowledge and awareness about the complexity of dual heritage relationships.

Black identity, racism and bringing up mixed parentage children

The most persistent issue for Black and white mothers during the group's life was the problems involved in bringing up mixed parentage children, with women using the group to work through their intense confusions. Lone white mothers needed support to promote Black awareness in their dual parentage children, but the group discovered little current service provision directly aimed at assisting white parents to meet their Black children's diverse needs (Thompson and Fleming, 1993). The group realised that whilst information was available to teach their Black children about self-pride and the nature of white oppression, this did not equip them with the necessary coping strategies when returning to a white household every night where the only significant parent was a white mother. Given the increasing complexity of racial, religious and cultural dimensions in family life, the group played a significant role in assisting Black and white women to gain knowledge of the multiplicity of challenges in identity development for dual parentage children. One woman had two younger mixed parentage children and an older white child, aged six years, who was struggling to understand why his siblings were a different colour to himself. He had a good relationship with their Black father whilst his own white father had rejected him.

The Black groupworker dealt with an African-Caribbean/white woman and her African-Caribbean/white son's denial of being Black by talking about negative images of Black women as bad mothers. Having witnessed the extent to which Black people experienced racism, both mother and son survived their poverty and hardship by identifying themselves as white. The group had to recognise the *hostility* of the dominant culture towards Black people and confront their own ethnocentricity to offer this woman a glimmer of an alternative perception of herself. Both mother and son gained a great deal from talking about his identity with the Black groupworker, who presented as assertive, was non-threatening, and had an ability to express herself well:

> She said to me, 'Let's stand up, we've got something to say'. She talked to me about not seeing myself and my son as Black, but she did this in a very easy way. It was alright, because it felt as if she was one of us, right there at my side. She didn't point the finger at me (African-Caribbean/white woman).

Such is the intensity of this issue that racist views were expressed in the group which had to be carefully tackled, with groupworkers using skills in *challenging* and *re-education*. The dynamics of oppressive behaviour and being oppressed were enacted during an incident where women were talking about confinement in hospital. One group member described 'This Black bastard' (sic) who was a nurse on the ward, adding, 'Well, I'm not racist, I've got Black friends'. She tended to throw out comments and then pull them back. Only one woman challenged her, asking how she would feel if she had a Black partner. The white groupworker took responsibility for confronting white women with their own part in the perpetuation of racism:

> I've got a big responsibility to listen for racism. I have to at least pick it up and see where the discussion goes. I challenged this incident by saying 'Are there any white bastards?' and then I commented on what it meant to others in the group to hear Black people described in this way (groupworker).

In terms of social action Aim 6, the groupworkers recognised that, at this stage in the group's development, they were holding responsibility for *challenging* instances of oppression whilst offering *protection* to vulnerable group members:

> We're the ones who *challenge* and we sometimes have to *protect* some women in the group, certainly from racism. Racism is a *big* issue. Sexism is there all the time and we have to highlight it. As yet, the women aren't challenging these things themselves; the women who are being hurt, say by racism, don't challenge, they keep silent. Unless you give them some space to talk about their feelings, the women are silenced. It'll be good when women members are able to challenge because they're very hurt by some of the things that are said (my emphasis) (groupworker).

The processes of domination in the group caused pain and distress, with antagonism and struggle replicating power relationships outside the group context. The ideology of 'putting women down' was played out by group members. The facilitators attempted to shift patterns of racism by enabling women to exchange points of view whilst empathising and respecting each other. In terms of interaction, the workers felt that this sharing was encouraging members to have more open discussions about racism and sexism:

> The group offers an opportunity to talk about all of this to each other and not just to us. There is now much more thoughtfulness in the group, especially around racism. There's much more of a willingness to pursue things at a deeper level (groupworker).

Money management, poverty and politics

A major priority for women's group members was the effect of poverty on the lives of their children, and their feelings of heavy responsibility for the economic survival of their families. Women were afraid of debt and its consequences and spent a great deal of time examining how they managed their money. Women's health and survival were constantly threatened as they juggled their limited income to secure the basic necessities of food, warmth and shelter. They experienced poverty in its most acute form through their management of the food budget. The weekly cycle of spending was shaped less by families' nutritional needs and more by other financial obligations such as rent, fuel bills, hire purchase and debt repayments. Food is often the main item on which women cut back to make ends meet (Graham, 1993). Running out of money was an ubiquitous experience for women.

During one session, women discussed how expensive food, household items and clothes were and the range of meals they made when there was no money and only a few tins of food left. At these times, women would either miss meals or eat smaller amounts and less nutritional items in order to protect the living standards of their children and male partners, especially when their menfolk expected 'a full meal on the table'. As a result, women compromised their own health to maintain the household. When material and practical resources were few and women's responsibilities many, smoking cigarettes provided group members with temporary relief from the grind of poverty. This small luxury both helped and threatened women's and children's health, but was a means of getting by on an income many would not think twice about spending on a restaurant meal.

The groupworkers commented on how resourceful and strategic they were. During the ensuing discussion it was decided to produce a leaflet for other women in the Shared Care Project, examining how to manage shopping economically, and produce meals which were tasty but cheap (Table 1 is a sample of this work). Women were concerned about their children's futures and their ability to confront these structural forces. As a reflection of social action Aim 4, discussions about money management led to a consideration of ways of breaking out of the poverty cycle in terms of training opportunities, employment and child care resources. Women wanted to return to work, to do something other than care for their children. The need for training was discussed as a means of earning a realistic salary. The group calculated that it would be impossible to afford child-care costs if they were in employment. Women were trapped in the paradoxical situation of being offered free nursery places when there were child care difficulties, but when they had reached the point of being considered 'good mothers' these places were no longer available.

Women were well aware of the increasing scale and intensity of their poverty and that this trend was shaped by wider social divisions, inextricably linked to political and structural forces. The provision of a forum for sharing ideas and experiences enabled women to express their anger and frustration about the political imperatives affecting their lives:

> We were talking about the difficulties of getting their benefits and that how much they get is determined by government. They swear about this and I asked how they can change things, but one said 'I don't bloody well vote for anybody'. Another woman said, 'Oh I vote, but I don't vote for this lot'. They're not daft, they know what's going on. We discussed how women are penalised by all of these policy decisions. We talked about where the government spends its money - they do talk at that level very easily (groupworker).

SOCIAL ACTION WOMEN'S GROUP LEAFLET
'All I've Got In My Purse Is Mothballs!'

'We don't like being dependent on the State. The children suffer through lack of wide experience, no holidays, and limited activities. It shouldn't really be like this, we should have more choice. We would like to work and earn our own money, getting more than we receive on Income Support.

All the government are bothered about are the rich. They don't care about the poor. Our benefit should go up, not down. The children deserve better than this'.

'All I've Got In My Purse Is Mothballs!'

So..... How to Live on Mothballs (with the kind permission of H.M. Government):

What I've discovered about shopping

'I used to do one big shopping, once a week, but found it used to go quickly - the more food you have in the house, the quicker it goes. Now I get about two bags on the Monday, and about Thursday or Friday I top it up, and whatever I don't have in the house, I just get. I find we are eating just as much, and can buy clothes for the kids. Whereas before, I was like buying one lot of clothes at a time and leaving two children out. Now I can buy three pairs of shoes, and whatever else I see for them.

Women like us still don't get enough money to give our children what they really need. I'd like them to go places instead of doing the same thing. You still feel bad because you can't give them what they ask for.'

Jobs and paying for child care.

They don't give you enough money to live on. When you get a part-time job, you have to pay for all these things:

Nursery places	Food
School dinners	Bus fares
Child minders	Clothes
Rent	Nappies
Bills	Fags

Table 1

Conclusion

At the end of this eight month period, the group had not reached the point where women could define *how* they were going to achieve personal, social and structural changes (Aims 4-5). However, the group's small-scale achievements in terms of understanding the *causes* of personal concerns were highly valued by the women, facilitating their movement through the project towards a recognition of their skills, strengths and belief in themselves beyond their parenting role. Within the timescale involved, the group made an impact on women in terms of their relationships; their self-care and desire to keep healthy; and their belief that going back to work was something that could now be contemplated rather than being seen as an impossibility. Men still remained shadowy but influential figures in a landscape marked out in terms of what women did for their families. The difference was that the group gave women permission to explore the humour, sadness and strains of family life, and no longer remain silent about these issues.

Group dynamics surrounding heterosexism and racism demonstrated the importance of not assuming an unproblematic, mutually exclusive boundary between the oppressed and the oppressors. Similarities between women were cross-cut by differences which were strongest when discussing dual heritage relationships and bringing up mixed parentage children. These major points of conflict made it possible for women to talk more deeply and in greater detail, such that feelings of powerlessness began to crumble:

> I don't think we've seen any big changes so far, but little things have happened. There is no doubt that it's a hard life for women, but they are much more prepared to talk in a more detailed way, rather than use throw-away comments, such as 'We can't change things' and shrugging their shoulders (groupworker).

Acknowledgment

The research on which this article is based was made possible through the financial support of NCH Action For Children. I am grateful to the Shared Care Project's management, staff and women's group members for their commitment to the research process and for their honest expression of feelings and perceptions.

References

Butler, S. (1994) *'Improving Our Lives': The Radford Shared Care Project.* Nottingham: Centre For Social Action, University of Nottingham.

Butler, S. and Wintram, C. (1991) *Feminist Groupwork.* London: Sage.

Fleming, J. and Ward, D. (1992) *'For the Children To Be Alright, Their Mothers Need To Be Alright'. An Alternative To Removing The Child - The Radford Shared Care Project. An Evaluation From the Participants' Viewpoints*. Nottingham: Centre For Social Action, University of Nottingham.

Freire, P. (1972) *The Pedagogy of The Oppressed*. Harmondsworth: Penguin.

Frost, N. and Stein, M. (1989) *The Politics of Child Welfare: Inequality, Power and Change*. Hemel Hempstead: Harvester Wheatsheaf.

Graham, H. (1993) *Hardship and Health in Women's Lives*. Hemel Hempstead: Harvester Wheatsheaf.

Jacklin, C. N. (1993) 'How my heterosexuality affects my feminist politics,' in Wilkinson, S. and Kitzinger, C. (eds.) *Heterosexuality: A Feminism and Psychology Reader*. London: Sage Publications, pp.34-35.

Mullender, A., Everitt, A., Hardiker, P., and Littlewood, J. (1993/94) 'Value issues in research', *Social Action*, 1(4), pp.11-18.

Mullender, A. and Ward, D. (1991a) *The Practice Principles of Self-Directed Groupwork: Establishing a Value-Base For Empowerment*. Nottingham: Centre For Social Action, University of Nottingham.

Mullender, A. and Ward, D. (1991b) *Self-Directed Groupwork: Users Take Action For Empowerment*. London: Whiting and Birch.

NCH Action For Children/Nottinghamshire Social Services Department (1993) *Joint Service Level Agreement for the Radford Shared Care Project*. Unpublished Report.

Parton, N. (1991) *Governing The Family: Child Care, Child Protection and The State*. Houndmills, Hampshire: MacMillan.

Thompson, F. and Fleming, J. (1993) *Nottingham Black Families Project: Background Study*. Nottingham: Centre For Social Action, University of Nottingham.

REVIEWS

Running A Short Term Activity Group
KATRIN FITZHERBERT WITH ANNE FORD
Barnados Childcare Publications, price £2.50

I am certain that any primary or secondary school teacher reading this booklet would wonder how they could get such a project in their community, especially but not only in the inner cities. Katrin Fitzherbert has ten years experience of setting up groups specifically for children of primary school age who are experiencing difficulties at home or school - the vulnerable children every teacher knows and is often desperate to get help for.

Arising out of education social work, the project called 'The Pyramid Project ' uses volunteers to run the two week groups with sound common sense and limited resources.

This booklet is intended as a handbook for volunteers and is packed with good advice, information, games and activities. It is well written, clear, enthusiastic and encouraging, all placed within a framework of basic groupwork theory. Individual case notes and comments by past leaders, along with the cartoons, keep the reader interested and involved, and the format is well produced and accessible.

The chapter on theory places these activity groups, accurately I feel, somewhere between counselling and psychotherapy groups and Brownies or other similar organisations. A clear warning is given about the dangers of straying into the deeper waters of psychotherapy, and the need for proper training, thus helping to define the activity groups and their boundaries. Aims are meticulously spelt out later. Fitzherbert displays a curious reservation, though, about children's psychotherapy groups, which are called 'talk groups and are described as 'intrusive and manipulative'. For me, the value of activity groups for children is unquestionable, and I do not have to be convinced of their serious nature and intent, so this judgement is unnecessary.

There are two short practice chapters: part one, 'Preparing for your group', and part two 'Running your group' - a courageous and successful attempt to cover the essential processes of group life in a practical and realistic way. There are ideas for activities based on what has succeeded in the past, which match with expected behaviour through the stages of 'Forming', 'Storming', 'Norming', 'Performing' and 'Mourning'.

Starting with the administrative structures for setting up a project, Fitzherbert gives important guidelines about leadership - skills, attitudes and recruitment. Missing for me though was any mention of the effect of leaders on children, the need for identification for black and Asian children, or role models for boys and girls for example. It is implicit within the text than an anti-racist stance was assumed, but I noticed that the term Christian names was used in an activity, and in my view a more assertive and conscious equal opportunities programme needs to be espoused, especially as this document is intended for people to emulate. I was please to see the value of consultation stated clearly and that some training was offered.

The claims made for these ten week groups may seem extravagant until you realise that group members are chosen from 'year' groups in school and so are already known to one another. A preparatory visit accelerates the process by engaging the children beforehand in the planning of the 'club'.

Good advice for would-be leaders is about selection, the need to be firm about who comes to the 'club'. This could be quite difficult for leaders, resisting the pressure from teachers and parents to include siblings, best friends or enemies, hoping for results impossible in the time available. The need for balance of membership keeps the leaders feet firmly on the ground, once again clarifying and limiting the aims.

Such good advice is often couched in questionable language, for example: 'your first task as leader is therefore to manipulate the eight or ten individuals presented to you at your first session into their very own unique club or secret society.' The advice following this statement is excellent, giving ideas of ways to bring a group together to begin the process of building up group solidarity. Manipulate is not a word I would use in this context, although it is clearly necessary within the aims of the project to be prescriptive. Throughout the text there are examples of language not quite doing justice to the intention of the project.

In the section entitled 'Rules and sanctions', 'everyone must have a good time' could be a bit misleading and really means that each member is to be equally respected and important. There are a lot of references to 'warm fuzzies', 'strokes', fun and good times, which may seem a bit sweet for some tastes. Children's groups do need all of these, but its not always that easy, especially for needy children such as these.

One word of caution regarding the notion that there is 'no such thing as a bad group'. It is tempting but simplistic to say that, as a way of encouraging leaders of groups that do not go according to plan. It would take a larger, more thorough account of groupwork theory to explain why groups could be termed 'good' or 'bad'. Leaders cannot always know what is going on for individuals in groups, and care must be taken in what is clearly a powerful experience for some.

The final chapter, on 'Games for every mood', is a must for experienced and novice group leaders alike, all well tried and tested and matched up with the groupwork process, except for one example perhaps - where in 'Wall Crash', a trust game, one player with eyes closed hopes he/she will be caught safely!

It is very encouraging to hear of a project which is so positive, offering effective preventative help for young children. Time was when many voluntary organisations and local authorities were committed to such preventative work to good effect, and its so sad now to watch them be squeezed out for lack of funding. If this publication stimulates some enthusiasm to follow suit, more children could be reached in this way.

ANN WALFORD
Independent Trainer and Consultant

Groupwork In Education and Training
MICHAEL REYNOLDS
Kogan Page, price £12.95 (pbk), ISBN 0-7494-1027-2

If you have ever wondered what it really means to be invited to participate in an experiential group; or what makes a difference in how groups may be enabled to contribute positively to learning; or how staff and students, or group facilitators and members may experience each other and what may affect their interactions; then this short book may interest you. Its focus is on using groups to facilitate learning.

The book has two sections. The opening three chapters provide some theoretical and methodological underpinnings. There are sections on the development of experiential learning groups, available group methods, and the rationale for using groups in education; on planning for and designing learning groups, including observation guides and ways of understanding and responding to group process.

The remaining five chapters focus on practice, and the implications of using groupwork for staff development. Questions of boundaries, values, taking account of a groups context, team development, and single sex groups are all discussed and illustrated. Chapters conclude with suggestions for further reading.

Written in an accessible style, the book contains clear expositions of elements of groupwork theory and practice, such as Bion's ideas on group processes, and pertinent critiques, such as of Tuckman's model of group development. The illustrations provide useful entries into complex group processes and into how trainers can create a climate for learning.

The book is directed at people who use or intend to use group methods. For those who are experienced in using groups in education and training, this book might be too general. Equally, for those who wish to adopt group methods, this book might provide an accessible entry into some groupwork theory and methods but will be insufficient since its focus is both somewhat selective and too general. Thus, whilst the book acknowledges and explores the complexity of group processes, this investigation has an introductory feel which in unlikely to take experienced groupworkers much further or, perhaps, to encourage the wary. There is a pertinent emphasis on groupworkers and trainers as facilitators of learning, but there is no reference here to self-directed, or to enquiry and action approaches to learning and work in groups. Social work trainers have made major contributions in these areas but the book neither acknowledges nor uses this work.

Nonetheless, as I prepare for the beginning of another academic year, worry about the future of social work education and training, and continue to strive to create an anti-oppressive environment in which staff and students can learn together, this book was a timely contribution. It reminded me, for instance, that values and beliefs are expressed through how one designs learning programmes, such that one's expressed commitments may not be reproduced in practice; and that the emphasis on competencies and outcomes should not exclude consideration of what is being learned and how. Some of the exercises are useful in enabling students to prepare for the challenges of professional practice. The books consideration of issues of power and influence connected me to the interface between staff and students, users and workers, CCETSW and social work practitioners and trainers.

If learning, as the book suggests, is a process of examining who we experience ourselves to be and what meaning different concepts have for that view of ourselves and our world, then reading this book prompted such an examination for me, at a personal and professional level. However, whether it would have encouraged me to adopt groupwork methods were I not already committed to using them, is another question and, whilst its clear presentation of ideas is helpful, I was left wanting both greater depth and breadth in the material.

Michael Preston-Shoot, Senior Lecturer in Social Work, University of Manchester. Author of *Effective Groupwork* (Macmillan).

Groupwork with Offenders
ALLAN BROWN AND BRIAN CADDICK (eds.)
Whiting & Birch, London, 1993, price £15.95 (pbk), ISBN 1-871177-41

Recently a colleague who had been working in a probation centre for the last 18 months with responsibility for organising groupwork programmes told me they were about to go on their first groupwork training course. A student, for whom I had arranged the opportunity to co-work a group with other colleagues, turned up for what he, and I, had thought would be the first planning session and found himself plunged into meeting the clients and co-leading a group session with no preparation being undertaken. Whilst I know these experiences are not universal, my experience of working for several probation areas suggests that they are not unusual. The contributions to this book reflect some of this diversity in training and preparation, some contributions making no mention of theoretical framework at all, others indicating a cursory nod to Tuckman's linear processes and some with clear models of approach with aims, programmes and evaluation procedures thought through and planned prior to the group beginning to look for members.

A considerable range of groupwork is considered with particular attention given to work in prison establishments and approved hostels as well as field offices and probation (day) centres. I am sure that those who, have experienced the marginalising of work they have undertaken in hostels and prisons, will feel pleased to have their contribution valued in this way. All of the groups considered are 'planned' groups which for me, suggests a devaluing of the more informal (although not necessarily unplanned) processes operating in reporting schemes, hostels (where a range of informal group processes operate in the residential environment) and community service schemes. The editors themselves identify a further shortcoming - no inclusion of the use of groupwork for black probation clients. Whilst nearly all of the contributors make some reference to anti-discriminatory or anti-racist practice some of this appears quite tokenistic. In a period when anti-racist practice has become more central to social work and probation training, both qualifying training and in-service, it is an indictment of the probation service that black clients continue to be marginalised, both in individual and groupwork, and a pity that this book perpetuates this marginalisation by failing to provide any proper consideration of the issues groupworkers should be tackling.

The book is split into 3 sections, beginning with a general introduction to the state of 'planned' groupwork in the Probation service. The next two sections look firstly at groups in prisons, hostels and probation centres, and secondly in field settings. I was concerned that hostels and probation centres were not considered as part of the provision of groupwork in community based settings, rather than grouped with prisons in what appears to be a section on 'institutional' groupwork. The inappropriateness of this chapter grouping is reinforced when the section on 'field settings' begins with consideration of a centralised group programme and included a report of a motor project, neither of which are based in a field office.

The introduction focuses on a survey by Caddick in 1989 which does little to add to the information in Despicht's much fuller review of a couple of years earlier. The political climate of the mid/late 1980s is set with Senior arguing that during this period groupwork developed as a major tool of control in the Probation service. Brown and Caddick also identify the influence of Priestley and McGuire, contrasting the individual pathology bases of both their Social Skills and Offending Behaviour programmes with the more community oriented 'Self Directed' groupwork of Mullender and Ward. Some comparison of the latter with the literature on community based work by Henderson and others would have been useful.

The most valuable chapters in the practice sections I found to be those which clearly identified their theoretical framework, with particularly useful contributions from Mistry and Cowburn who both identified an explicit value-base for their work and showed how this affected their choice of framework. This was a feminist model of groupwork with women from Mistry, and work with sex offenders in Cowburn's case.

Jones et al. and Thomas look at how informed by both a 'feminist' and 'welfare' perspective, they developed a model of work for women which is suggested as empowering women both as workers and clients, in a way which echoes Ahmed's identification of using groupwork as a process for empowering black social work clients.

The chapters covering probation centres compare how the political climate has affected the approach of one centre transferring its approach from a more caring self-directed environment to a more controlling one, with others identifying how in the same climate they have managed to move in the reverse direction in one case, and maintain the original ethos in the other. Again the clarity of theoretical framework is important in this and the argument that political influence has affected groupwork approaches is again challenged by Mackintosh who demonstrates how a commitment to voluntary attendance on an Intensive Probation Programme is accepted by sentencers when they more clearly understand the basis the groups operate on.

The approach to groupwork with violent offenders is explicitly based on McGuire & Priestley's *Offending Behaviour* whilst Cowburn's exploration of principles for practice with male sex offenders also identified individual responsibility as a major emphasis. Cognitive behavioural approaches have developed and the primary model of work with sex offenders, but, as already indicated, Cowburn's explicit statement of values gives a clearer explanation of why this approach is chosen from those available. It is one of the failings of the book that there is no further exploration of cognitive-behavioural approaches and the debate they have generated over the last few years.

The chapters on hostels also provide a clearer explanation of their theoretical framework and Mulvie and Sapsed also make a positive link between the informal group processes in a residential environment and the formal groupwork, however the chapters on work in penal settings and a motor project are among those with least reference to any theoretical basis or working model.

It is a pity that, when commissioning the contributions, the editors appear not to have identified a framework for covering particular issues. This limits the usefulness of a number of the contributions, as does the datedness of the material included, it all being written prior to the introduction of the Criminal Justice Act 1991. The prominence given to hostel and prison work is important, however, and the learning to be gained from the clear examples of preparation process, choice of models of work, theoretical framework and values underlying these, provide a valuable resource both for those involved in planning and running groups, and those involved in developing training for groupwork in the probation service.

Nick Wood, Senior Probation Officer/Practice Teacher Co-ordinator

Systems Thinking for Harassed Managers.
N. McCAUGHAN AND B. PALMER
Karnac Books, price £13.95 (pbk), ISBN 1-85575-055-4

'Conversations about Consultancy' could have been another title for this book. In an almost everyday language, the authors share their experiences of running courses for social work managers. During these courses they have encouraged participants to adopt the view of systems developed by the Milan team. Now they share the experiences and the thinking behind them. First, the purpose is stated. It is threefold: to outline the elements of systems thinking, to describe a procedure for addressing situations that cause managers problems and to provide examples of managers using the procedures so that readers could work in this way themselves.

The authors then construct the contents according to the process of consultation. They introduce some quite basic ideas first. Then problems are examined in systemic terms. Once these terms are understood, assessment is explained as a way of 'asking the right questions'; that is, the ones that highlight mutual influences in the organisation, and the behavioural patterns that connect them into a whole. Such questioning enables practitioners to construct 'hypotheses'. These are the practitioners' guesses about patterns that sustain the problems. Having arrived at such rather educated guesses, the practitioners can then suggest 'a new course'; what can be done and particularly what can be avoided if the problem is to be removed. At each point, ideas from the Milan school of thought are rather briefly introduced.

Only after sharing the whole processes during the five chapters, is a 'theoretical postscript' offered. This sixth chapter briefly elaborates some of the ideas suggested during the previous five. I found the Appendix particularly illuminating. At the very end, the authors actually describe how they construct their courses. Systemic thinking is hard to teach, as this discourse can easily become rather abstract. I felt I was learning from the authors' extensive and well recognised experience about pacing the material and about connecting head and heart.

Unlike others, the authors also describe 'where we are coming from': their professional development. Respecting their constructionist perspective, perhaps book reviewers should also acknowledge their biases. I *am* a great admirer of the ideas developed by the Milan team which have influenced my practice and my thinking considerably. Yet, I am not convinced that any systemic style (and there are many of them) is enough on its own. It follows that I have not embraced the Milan approach to the exclusion of others. It is only from an integrative perspective that I can offer any comment. Still, I have been asked.

I found the book very easy to read. Perhaps being somewhat familiar with the theory helped. All the same, I was taken by the lively fresh style. I felt I was involved in a conversation: sometimes I was slightly thrown by certain strong expressions, often I wanted to know many more details about each case. Yet, I always wanted to read on. As the authors say: I was 'hooked'.

My interest came to a head with the section 'mapping dilemmas' (pp.112-116). These four pages, almost at the end, focused my experiences. I realised that for me the main impact of this book was to highlight dilemmas. From an integrative point of view, I warmed up particularly to those sections which dealt with dilemmas. Examples of these were the dilemma between listening and intervening (pp.30-31), and between listening and clarifying (pp.33-34). Also, I was relieved to see feedback processes, patterns, and power each presented *separately* (pp.37-42), rather than lumped together as in other sources. This separation could enable practitioners to pinpoint the abuse of power.

I have to say that at other times I wished the authors handled the material in the same way instead of splitting. An example, is the split between the 'open systems model' and their own 'recursive systems model' (pp.16-18). My own perception is actually that each has serious limitations when applied on its own. I have been won over by the hard work of the team led by James Durkin (1981). That team offered a synthesis of the two models under the umbrella of 'general systems theory'. I appreciate that had the authors drawn on that volume their discourse could not have remained as evocative and engaging. It would have led to 'the heavy stuff' (p.96). What harassed manager would have continued to read? Yet, this split seems to be at the root of other difficulties.

On page 82 the authors recommend that managers 'examine the possibilities of straight or direct interventions, before assuming that only paradox can move things along'. I found this most refreshing. Alas, two pages later the authors retreat. Having proposed such a direct intervention, and having seen it help, the authors comment that they 'did not regard this as a systemic intervention; it seems to be logical advice, given the situation.' (p.84). Now, for an integrationist, this *is* difficult. The statement implies that logic and systems thinking do not go together. It suggests that direct linear responses are somehow less systemic. The difficulty is that such as interpretation may lead practitioners to ignore the initial recommendation and 'paradox people' regardless of their relationship with them. I have seen it happen and the results have been alarming. I would suggest that as long as any partial influence among people is concerned with the pattern as a whole it IS systemic, and equally important. Such direct linear influences are simply a different type of change, called 'first order change'. Yet, involving people with the complexities of the interplay between first and second order change may lead them to the detailed examination of the relationship between analogue and digital information...You see what I mean? Who would survive?

There were other points where a more complicated discourse might have prevented potential problems; for example, the definition of positive feedback (pp.61-63). Further clarification of the difference between Klein and Fairbairn might have prevented the split between the systems approach and psychodynamics (pp.105-108), and in turn prevent the potential for 'oscillation between opposing configurations and for debilitating conflict which rumbles for ever'. (p.116).

So, I continued to struggle with my dilemmas, and these included also ethical and moral questions that others have raised about the purely Milan approach. I shall probably continue to struggle for quite a while. A book that stimulates such a struggle is certainly a worthwhile book. As for achieving its goals: I anticipate that many managers will feel warmly engaged. I hope only few will simply read the book and begin to act on it. I trust most will be inspired to enrol on courses such as the ones offered by the authors where they learn even more of 'the real stuff'.

Oded Manor, Principal Lecturer in Social Work, Middlesex University

References

Durkin, J. (ed.) (1981) Living Systems: Group Psychotherapy and General System Theory. New York: Brunner/Mazel Pub.

NOTES ON CONTRIBUTORS

Sandra Butler is Lecturer in Social Work at the University of Nottingham and is co-author with Claire Wintram of *Feminist Groupwork* (1991, London: Sage Publications).

Kerry Chamberlain works in administration in the National Health Service. She runs a home and is a very active member of the women's group she writes about.

Deb Dobbin is a social worker; she is particularly interested in supporting women who find themselves in difficult circumstances.

Sarah Evans is a social worker; she is particularly interested in supporting women who find themselves in difficult circumstances.

Judy Fawcett is a qualified teacher and social worker who has worked in both the statutory and voluntary sectors as a manager and practitioner. She is now an independent consultant and trainer and acts as a groupwork consultant. She has set up support groups for women managers and runs seminars and workshops on gender issues and women in management. She is currently Deputy Chair of BASW.

Marcia Francis-Spence is a Lecturer, Centre for Applied Social Studies, University of Durham.

Barbara Becker Holstein is a psychologist in full time private practice in Long Branch, New Jersey, USA.

Marlene Kuhn is a qualified midwife. She is currently engaged in teaching on behalf of the British Red Cross. She is a woman with a disability and belongs to a support group for people with disabilities.

Doreen Laperdon-Addison MA, CMA, RMT is a movement educator, choreographer, and professional dancer.

Olive Otway is a Lecturer in Social Work, Keele University. She has been involved with groups for women and children who have experienced abuse. She is engaged in a research project on groups for abused children.

Anne Peake is a Principal Psychologist based in Oxfordshire who has published widely in the field of sexual abuse.

Jo Smith is a woman with a disability and is very active in support and campaign groups in Leicester for people with disabilities.

Claire Wintram is an independent trainer and groupworker, based in Leicester. She facilitates many women-only courses, includng Counselling Skills, Women and Health, Women and Paid Work.

NOTES FOR CONTRIBUTORS

Potential contributors
Articles are welcome from all who have an interest in work with groups (whether as practitioner, trainer, researcher, user or consultant) and who wish to contribute to the development of groupwork theory and practice.

Types of Articles
The journal will publish two main types of articles:

i. practice-based papers
ii. theory-building papers

Although these two types of article will differ in emphasis and perspective, both are seen as equally important. The intention is that the practice papers will draw out general principles and the theoretical papers will indicate their relevance to practice.

i. PRACTICE-BASED PAPERS

These articles will be based directly on groupwork practice experience, but written in a way which is evaluative as well as descriptive. The material will make a direct contribution to practice theory in a way which will enable groupworkers to learn from it, and to develop their practice competence. The journal would like to receive articles from groupworkers from a wide range of settings working in different ways with people having fieldwork, residential, daycare and hospital settings; members of diverse age, race and gender; and methods varying between discussion, structured activity, therapy and action. We recognise that many practitioners may not be familiar with writing for journals, and we wish to suggest the following guidelines to assist in this process:

(a) A brief summary of the contents of the article (100-150 words), drawing attention to any particular theme or emphasis.
(b) Background to the group, the context, e.g. agency setting, type of group, workers and members; group aims and objectives; and the theoretical/philosophical perspectives i.e. any particular principles or values central to the approach taken.
(c) A brief review of the group, content, methods and process.
(d) Outcome and analysis, specific topics of interest relevant to the focus of the article, e.g. key issues arising from this piece of practice; and evaluation of the group drawing out learning points for other practitioners.

ii. THEORY-BUILDING PAPERS

Each issue will carry several theoretical papers ranging over groupwork concepts, theory, research, issues and values. These papers will have no set format, but contributors are asked to begin with a brief summary of the contents of the article (100-150 words) and to include a section at the end which indicates the specific implications of the theoretical material for groupwork practice. Papers on the following topics would be especially welcomed:

(a) The current 'state of the art' of groupwork.
(b) Papers analysing the significance for the groupwork process of race, gender, class, culture and other social factors.
(c) Papers analysing key group concepts and issues.
(d) Papers from different countries, sharing current developments and theoretical concerns and preoccupations likely to be significant for groupwork practice in Britain and elsewhere.
(e) New sources of research evidence.
(f) Groupwork training and skill development, consultation/supervision.

We recognise that some contributors may wish to write papers which do not fall neatly into one or other of these categories, e.g. papers drawing out general principles from groupwork practice programmes. Such papers will, of course, be just as welcome in the journal.

Length of papers

The normal range will be 2,500-4,000 words, with practice accounts normally not longer than 3,000 words. Exceptionally, longer articles will be accepted and there will be a place for briefer contributions on new developments, responses to previous articles and other material of special interest.

Form of Submission

Articles should be submitted in one of two ways:

i. typed on A4 paper, 3 copies, double-spaced with wide margins
ii. on computer disc. Authors who have prepared their material by word processor are asked to provide a copy of the computer file on disk. Most Macintosh, IBM-PC compatible and Amstrad word processing programs can be read.

References

These should be quoted in the text by giving in brackets the author's name and year of publication. They should then be listed in alphabetical order at the end of the article as follows.

Books - author's surname, initials, date, title of book, place of publication, publisher's name, page if relevant.

Articles - author's surname, initials, date, title of article, title of journal, volume and number. Only those references which occur in the text should be listed. Where appropriate, additional resources may be listed separately as further reading.

N.B. It is important that punctuation and the use of capital letters should accord with the style used in *GROUPWORK*.

Assessment for publication

Articles submitted will normally be passed to members of the journal's panel of assessors, and decisions as to publication made by the editors in the light of the assessors' comments.

Publication

The journal will be published three times a year.

Abstracts and information section

Any information for inclusion in this section, e.g. notification of conferences, network meetings, recent groupwork publications of particular interest, should reach the editors not later than two months prior to publication of the relevant issue.

Authors

Authors should include brief information - two or three sentences - about themselves and their background.

Enquiries

Any potential authors who would like to discuss their ideas prior to writing or submitting an article are welcome to contact either of the co-editors ...

Allan Brown, Dept of Social Work, University of Bristol, 8 Woodland Road, Bristol BS8 1TN. Tel: 0272-303030, ext. M208

Nano McCaughan, 12 Barr Beacons, Canonbie Road, London SE23. Tel: 081 699 8438

ALL TYPED ARTICLES AND INFORMATION FOR THE ABSTRACTS SHOULD BE SENT TO ALLAN BROWN.

ALL MATERIAL FOR REVIEW SHOULD BE SENT TO NANO McCAUGHAN.

GROUPWORK

Volume 7 Number 3 1994

SUBSCRIPTION, ADVERTISING AND BUSINESS ENQUIRIES
Should be addressed to the publishers, WHITING & BIRCH LTD, PO Box 872, Forest Hill, London SE23 3HL. TEL: 081-244-2421 (Int'l +4481 244-2421). FAX: 081-244-2448 (Int'l. +4481-244-2448)

SUBSCRIPTION RATES
British Isles £35.00, North America US$80, Elsewhere £45.00
Special reduced rates apply as follows: Individuals to private address: £19.00 British Isles, North America, US$35 Elsewhere £22.00.
Special reductions for members of AASWG and Groupwork Exchange Network. Groupwork is published three times a year.

PAYMENT
Should accompany order. Cheque or banker's draft (made payable to WHITING & BIRCH LTD) may be in any convertible currency to the relevant amount. Direct transfer can be made to our Girobank account (no. 5440564). The following credit cards are also accepted: Access/Mastercard, Visa, Diners Club, American Express. Quote card number, expiry date and give cardholder's name and address if different from delivery address.

GROUPWORK is cited in: *Applied Social Sciences Index & Abstracts, Sociological Abstracts, Bibliographie Zeitscriftenliteratur aus allen Gebieten des Wissens, Social Care Update, Social Work Research & Abstracts, Special Educational Needs Abstracts*. and *Studies on Women Abstracts.*

PUBLISHED BY WHITING & BIRCH LTD, LONDON. ISSN 0951-824X
Printed by Antony Rowe Ltd, Chippenham, UK

EDITORIAL

In this issue we include six contrasting articles, each of which in very different ways extends the frontiers of our understanding of the possibilities of groupwork. The range includes new conceptual thinking about the meaning of silences in groups; a journey deep into group processes and empowerment in work with adults with learning disabilities; the case for new kinds of groups for parents of young offenders; creative use of literature and film in understanding groups; group continuity across the birth event for young mothers; and the development of techniques for formal evaluation of anger control groups for men in prison.

We believe Janet Batsleer's paper makes a breakthrough in our understanding of the links between silences in groups and the oppressive life experience of individual group members. Hitherto the literature on silence in groups has tended to seek explanations within the group dynamics: Batsleer makes the connections between these intra-group processes and the force of structural disempowerment which affects, for example, the group participation of many lesbian women and black people.

We are pleased to publish a second article by Helen Gobat (see 6[3]) on her groupwork in the field of learning disability. Here she accomplishes the difficult task of sharing group life with the reader, in a way which relates practice to theory (psychodynamic and empowerment), whilst portraying vividly the group experience of individual group members, and the remarkable progress made. Interestingly, in discussing the need to overcome what she refers to as members 'secondary handicap' (non-verbal adaptations for self-protection in the face of discriminatory attitudes to learning disability), Gobat is addressing the same basic theme as Batsleer - the structural discrimination which inhibits full and equal participation in a group.

Caroline Norman outlines a comprehensive programme of groups for very young mothers which starts with a Pregnancy group, and continues after the birth with a group for mothers and babies together, complemented by groups for the mothers alone. So often people enter a group for a few months as an isolated event in their lives: for some this is enough, for others continuity is essential. Mark Drakeford's paper is rather unusual, in that it makes the theoretical case for a particular type of groupwork to be undertaken: with parents of young offenders. He has identified this apparent gap in group provision in the criminal justice arena, and we would be interested to hear from any readers who either already run groups of the kind he envisages, or have been inspired to do so by his article.

The last two papers could not be more different in their theme and treatment. Jeremy Weinstein writes about the rich learning about groups that is available from literature and film, reminding us that we need to look more widely and creatively in our ways of learning and teaching about groups and groupwork. Graham Towl and Polly Dexter attempt the systematic evaluation of groupwork. This is an area from which many of us shy away, whether because of our unsubstantiated assumption that a 'good group experience' is proof enough of its intrinsic value, or because we are deterred by the sheer methodological complexity of evaluation, both quantitative and qualitative. They share with the reader their clear thinking about method and their attempts to obtain meaningful information about the degree of success they and their colleagues are having in achieving the objectives of anger control groups for men in prison.

Allan Brown and Nano McCaughan, Editors

Silence in working across difference: groupwork in a youth and community work training context

Janet Batsleer

This article focuses attention on the links between silence and oppression. It argues for the need to pay careful attention to silence in groups as an aspect of anti-oppressive practice. The groupworker needs to pay attention to the silences between group members, the silences imposed by the institutional setting and the patterns of silence in the wider society. The author draws on her experience of working with groups in youth and community work training to illustrate her argument.

> We can learn to work and speak when we are afraid in the same way we have learned to work and speak when we are tired. For we have been socialised to respect fear more than our own needs for language and definition, and while we wait in silence for that final luxury of fearlessness, the weight of that silence will choke us. The fact that we are here and that I speak these words is an attempt to break that silence and bridge some of those differences between us, for it is not difference which immobilises us, but silence. And there are so many silences to be broken (Lorde, 1984).

Some instances of silence

We have been watching a video on the subject of racist attacks and the self-organisation of Asian communities who are resisting those attacks. We break for coffee without discussion, as it seems appropriate to allow the powerful images some time to settle. The two Black women who are in the group - very different people in terms of their history and experience - linger behind. The gap of understanding and experience aches between their experience of watching the video and that of everyone else on the course (including mine). I try to acknowledge that I have seen the gap, heard the silence. Six months later, one of the Black women challenges us about non-communication. We are writing poems, at her instigation, about our experience of racism. 'You have been silenced by guilt', she says.

Every year I have worked with this course, I have worked with lesbian students and once or twice with gay men. I am not a lesbian. I listen as each year lesbian workers struggle to find a voice that will not leave them vulnerable to attack. One woman announces herself with pride at the beginning of the course. She is labelled by the group and punished by the group, who do not listen to her. Another woman carefully and discreetly allows her identity to become known. She is subject to such intense scrutiny and questioning by her colleagues that she chooses to pursue her studies in increasing isolation.

A third group is made up in the main of white women. The few men on the course have powerful voices but are not entirely dominant. The one Black worker, who is a woman, is marginalised. There is tremendous conflict and division among the women. This is being talked about as a conflict over class. Some women -seen as working class - being mouthy and aggressive. Other women - seen as middle class - being quiet and withholding. Silence and speech, talk and writing are the place the battle is conducted among the women in this group. The lecturer, who is a working-class woman with a middle-class education, or if you prefer, a middle class woman with a working-class background, wants to value them all.

During the last ten years the training of youth and community workers has involved an increasingly explicit commitment to a process of empowerment (NYA, 1990). Groupwork is seen as the major tool of practice and the aim of such work is to assist those who face discrimination and oppression to develop strategies, methods and actions which assist the development of their true potential. It usually takes place in informal community settings and the worker has to be a 'resourceful friend' skilled in both methods of working and in a knowledge of the social problems facing the community she is employed to work in. The training of youth and community workers therefore offers a powerful focus for many of the conflicts and differences which enrich the practice of community work itself.

The purpose of this article is twofold. First, it is to explore the connection between observations of silence I have made in different groups I have worked with. I believe that silence is often related to the operation of power and is a sign of the existence of conflict. I see identifying such common features of oppression as a way of moving beyond the tendency of a great deal of professional literature to list the competing claims of different interest groups: the familiar litany of gender, race, sexuality, disability and, occasionally, class. I believe it is possible both to develop a very concrete and contextualised understanding of oppression in all its diversity and to find focuses for work which will enable alliances to be made. I see the analysis of silence as a very important place to make some connections. In *Pedagogy of the Oppressed*, Freire claims that silence is the single great theme of emancipatory education, and this claim has been developed in many places since. The breaking of such silences and the entry either into dialogue and conversation or into rage and violence are the starting point of liberation movements everywhere, it seems (Freire, 1972; Fanon, 1967; Rowbotham, 1973; Wilson, 1978).

Secondly, I would like to contribute a little to some further discussion about the place of the small group in the social formation. This has been a theme, usually quite understated, of youth work literature since the 1960s. Joan Matthew's pioneering work *Working with Youth Groups* promoted social groupwork with adolescents as a method of developing citizenship (Matthews, 1966). Community work is very much concerned with methods of small group organising, with networks and organisations in which small groups have a central role. When community workers write and speak about empowerment, I believe that they are largely concerned with the dynamic between the work of such small groups and society wide patterns of regulation and resistance. Currently the literature which explores this relationship in detail is rather small (Mullender and Ward, 1991) Here I wish simply to offer some reflections on the possibility that the silences of small groups that are sometimes seen as 'problems of group dynamics,' and the silences waiting to be broken by emancipatory education, are the same silence.

Silence and its related anger can strongly affect communication and learning in a small group especially when the silence and the unspoken conflict are perceived to be connected to wider patterns of oppression and domination. Groupwork theory often focuses on the nature of the roles that are taken by participants and by the group leader especially. Group dynamics are thought to derive mainly from the strong internal life which groups develop, and may be considered almost completely autonomously from wider social or political analyses. For example, questions of leadership style, patterns of confrontation and conflict, selection and open and closed membership of groups are thought worth discussing. However, the discussion occurs with little or no attention to the impact of social inequality in the membership of the group.

In discussions of groupwork, there is sometimes reference to external factors which are perceived to be 'distorting': such factors as poverty, racism or sexism. It is felt that these 'must be taken into account. 'The trouble with this too simple division between 'internal' and 'external' factors is that the interpretation of group dynamics can become very skewed and ill-informed. Although, for example, racism can never be understood only by reference to interpersonal dynamics, it is equally false to understand racism as a problem that occurs 'out there. ' The experience of racism is indivisible and, for example, 'shunning' behaviour by white members of a 'racially' mixed group will inevitably be interpreted by Black group members in the context of a lifetime's experience, not simply in the context of short-term groupwork. A familiar example of this is in the differing interpretations of the 'quietness' of Black girls in British schools, which white educational institutions often perceive as either 'docility' in Asian girls or as 'dumb insolence' in African Caribbean girls. This racist interpretation is challenged by Black writers, for example the authors of a collection of writings by Black women who recognise this quietness and name it the silence of 'Watchers and Seekers' (Cobham and Collins, 1990). Thus their perceived silence is reinterpreted in the context of an experience of being made outsiders as a result of racism.

The mirror image of interpretations which have too firm a division between internal and external factors is the tendency to read off society-wide patterns directly from events in groupwork. All interpersonal interaction in this model is explained by reference to people's ascribed social position within a hierarchy of oppression. A conflict between a man and a woman may be read as sexism, the silence of white workers on the subject of race may be read as racism and so on. Judith Katz's work *White Awareness* (1978) is a significant example of this tendency.

It contains a number of exercises for use with small groups, many of which are very imaginative and interesting. The power of group exercises, especially those which involve values clarification, can however lead at times to an overidentification of systemic patterns of oppression with personal choice. Overstating the case, the interpretation works something like this:' your support for this character in the role play indicates your personal collusion with patriarchy. Patriarchy is the sum of these personal collusions.' Although this method can produce an immediate 'shock' of enlightenment for some group members, it also is too simple and can lead to a tendency to view group members as representatives of a particular social group rather than as making individual, personal contributions to a group process in a rather more complex way. (This approach to training has received powerful criticisms from writers such as Sivanandan (1990) and Ahmed Gurnah (1985) who are concerned with the development of effective strategies to combat racism.) It seems particularly to have a damaging effect on group members who are already marginal: it is a common experience for the only Black member of a mainly white group to be taken as speaking 'on behalf of Black people'.

There is a third approach which does not refuse to recognise the total reality of oppression yet which still attempts to give specific weight and attention to interpersonal communication. It is possible to acknowledge the society wide and historical patterns of inequality having an active impact in groups and to acknowledge explicitly the barriers to communication these create. In Youth and Community Work training we have developed an approach which begins with issues of 'working together as equals across difference' and allows participants to name the barriers that have to be overcome from the very beginning. In doing this, it is possible to validate outside agendas.

Psychological theories of group dynamics often point to the impact of internalised agendas, particularly those drawn from the small theatre and small group of family life. Cultural studies offer us an alternative approach to group processes, with the combination of respect for and attention to the particularities of social life, and the impulse to locate identity and interaction in a wider social history. In the field of cultural studies the work that has developed from ethnography is particularly interesting (for example, Griffin, 1993; Willis, 1990).

The discussion of silence in groups offers a focus for further reflection on 'anti-oppressive practice'. Is silence a groupwork problem? How do we interpret 'the external environment'? Does silence in a small group connect with 'structures of feeling' in the society as a whole ? And what does it mean to be a facilitator who is attempting to break that silence?

What does silence mean?

Silence in a group can make everyone very uncomfortable. It can also be a place of warm connection which precedes powerful communication. When it is making people uncomfortable, it is often acknowledged that the group leader needs to intervene.

Gaie Houston's little *Red Book of Groups* (1990) which is a good example of the kind of material that students and groupworkers can turn to, is very clear on this matter. Houston acknowledges that the group leader's method of handling power and authority affects the climate and dynamics of the group. She talks about ways of handling a 'stymie' and the ways in which silence can be experienced as very threatening and withholding by the group leader. Silence is acknowledged as a source of power and is linked to 'white anger': a way of dealing with conflict without contact, a withdrawal from communication and a refusal of intimacy. Silence is clearly a signal that all is not well but the focus is very much on how to enable the individual concerned to acknowledge and deal with the silence.

Asking individuals to articulate the reasons for their silence can at least help prevent the fears and fantasies about that silence building up out of all proportion. For example, silence might be perceived as hostility, animosity or rejection of the subject under discussion or of the people who are passionately engaged in it. It can also appear to be about 'taking' and not 'giving' in the context of interpersonal communication. However, the person who is silent may when asked, explain that they are silent because they are confused about the subject and fearful of giving hurt or offence to others to whom it matters passionately. This kind of clarification can help enormously.

Tom Douglas' work on groupwork (1976) is widely read and consulted by practitioners and is particularly helpful on many aspects of the group process; the need for clarity about aims and purposes; the establishing of appropriate roles; and the creation of a structured and purposeful ethos for groupwork are significant themes which are very important for youth and community work. The silence of his work on the theme of silence comes therefore as a great surprise and it may be linked to a more general reluctance to acknowledge wider social factors.

Among recent writers, the authors of *Feminist Group Work* make significant progress in developing an understanding of silence in relation to a more general context:

> The weight of silence in the group may be oppressive embarrassing, uncomfortable. Usually it is assumed that silent members negate the purpose and direction of the group by exercising a subversive form of power and influence. Yet women have had more practice in keeping quiet, backing off, or retreating than in standing ground and demanding to be heard (Butler and Wintram, 1991).

The example they give of a woman psychiatric patient who breaks a long silence in a group by joining in a discussion on housework with the words: 'I'm on strike,' indicates an interpretation which locates events in the group in the context of particular lives, while retaining a powerful attention to the dynamics of each particular group.

Questions about silence in groups have also been asked from a Black perspective and here again discussions often relate to the role and work of the leader. There is a developing literature about 'race' and racism in group dynamics, as there is a developing literature about male dominance of women in groups and about the empowering potential of women's groups. Here there is a helpful focus on styles of leadership, expectations of groupworkers, and on the ways in which the authority and power of co-workers are expressed. For example, in the literature on Black and white workers co-working there is a recognition of the different impact of challenges about racism and about silence and collusion, when they come from the Black worker or the white worker (Mistry and Brown, 1991). As a white lecturer, I have often experienced positive feedback from both Black and white students when introducing sessions on anti-racist strategies. I have also seen Black colleagues perceived as involved in 'special pleading' or as 'having a chip on their shoulder about their colour' when introducing identical work.

In writings about feminist practice there has been much helpful discussion of the extent to which women who are in the position of groupworker do or do not share their own experiences, for example in relation to sexuality, and as with the example of racism, speech and silence are taken very differently from women who declare themselves lesbians, in contrast to the speech and silence of women in the socially more powerful position of non-lesbian (Hearn, 1989). Feminist and specifically lesbian writing has been insistent on situating group dynamics in the context of society-wide power relationships (Hanmer and Statham, 1988).

What does the 'external environment' mean? Education and another brick in the wall

It is of enormous importance for the groupworker to analyse very carefully the impact of the setting in which groupwork takes place. Discussion of youth clubs and classrooms as an external environment can become trapped in discussion of fixtures and fittings, furniture, equipment, pictures on the wall and so on.

But beyond this, the institutional location of groupwork determines or shapes whose voices are privileged and whose speech marginalised. In *Feminist Groupwork* (1991) Sandra Butler and Claire Wintram discuss the impact of the Social Services setting on their negotiations for setting up groups, and they explore in some detail the impact of their role as workers on their capacities to identify common ground with women in the groups they work with. The 'external environment' should be understood as a powerful group member in its own right and certainly as a force that is shaping the patterns of speech and silence. From some theoretical accounts of the nature of power in the social formation, it is even possible to argue that all communication that is happening in groups is an effect of these powerful formations: even antagonism and resistance derive from the system of regulation that is in place. A less determinist position than this can recognise the nature of the 'pressure' on language and communication exerted in particular settings: the way the boundaries of what may or may not be spoken about are implicitly and informally regulated and controlled.

Recognising the influence of the formal education setting makes one of the major difficulties which besets youth and community work training apparent. At the heart of the practice is an approach to working with groups in a community setting, to enable self-direction and empowerment. The 'training process' in college is often understood as needing to emulate in some ways groupwork in a community setting: certainly, ideally it is expected to share some of the same values and there is an expectation that the trainer/facilitator will be an experienced and skilled groupworker. But the patterns of mutual support and challenge, linked to personal and community development, are cut across by patterns of assessment and judgement of a quite insistent and controlling kind. Non-judgmental approaches to groupwork are taught in a setting replete with judgement; non-discriminatory practice is taught in a setting in which the art of 'discrimination' (between a 'pass' and a 'fail', between a '60' and a '58' for groupwork assignments) is highly developed.

So the questions: who is speaking? who is listening? and who is being spoken about? become important questions to address not just within the training group but also to the institution which is framing the work. In higher education based youth and community work training, there is both a process of accommodation and a constant struggle to recognise and name the silences being imposed by the institution. This moment of analysis really merits an article in itself, but the following may give some indication of their key mechanisms that are in place:

1. The idea of 'individual merit' and personal achievement make the expression of any shared collective disadvantage and

grievance difficult. Individuals speaking for themselves can in many settings be an integral part of community building, but in institutions whose ethos is profoundly shaped by competitive individualism 'speaking for yourself', can all too easily become speaking against rather than with others.

2. The pattern of assessment validates some forms of speech and writing and some subject matters as appropriately professional, while others are discredited as overly personal and subjective or else as overly political or both. A matter of class, codes and control?
3. The aspiration towards universality as a mark of higher education. This seems to permit the dismissal as 'anecdotal' of much knowledge that is rooted in particularity and in the concrete expression of difference. 'Universal' perspectives often turn out to be those of the European 'enlightenment'.
4. Bureaucratic patterns of relationship which either imply asexuality (which women cannot aspire to) or else the clear ascription of male and female roles involving the subordination of female roles. This is a way of silencing much that women may want to say and of constructing a closet for gay men and lesbians.
5. Teacher speaks, students listen and write only at the request of and in the form provided by the teacher.

Youth and community workers in training always bring with them sharp memories of such mechanisms from their experience of schooling or other higher education experiences. It is often their critique of these processes that has impelled them to become involved in youth and community work in the first place.

Our students are often people who have 'spoken out of turn', or who have not spoken 'properly', or who have learned carefully exactly when to speak and when not to speak in order to please the teacher, or who have become afraid to speak in this setting for fear of being spoken about as a problem or in even more hostile and denigratory ways.

Without some analysis of this relationship to educational institutions, the groupworker can seriously mistake the meaning of both silence and speech. Formal educational settings evoke schooling, and the hostilities and complicities that have been experienced in schools and colleges become part of the groupwork. Early on in our training we work explicitly on questions of power and difference in educational settings, making explicit use of students' own memories of schooling, in order to allow some shared analysis to occur.

Consciousness-raising does not in itself overcome the problem, but it does make the problem shared and explicit. This process of 'making the familiar strange' is one that has to be returned to continually, as new conceptualisations of the impact of power and of diversity are made.

The problem of silence in the whole society

> 'We've come to listen...'. The problem is the absence of authentic conversation. If there is no real conversation, the language games are kept in isolation. This means, especially for those who hold political, economic, social and cultural power, the simple possession of the power becomes its own claim to legitimacy. The rest of us become Aristotle's 'idiots' as understood in the Greek, people who do not or cannot participate in the 'polis' or the 'good' of public life. We are beings without a public voice, banished into silence as to a place which is our inherited condition of life.
>
> One of the more depressing sides of British public life today, not to mention countries at a distance politically, economically, socially and culturally, is the amount of simple listening or talking about which permeates our social existence. The rich talk about the deserving and the undeserving poor and from time to time listen to them; whites talk about blacks and from time to time listen to them; males talk about females and from time to time listen to them; the well salaried talk about the benefits of the unemployed and from time to time listen to them; stable families talk about unstable families, as they are called, and from time to time listen to them. In such an atmosphere we are forever being sucked into a vortex of violence. if you are constantly talked about, you will eventually explode (Smith, 1985, p.39).

Austin Smith, who wrote this response to a policy document, is a priest whose whole life has been spent in the inner city areas of Liverpool. It is one of the most accurate expressions I know of the ways in which silence presses on people who are not powerful in society's terms: not economically successful or occupying positions of high status. I think this level of silence also has be interpreted by the groupworker involved in youth and community work training.

This entails, as a minimum, recognising first that each participant on the course has a personal history which has been socially constructed (we need to acknowledge 'where people are coming from'). It also means acknowledging our shared participation in a social history that is happening within us and around us ('in here' and 'out there') throughout the work of a group on a training course.

How would you interpret silence in a group of youthworkers the day after the news of the brutal murder of James Bulger? There is reporting of racist attacks increasing locally and nationally. What do silence and anger mean then? From white people? From Black people? There is a post advertised with new funding for crime prevention work with young men: it is a fulltime, well salaried post. The sessions for work with girls and young women and the sessions for arts and drama work have been cut. Our groupwork means that we are involved in a 'structure of feeling', connected through our experience and our history to key dynamics of the society. This structure is a process, a pattern, a pressure on our communication.

There is a common groupwork strategy which requires people to 'own their own speech' in groups. This is done to clarify communication. Sometimes however the emphasis on 'I' seems to overpersonalise. It can also be useful to help people understand their membership of particular speech communities and to explore the field of meanings and conflicts over meaning for key themes in the group's work. I have done this with terms such as 'professional', and 'marketing', exploring their significance for different social and cultural groups. It is also important to do this exercise with key connecting terms within 'structures of feeling'; words that connect the participants on a course to a wider stream of social life. Mother. Race. Anger. Sexuality. Participants can name their own 'connecting themes' very accurately.

This level of analysis then allows a shift away from a goldfish bowl approach to groupwork in which the interpersonal dynamics of a group are seen as directly mirroring or straightforwardly implementing the social patterns. Some models of awareness training mobilise powerful interpersonal dynamics in groups to highlight personal collusion with oppressive systems and personal responsibility. I am suggesting that these same powerful dynamics can also be used to move away from the individualising of issues towards a greater participation in understanding shared and collective processes.

The silent facilitator?

Many versions of group facilitating suggest that the groupworker's role is essentially neutral and involves acting as a catalyst to facilitate communication among group members.

Following a model established in psychoanalysis it is seen to be important that the worker reveals nothing of themselves that might interfere with the process of communication. This practice has been challenged by writers who consider the powerful messages that the facilitator conveys to the group to be part of the process of recognising the meaning of difference in groupwork settings. If communication is to move away from the pattern of locating 'difference' and 'otherness' in relation to the still centre of the silent 'norm', this concept of the neutral and silent facilitator must be challenged. The facilitator must accept the challenge of finding the right words to intervene.

She needs to be able to acknowledge her own specific agendas, her passions, her own fears and difficulties, and she must be able to make connections. And all of this must be connected with the purpose of the group, so that the primary purpose of self-revelation is the facilitating of group development. (However, it would be foolish to deny the very real personal gains that are a common by-product of this apparently rather risky way of working) (Hanmer and Statham, 1988).

I have used the examples from youth and community work training to offer some reflections on the power of silence in groups.I want to develop our understanding of the connectedness of apparently quite different forms of oppression, and it seems that the theme of silence does offer one important point of connection. The connection can only occur in practice however when the silence is broken by speech, and here, in common with all groupwork theory, I see the role of the groupworker as a crucial role. The reflections on the theme of silence have led me to suggest that the worker must be prepared to act as an interpreter as well as a facilitator. Someone who can listen, hear and speak. Some-one who can 'read the signs of difference' as well as 'read the signs of the times'.

The interpreting however does not happen from the standpoint of superior knowledge of a 'universal language' which can overcome difference and conflict: a kind of Esperanto of groupwork. It is much more a matter of 'diving into the wreck', searching for jewels that can be imagined as part of the same treasure trove. Success in interpretation also involves a shared commitment from all participants to be attentive to silence, to acknowledge the impact of different personal histories, to recognise and try to understand the force of the institutional setting, and to analyse the currency of speech and silence on key social themes.

It also involves an enormous amount of laughter, pleasure, intuition, courage and luck and fortunately, since the enterprise of breaking the silence is a difficult and hazardous one, these are not in short supply among youth and community workers.

Acknowledgements
I would like to thank Julian Batsleer, Margaret Beetham, Kate Kirk and Ken Leech for help with this piece.

References

Butler, S. and Wintram, C. (1991) *Feminist Group Work*. Sage.
Cobham, R. and Collins, M. (eds.) (1990) *Watchers and Seekers*. Cambridge University Press.
Douglas, T. (1976) *Groupwork Practice*. Tavistock.
Fanon, F. (1967) *The Wretched of the Earth*. Penguin.
Freire, P. (1972) *Pedagogy of the Oppressed*. Penguin.
Griffin, C. (1993) *Representations of Youth*. Polity.
Gurnah, A. (1985) *Racism Awareness A Closer Look*. JCARP.
Hanmer, J. and Statham, D. (1988) *Women and Social Work*. Macmillan.
Hearn, J. (1989) *The Sexuality of Organisations*. Sage.
Houston, G. (1990) *The Red Book of Groups*. Rochester Foundation.
Katz, J. (1978) *White Awareness*. University of Oklahoma Press.
Lorde, A. (1984) 'The transformation of silence into language and action' in *Sister Outsider*. The Crossing Press.
Matthews, J. (1966) *Working with Youth Groups*. London University Press.
Mistry, T. and Brown, A. (1991) 'Black and white co-working in groups', *Groupwork*, 4(2).
Mullender, A. and Ward, D. (1991) *Self-Directed Groupwork*. Whiting and Birch.
National Youth Agency (1990) *The Youth Service Statement of Purpose*. Ministerial Conference.
Rowbotham, S. (1973) *Women's Consciousness, Man's World*. Penguin.
Sivanandan, A. (1990) 'RAT and the degradation of Black struggle' in *Communities of Resistance*. Verso.
Smith, A. (1985) 'After reading a document' in Leech, K. (ed.) *The Bishops and the Economy*. The Jubilee Group.
Willis, P. (1990) *Moving Culture*. Calouste Gulbenkian Foundation.
Wilson, A. (1978) *Finding a Voice: Asian Women in Britain*. Virago.

Ourselves and others

Helen Gobat

This is an account of two groups of adults with a learning disability, which ran for two years at a social services day centre. They focused on personal relationships and interaction.
The features of working with this particular client group are considered, and the progress of two members are used as an evaluation. The author also examines how her increased understanding of a psychodynamic approach affected her work, and makes some links with the work of Sinason and her colleagues at the Tavistock Centre.

I began working two years ago as a tutor with two groups of adults with a learning disability. These groups were held weekly at a social services day centre, and were jointly funded by the Local Authority's Social Services and Education Departments. Simultaneously I pursued a psychodynamic approach at the Tavistock Centre, in training courses set up by Valerie Sinason and Sheila Bichard and their colleagues. This undoubtedly influenced my groupwork; what began as educational groups served a therapeutic function for the members, and for me acquired a much richer meaning.

In this paper I shall give a practical account of these groups over the first eighteen months, explore the features particular to groupwork with this client group, and evaluate the experience for two of the participants. I have also looked at any parallels between my experience and those of Sinason, both in her individual and her groupwork. Unfortunately in this space I cannot attempt to compare the groups, or to explore whether it was the aspects of self-advocacy and empowerment in the experience which account for the results, rather than my psychodynamic approach.

Introduction to a psychodynamic approach

Sinason (1992) has based her work on the premise that a person with a learning disability has an emotional life which is accessible through psychotherapy. 'However crippled someone's external functional intelligence might be, there can still be intact a complex emotional structure and capacity' (Sinason, 1992, p.74). Everyone's capacity for handling emotional experiences is affected by their

Groupwork Vol. 7(3), 1994, pp.210-222

experiences of the outside world, but unlike the `normal' population, these experiences for a person with a learning disability may have been impoverished and confused. Bicknell (November, 1992), in a lecture to students at the Tavistock Clinic, on Psychodynamic Work in learning disability, indicated his belief that this may mean that a person's inner world and defence mechanisms are skewed and the ego's ability to test reality is not so effective.

These and other factors mean that the process of psychotherapy is different, and can take longer. Sinason has found her work during the first year of therapy achieves a reduction in what is referred to as 'secondary handicap' - the non-verbal idiosyncrasies and mannerisms, the `handicapped smile'- which act as defences against the larger more permanent learning disability. When this stage is reached, depression arrives. If the person continues in therapy, then they address five areas - grief and loss, sexuality, `the handicap spelt out', dependency and fear of being murdered. Beyond this stage, the person enters `ordinary' psychotherapy. These stages apply to a person of any age or degree of learning disability (Sinason, 1992).

Professor Sheila Hollins (in her inaugural lecture May 1992, St. Georges) believes that there are four secrets kept from a person with a learning disability - sexuality, dependency, handicap and mortality. It is thus not surprising to find that people given a safe place want to explore these hidden issues.

There are many groups now which address relationships and sexuality, and even sex education in some schools, but there are few therapeutic groups for people with a learning disability. At the Tavistock, Sinason and Lusada have one such long-term group, and Sprince and Usiskin held a group which ran for two years. Although my groups were not set up as therapy groups, my increasing awareness of the emotional meaning of what took place, and an acceptance of the emotional intelligence of the participants, affected my attitudes and made me respond differently as a leader.

Aims of the group

The 'Ourselves and Others' course was designed by West Surrey Extended Education Centre 'to encourage the development of self-awareness, the ability to express personal views and the ability to relate to others...based on a broad view of each individual which includes their emotional and sexual development'. Although the course might produce improvements in specific social skills, the expectation was that these would develop through group interaction, rather than in a direct way.

Methods

The course stated the methods to be firmly based on groupwork, 'encouraging group cohesion and interaction between individuals'. From early on in the planning process, I felt these aims would be achieved not just through following the Course Units, but by allowing members to bring material from outside that was important to them, and to allow time to stop and explore what was happening in the sessions between members as we went along. No direction was given as to the model of groupwork to be used. What developed was a mixture of psychotherapeutic and group discussion models, where a person's self-concept and relationships are strengthened, but learning and change are also on the agenda.

We met on a weekly basis for about 12 sessions at a time, following three academic terms a year. Planning was done week by week in order to be responsive to the needs of group members and the events of each session. The normal mode of the groups was discussion, and for a set of people who are not normally expected to have a long concentration span, tolerance of lengthy discussion was high from an early stage. We also used group exercises around themes, rather than 'games' as I considered games to be inappropriate for adult groups. We used an audio tape and video camera, did role play and some writing and drawing. The participants kept a folder for their work, and were given a record of any group brainstorming done on a flipchart. Sprince and Usiskin found in their groups that the process of recording meant that the members felt they were being heard, and that they were considered intelligent (comment made in a seminar at the Tavistock Clinic, 1992).

Course material

There were eleven units in the course. The first four had to be covered before the groups selected the next unit. It took a year to cover these four units - *Who am I; Friends; Feelings and Communication.* Both groups followed on with *Family,* then chose *Handicap and Sexuality* for two more terms. *Conflict, Rules, Groups and Values* remained. Within each unit, we focused both on group members being both heard, and on listening, as a basis for being valued within the group.

There is a wide range of resource material today, and several useful publications by Craft and Dixon (1988). Whatever is used, it needs to be constantly adapted and modified for the group and must bear in mind the leader's particular capabilities.

Venue

We met in the staff room at the day centre, and had comfortable chairs and a table to sit round for written work. The room was too small for the numbers, and did restrict activities, but it was important to keep the sessions in the same place, which then became secure for the members. This was even more important when the centre underwent a massive refurbishment, and all familiar territory was disrupted. It would have been ideal to meet at an independent location, but transport would then have been a problem. I concluded that the venue was probably more an issue for the leaders than the participants. This was either a reflection of the success of the groups, or the fact that this set of people are used to having little chance to exert choice.

Membership

The group members were originally pre-selected by day centre staff, who knew clients better than I did, and we sent out letters of invitation to those proposed. Criteria included a certain level of articulacy and comprehension, and a few people were also referred who presented 'problems' in personal interaction. All lived in the community, either with families or in a social services hostel. All members were white and of English origin.

We decided to have an even number of men and women, and this has been maintained. At first we had eleven members in each group, but ideally eight with two leaders would have been better. As attendance was high we were often twelve in the room. Within the groups we had several people who suffered from epilepsy, one man electively mute, another with muscular dystrophy and failing eyesight and mobility, one man almost blind, and several with speech impediments. Three men with Downs Syndrome were in one group, by chance. (Sinason (1992) has found that being the only person in a group with this condition is intolerable for the only one with the visible 'mental handicap'.)

The first group were all in their twenties, and contained several individuals with identified problems in their personal interaction. The second group was older, their ages ranged from 22 to 53 years. Their mood was more sedate, but less flexible.

The groups were closed after the initial intake, and we resisted approaches from keyworkers with recommendations from reviews for additional members to join the groups. If it seemed appropriate, then we introduced a new member at the beginning of a new term, and with the agreement of the whole group. Overall, only four people left, and four joined. The groups only met together for an end-of-year outing.

Leadership

Initially I had two co-leaders, one for each group. They were staff members of the day centre, who had offered to work with me. Keeping boundaries for them was always a problem, and if called upon to cover the work of the centre they would have to be absent from the groups, so I was often alone. The sessions at first ran one after the other with a short break in the middle to unwind and plan. I felt split between the two co-leaders, and it was a great relief in the second year to have the same person co-lead in each group. She could share the whole experience, and we could look constructively at comparing the groups. I knew none of these leaders well beforehand, and their professional background and theoretical perspectives were different from mine and from each other. We did not have enough time to cover these issues in pre-planning, and as time went on, even less time for joint planning as their work schedule was very full. This meant that I did the recording and most of the detailed planning for the groups, and the groups remained 'my' groups.

Joint planning leads to joint leadership, anything less than that leads to unequal leadership and rivalry. We did all share a long history of commitment to working with people with a learning disability, but from different value bases. I had never had a caring role for these users and therefore power was not an issue in the same way for me that it was for the centre staff and the users in their day to day care. I felt strongly that every individual in the group had an equal right to be heard and valued.

My function throughout was as chief planner and facilitator for the group but I also played both maintenance and task roles as the need arose. In Kindred's words (lecture at the Tavistock Clinic, 1992): 'The task is what the group comes together to achieve and the maintenance is concerned with building up and nurturing relationships'. The latest co-leader has a sense of lightness and fun which the groups appreciate, but even more important, she picks up and reflects upon group feelings and atmosphere. A major role for the leaders was that of modelling appropriate adult behaviour, not interrupting, giving adequate space, checking out how people were feeling and using their own feelings to illustrate a point.

In the ethos of the day centre, 'users' often behaved and were treated like children. Thus it was not surprising that these groups sought a directive form of leadership. Lusada and Sinason found in their groups that the leader acted as the 'transmitter and receiver', and the members thus communicated with the leader dyadically. Lusada speaks of the problem as leader of transacting between the 'handicapped world' and the 'real world', an unequal task because the leader already comes from a position of greater power than the members experience. In each group there was a pair of members who acted as co-leaders, maybe transacting more effectively than we did!

There was a strong level of competition for the leader's attention throughout the life of the groups. Whether this was in response to general deprivation for the members, or a reflection of envy for the more powerful and articulate leaders, I do not know. Direct interaction between members remained limited, and the dependence on leaders high.

It seemed of immense importance that the leaders created a safe place for the group members to explore personal issues not dealt with elsewhere. The outside world was kept at bay, and consistency and continuity were maintained.

Stages in the life of the groups

Tuckman's model of group life (1965) suggests that groups can pass through five stages, sometimes sequentially, sometimes 'backwards and forwards' and can also be seen to occur in any one session. These stages could be identified in the life of these groups over time, but because of the end-of-term breaks, there was a start-up stage each time.

Forming and storming

These two stages seemed to run into each other. Members would enter and urgently demand attention. The loudest and most vociferous man in the first group was scapegoated outside the group, and one of our aims was to address this in the sessions. Whatever he said was not considered worthwhile by his peers, and his personal problems were discounted. His over-loud voice would provoke either a competing set of tales, or negative reactions such as covering one's ears, or he was attacked verbally. He did get the group started! The second group did not have such a person. They were usually quieter and much slower to start. This process in each session felt equally like storming, and though it reduced over time, would happen as strongly after a break. Another manifestation of storming was starting late, which recurred at the beginning of a new term.

In each group we allowed time for people to settle and get used to being in the group. The first group had coffee, which sometimes was an excuse for delay. This was later resolved along with the problem of one late arrival, by having him make the coffee. Once seated, people were reluctant to move or help actively. There was both an expectation of things being done for them, and a reluctance to be the sibling to do the job asked.

The Forming stage included a large exercise on paper on group rules and boundaries, to which the groups often referred. During this stage, we covered the topics *Who am I?* and *Friendship*. This meant we started from the individual, and it was a valid reflection of the early needs of the group members.

Norming

In the life of the groups as a whole, the norms and identity were fixed after about twelve sessions. The mood and atmosphere of each group became consistent, though different. The members of the first group were younger, more able to look at things with a fresh approach, and sometimes surprised us with the amount of material they could process in one session, compared with the second group. The atmosphere could be volatile, but was always lively.

In the second group were members who had lived in the same situation for years, doing the same things. They had fixed patterns of coping behaviour and attitudes, often reinforced by parental pressure. The atmosphere could be heavy, denial palpable in the air. There was resistance to paired exercises and to physical touching in both groups, so we did not push these.

The groups developed cohesion at this stage, a regular and predictable 'flow' to the sessions whatever the tasks, and a definite identity. The groups felt for the most part `We can do it' (Tuckman 1965). In spite of sharing the same label of `handicap', (otherwise they could not use the centre), group cohesion was not easily attained.

It was during the second and third terms that Norming was the most prevalent feature, when we covered *Feelings* then *Communication*. These themes remained with us for the rest of the life of the groups.

Performing

The groups felt like they took off with their own momentum at the beginning of the second year. The roles which people had adopted, or which had been ascribed to them, became constructive, and the groups functioned well. One person in each group identified with me and helped prompt and direct the group toward achieving the tasks for which they had been set up. The person scapegoated in the first group lowered his voice volume. Adverse reactions to him reduced. The woman in the second group who had led in a destructive manner became less powerful.

At this stage, as Sinason found, 'secondary handicaps' were much reduced. The woman who would not try writing, found she could spell. The mute man tried to speak. Expression of feelings and their comprehension increased dramatically. Articulation for the three women with indistinct speech improved, and they were usually understood. Of two men in the first group who found it difficult to make themselves understood, one became chief coffee-maker and I found I understood the other man better if he sat closer to me. In one session I responded to his underlying message and offered an interpretation which evoked his response: 'You got it'.

At this time, both groups chose *Handicap* as a topic, then *Sexuality*, both taboo subjects. The highlight of performance of the groups came during this stage. The members interacted more with each other, and directed the sessions. Discussion of these topics were the most meaningful. The second group managed to support a woman whose mother died, so mortality was a real issue.

Ending

In the fifth term I learnt that the funding for the groups was about to end, as it was for a fixed period. Ending became for me a dominant theme if not an obsession. I felt very defensive on behalf of the groups. Here were two committed sets of people, with little opportunity for this kind of experience. They were clearly performing well, and it was another confirmation of their low status that something good could be taken away. We were discussing sexuality, and their denial and resistance were being reduced dramatically. My dilemma was, do I tell them we shall definitely end and spend precious time on that, or do I delay until the end is inevitable?

I decided to fight for continuation, and prepared reports and begging letters to case managers. We had a session in which the whole group wrote to their case managers. Not only did the group construct the letter, but every person was able to copy it from the flipchart, irrespective of their literacy skills. It was a very powerful occasion. The following week, the man who is mute was the first to respond when I asked what we had done the previous week: 'Letter to case manager'. This was a confirmation of the power of this action, and the powerful feelings it left for the groups. It could not have happened earlier in the life of the groups.

I heard in the last fortnight, that the funding was assured and then ironically, was told that half my group members were going to be offered a six month pre-employment course. I might have seen this as a positive result of the group experience, but it felt more like sabotage! I did what I could to prepare those members for leaving the group, and most took up the course offer. Some of the second group decided not to continue with the group. It may have been that the topics became too threatening, or their dependency on the group may have felt too frightening, or maybe they preferred to 'kill me off' before I 'killed' them. The groups served a purpose for some of the members, they had gone as far as they wished to go. Although all their reasons for finishing were not clear, I felt that they should be able to exert choice, and to find that they were not punished for it. Groups have a way of reaching a point of achievement and then their life is over, and I had to accept that. (The groups have continued, but with changed membership and smaller numbers).

Special feature of all these groups

Attendance

The groups were uniformly well-attended. From an early stage the group expectation was that you could only miss a session for a good reason. In the absence of formal evaluation, attendance can indicate success of a group. Though there is a possibility with this client group that they are over-compliant, I did see them develop choice and consider carefully before embarking on something new.

Leader / led

It was a difficult balance to manage the group, to acknowledge the continued dependency without reducing choice and the rights of the individual adult, and resist being over-protective. I think it is a feature of people who have never been given power that they are looking for safe leadership, and I certainly responded by maintaining and guarding the boundaries between us and the outside world.

Articulation / communication

It can be daunting working with a set of people with variable speech and articulacy. People spoke without checking that they were understood. We leaders often found that we understood less than the rest of the group, who were accustomed to unusual speech patterns. The group helped us, by prompts to use a speech board, or by re-phrasing. I sometimes acknowledged that it was I who was stupid for not understanding, and this was well received. The group would wait for ages for the mute man to speak. The favourite exercise was audio - taping, when the groups waited patiently for each member to have their turn.

Conceptualisation

One could assume that people with a learning disability cannot conceptualise as well as a person of 'normal' intelligence. Whilst I found their connections to be different, once I opened myself to the underlying emotional messages, new and valid material emerged. I had to be creative regarding how to convey an idea, adapting and sometimes jettisoning an exercise. I was conscious that I often went too fast, and I needed the co-leader to check me. The gap between us as more 'intelligent' leaders and the group as less able intellectually, tells more about power than ability, and is a reflection of the world's perception of this client group.

Staying with the task / avoidance

It was important that everyone participated in the group exercises, but some members never liked role play or physical touching. Even though this meant escape within the group, no-one ever left the room, except for one man who occasionally went to the toilet. One member might change the subject if a topic became too difficult, but the rest of the group did not necessarily follow. I had the feeling that here was a set of people who had to struggle hard to hold onto what they had achieved, and if this meant they could only cope with their own responses and behaviour then that was a feat in itself.

Literacy

We often used a flipchart to do a group exercise, and written work round the table. It soon became clear how much help individuals needed. They enjoyed both tasks, and as the groups matured, the more able helped the less able. It was remarkable how their skills improved after the first year.

Expression of emotion

It was clear that group members had had little opportunity to identify and express their feelings. At first the only feeling acknowledged was 'happy'. Sinason talks about 'the handicapped smile' which is expected of disabled people: a defence which appeases the rest of the world. Anger was hard to acknowledge, though live examples occurred, and we used them. Caring for each other was difficult, and not always appropriately directed. The quality of empathy may be different for a person with a learning disability, not because they are uncaring, but because no-one empathises with them. Attachment theory may have some relevance here: a child who is securely attached also has higher self-esteem and better emotional health (Ainsworth, 1985). The processes of development of attachment behaviour may be complicated for a person with a learning disability. Only two members of the groups were in a loving relationship. Physical demonstrations of affection were not always appropriate.

Examples of group members and their development over time

Jo is a woman of 35, who has a slight speech impediment and suffers from epilepsy. She was living with her foster-mother when the groups started, and had previously participated in a counselling group I held. Jo's relationships with others were ambivalent and she found it hard to have close friendships, particularly with men. She had a strange mannerism of clutching at your arm with excitement, but I always felt there was an element of suppressed anger in this gesture. If you said something apparently non-loaded like: 'How are you?' she could respond appropriately or just as often say: 'Don't ask me that', and turn away.

Jo would arrive at the group early and eager, but was uncertain about doing the right thing, needing reassurance. She actively turned her face away from any exercise which showed people undressed or touching. Over time, Jo became an active contributor, sharing her own experience for the benefit of the group. Jo was at first very slow with written work, but her literacy skills and confidence grew so that she became the group scribe, asking only for help with spelling. The group would wait patiently for her to complete the task.

At the beginning of the second year, Jo's mother became ill and was hospitalised briefly. Jo had been going to a hostel for short breaks, and we discussed independence in the group. Jo admitted that she felt freer there. During the half-term break, her mother died, while at home with Jo. Jo had gone to a neighbour to call the hostel who set things in motion. She moved to the hostel that day, attended her mother's funeral and was back at the day centre after the break. This is a typical response for people with a learning disability, no time is allowed them for grieving.

Jo then came to the group. We were looking at feelings in families, and Jo's foetal position and deep grief disturbed us all. By the next week, Jo used the group to explore her feelings, to examine what her life would now be like. I realised on referring back to my notes, that Jo had in fact been preparing for her mother's death which occurred at that time. Over the next few months Jo managed to lead the group through the topic of *Handicap*. She was sensitive to being thought of as 'stupid', and loved catching me out if I forgot something. She opened up to new ideas on sexuality, owning her own potential. The progress was phenomenal. Jo moved to a Group Home in another area, whilst attending the same day centre. She then decided that 'someone else should have a turn' and left the group. I do not believe Jo could possibly have made such progress outside the group.

Fred by contrast is an older man of 50 with Down's Syndrome, who lives with aged parents. He likes routine, his parents have always cared zealously for him without a break, and he has been at the day centre since it opened. He is hard of hearing but will not wear his hearing aid.

Fred likes to do simple assembly work, the supply of which is decreasing. He is very attached to his workshop manager, and has never participated in any other activity at the centre. Fred has definite likes and dislikes but no special friends, though he says he would like to get married. He chose to join the group, and obviously enjoyed the experience, in particular role play.

I never discovered why Fred kept coming to the group. His interaction with the other members was limited, though he would verbally attack the man who spoke too loud and too often. He also shared his own distress at all the changes at the centre. Maybe there was a quality in the group experience which he relished, or the groups might have offered stability in his changing routine. He did not change much over time, but we have to accept that change is not on everyone's agenda.

In conclusion

I am still processing what the groups meant for me, and why they worked, but I am sure that a psychodynamic background was a contributing factor, as much as valuing the individual in the group and respecting their rights as adults. It was significant that 'secondary handicaps' disappeared after the first year. Maybe this was a direct result of recognising the emotional intelligence within each individual, which was a new experience for group members. It was also a measure of group cohesion that taboo topics were eventually tackled.

The content of the course was relevant to all aspects of personal interaction, and even if all members did not use the group to the same degree, they acquired something special from the experience. The groups are continuing, but with an agenda which is more responsive to themes which the groups bring forth, rather than a 'course outline'.

Groupwork is predictable, and yet simultaneously it keeps you guessing. I hope that this paper may encourage other people to do similar work, and to appreciate that people with a learning disability can use groups effectively.

References

Ainsworth, M.D.S. (1985) 'Patterns of infant-mother attachments: antecedents and effects on development', *The Bulletin of the New York Academy of Medicine*, 61(9).

Craft, A. and Dixon, H. (1988) *Sexuality and Mental Handicap: An Educator's Resource Book*. FPA Education Unit.

Sinason, V. (1992) *Mental Handicap and the Human Condition*. Free Association Books. Also in lectures attended by the author during a recent course at the Tavistock Clinic.

Tuckman, B. (1965) 'Developmental sequences in small groups', *Psychological Bulletin*, 63(6).

Groupwork with Young Mothers

Caroline Norman

The article describes the background and experience of running Pregnancy Groups for young women and the follow-on support groups for young mothers and babies over a period of two and a half years. It looks at the particular needs of the client group, the style of group leadership, the process of the group, and the issues involved in addressing therapeutic needs in a daycare setting.

St Gabriel's Family Centre is a Children's Society project in Brighton, England (joint funded by East Sussex Social Services Department), which works in a variety of ways with children, young people and families.

The work of the centre has changed over time, particularly in its day programmes, from individually focused work to a groupwork model. We have learnt that individuals gain more from sharing experiences with each other in a group setting than from one to one work. Also, the staff team regularly examines its own group process with the help of an outside facilitator.

The subject of this article is the work St Gabriel's has been doing with young mothers, from the state of pregnancy through to the point at which their babies reach toddlerhood.

It may be helpful to describe the background to this work before discussing the groupwork programme. At the beginning of the 1990s, St Gabriel's began liaising with Marina House, a residential project for young women leaving care. Part of their work involves running pregnancy support groups; we became involved in co-running one of these groups with the aim of providing longer term support for the women after the birth of their babies. Our research indicated that local services for vulnerable young women who are pregnant are poor and inappropriate to their specific needs; most antenatal classes being aimed at older women in stable relationships. As a consequence, these young women often miss out on important information about pregnancy and labour. Their age and circumstances may also mean that they are isolated from their peer group, and are dealing with family tension at home.

The pregnancy group

The Pregnancy Group, which is jointly run with staff from Marina House, is the first stage of a two stage process. Stage two, is a group for mothers and babies, following the birth of the babies, and is held at St Gabriel's. To date this has meant a female worker (myself) from St Gabriel's working with staff at the other project, from the referral stage onwards. Working together in this way is both challenging and rewarding since each of us brings different ideas and attitudes to the task.

One of the key differences between the two agencies is that Marina House is an all-female project staffed by and for women, whereas St. Gabriel's has always employed male workers, believing that a gender balance amongst staff is of key importance in work with families. Male workers, actively involved in work with children in the playroom as well as co-facilitators of groups, provide a positive role model for both the children and their mothers by demonstrating that men can and should be involved in all aspects of child rearing. That men can be nurturing and tender with children helps to challenge stereotypes and gives women higher expectations of their partners. This is of course a political as well as a cultural statement and may lead to conflict for some women, but if their own confidence and self esteem improves over time, they are better equipped to make demands on their partners - or to separate from them if this is the alternative to staying in an unsatisfactory relationship. Gender issues have not been a problem in the joint work with Marina since we are in agreement that the Pregnancy Support Groupwork is more appropriately facilitated by female workers, and that the same pair should continue to run the follow-on support group at St Gabriel's. Male workers are however involved in other parts of the work with young mothers; for example, two of them regularly staff the morning session with mothers and babies.

Referrals

Referrals for the Pregnancy Group are made from several sources; the maternity social workers at the local hospital, the education tutor at the school age mother's unit, as well as other pregnancy advisory services. To give an idea of the range of young women who are referred, I shall describe the background and circumstances of a number of those with whom I have worked. At the time of writing, the second Young Mothers Support Group has just finished. I refer to both groups throughout the article since the work with the first group has influenced the current work in a positive and beneficial way.

Group members (all white)

K aged 19, left home at 16, moved to a new town to avoid violence from her father. Positive about the pregnancy and determined to make a go of things on her own. Some support from the baby's father.

P aged 14, living at home with her mother, mother's partner and younger brother. P had had a turbulent early adolescence involving alcohol and drug abuse and a period of living with an older man who at the time of her pregnancy was in prison. P had already had a termination and was still distressed about this and keen to continue her present pregnancy. Although P's age made her in many ways the most vulnerable, she attended the group regularly and contributed a great deal.

S aged 15, living at home with her mother and younger brother, in regular contact with her partner and planning to live with him and the baby. S was difficult to engage and her attendance was sporadic and unpredictable, but when any contact with her was achieved she always spoke of her intention and desire to return to the group. S eventually dropped out altogether and did not attend the St Gabriel's support group.

T aged 15, living at home with mother and younger sister, in contact with baby's father, but relationship very volatile. T was particularly vulnerable in a household where the mother's lifestyle was chaotic and unpredictable and could not provide any boundaries for her children. T enjoyed the group and brought humour and liveliness to it. Unfortunately due to complications in her pregnancy she was unable to attend the last few sessions of the pregnancy group but we continued to work with her after her baby was born.

K aged 17, living alone, following the death of her mother when she was 14. K came from a large extended family who offered some support but she was still grieving her mother's death and 'looking after' her father. K was no longer in a relationship with the baby's father but very positive about the pregnancy. She attended the Pregnancy Group regularly but found it difficult to join in or offer her opinions until much later in the Young Mothers Support Group.

B aged 18, living alone but with the support of her boyfriend, whom she subsequently married. B was in many ways the most needy, having been in care for most of her life and having no contact with her family. She was very attached to the group and attended regularly.

J aged 15, living with mother and younger brother and in contact with baby's father. She was angry about the disruption to her education, and expressed some ambivalence about her pregnancy. J's baby was due later than the others in the group and she eventually stopped attending so that she could pursue her studies.

F aged 15, living at home with mother and two sisters. Her boyfriend was still at school, and subsequently moved in with F after baby was born. After living in cramped conditions for several months, F and her partner moved out and they now rent their own place. All three, including baby, suffer from asthma and F also has severe eczema.

Six young women attended the first Pregnancy Group, four of whom continued to attend the Young Mothers Support Group at St Gabriel's. The same number started in the latest group, five of whom stayed throughout the support group.

The Pregnancy Group is a fixed term (8 or 10 weeks) closed group with a specific focus, i.e. pregnancy, hence the need for a structure which can incorporate information giving *and* support. The aims are: to increase understanding and knowledge of pregnancy, labour and birth; to enable group members to improve their self-care during pregnancy; to learn how to seek help, advice and information from appropriate sources when they need it. The personal development aims are: to increase self confidence and self awareness; improve their social skills; to have a voice and feel heard by others. The Pregnancy Group gives the young women an opportunity to be with others in similar circumstances in a supportive environment. This is fundamental to the group's success and the factor most often mentioned by group members. Having their pregnancy acknowledged and validated by others is an important starting point when much of their previous experience may have been negative and judgemental. Research into the effectiveness of groupwork indicates that it can be particularly helpful to individuals:

> ...experiencing powerlessness, alienation and hopelessness; being victimised, not feeling understood in their current human relations; and/or feeling inadequate in changing systems of which they are a part (Anderson, 1979, p.291).

This is particularly pertinent to young mothers, as they are increasingly scapegoated by the government and blamed for all society's problems. For example, in the period July-October 1993 the Independent newspaper printed 90 articles on the subjects of teenage parents/young mothers, reflecting the number of (critical) government statements made at the time on welfare and social policy issues relating to young mothers.

Group leaders

The group facilitators aim to provide a model in the way we approach and address issues and feelings, each other and group members, by conveying an attitude of acceptance and respect. At the start of the group we discuss 'group rules' which endorse this, e.g. listening to others, arriving on time, letting group leaders know if it is not possible to attend. We work as a consistent pair throughout the Pregnancy Group and our role extends beyond the boundary of the group session into greeting, coffee-making, preparation and serving of lunch, and home visits. Indeed, home visits are given a high priority, both in the engagement process and during the life of the group when attendance is poor or when a visit is requested.

At the first session we contextualise the group setting by comparing it with their (everyone's) first experience of being in a group i.e. the family. We acknowledge that this may have been an unhappy or abusive experience and that subsequent group situations may have unpleasant resonances. Many of the young women we work with have also been unhappy at school; becoming pregnant can be a further disruptive experience which separates them from their peer group and leads to isolation. The Pregnancy Group can be a positive group experience offering a safe space with firm boundaries, where the rules are negotiated and respected, perhaps recreating a 'good family'.

Adolescence

It is important to see the groupworkers' relationship with the young women in the context of working with adolescents. Adolescence is a life-stage during which the relationship between the emotional, physical and intellectual aspects of the self are often in conflict, resulting in fluctuating moods. When this process takes place within a well functioning family there can be gradual disengagement from parents and space given to the child to find her adult identity. If the family is dysfunctional or the child is separated from her parents, the adolescent may feel overwhelmed and fearful of the physical and emotional changes taking place. Pregnancy at this point catapults the child into adult responsibility and confers an immediate adult identity. This can of course seem to satisfy the wish for a viable identity but the losses involved also need addressing.

The groupworkers' task in working with pregnant adolescents is therefore complex and needs to integrate their conflicting needs by providing firmness and containment, on the one hand, and enough freedom, on the other. Hence, some form of structure is needed that satisfies those needs. Turn-taking, i.e. having an opening round at the beginning of each session, when each individual is given space to say how they are feeling, seems to provide this. It allows people who may be carrying problems from experiences during the week to voice them before the 'learning' part of the session begins. We do however try to leave spaces within the 10 week plan where a whole session is available for discussion of feelings or particular issues e.g. domestic violence, other experiences of abuse etc.,

Themes

Certain themes emerge during group sessions and it may be useful to look at how this affects group process. For example, the issue of male power, either in the form of violence or as a denial of responsibility for parenting, recurs frequently. Many of the young women we work with have experienced abusive and disrupted childhoods with resulting low self-esteem. However, it would be wrong to generalise the effects beyond this; each individual in the group brings different ideas and responses. At first, when group members took turns to speak, the others would listen passively, occasionally commenting or advising. As the group matured, individuals became more reactive; sometimes overly critical. For example, one young woman described her partner's violence towards her whilst she was pregnant. This brought an immediate reaction from several in the group, one of whom said she thought it was completely out of order and that she should leave him. Others contributed with anecdotes describing similar experiences. As group leaders we comment on the universal nature of the power imbalance between men and women, to enable them to see their situation in a more political context, not just as victims of individual acts of injustice.

Another theme which frequently comes up in the group (usually in the Pregnancy Group) is that of consent - i.e. to sexual intercourse. We made space to discuss this more fully following a talk on contraception by an 'outside' professional, in which the speaker assumed that there was at least some negotiation between a couple before intercourse. It was clear to us that some individuals had not engaged in any discussion about contraception; very few group members had ever been in relationships where their boyfriends had taken responsibility for contraception, and very few have the confidence or power to encourage their boyfriends to use condoms, let alone insist that they do. We are conscious that this important issue needs to be looked at frequently, particularly once the babies have been born and the young women are at risk of further pregnancies. Clearly there is some difficulty in addressing this whilst the group are all still pregnant and the risks seem remote compared to the immediacy of the birth. The subject can be addressed later, in the context of learning how to take control.

Practical support

Another important aspect of the work with young women is the practical support we give in the form of benefits advice and liaison with other agencies e.g. housing. This is usually performed when group members first arrive and are settling in over coffee. It also helps to free them up for the group if a pressing practical problem can be dealt with before the session begins.

The objective of the Pregnancy Group is to prepare each young woman for the birth of her baby, with adequate understanding of the physical process and the emotional support to deal with the demands of a new baby and the feelings engendered. It is hoped that information and advice combined with a growing sense of self esteem will enable each young woman to make a reasonable start in her new life as a mother.

The young mothers' support group

Acknowledging the difficulties inherent in providing such a package of support and advice to a vulnerable client group within a fixed time limit, led the team at St Gabriel's to plan a long term support group which could cater for the young women's emotional needs as well as offer practical support and information about motherhood. We believed this could best be achieved by running two, differently focused group sessions, over the course of one day. As a family centre we are fortunate in having a large staff team and experienced voluntary creche workers. We were aware that working with a group of mothers and their babies would be staff intensive and require careful timetabling.

Timetable

Using a combination of our own minibus and social services transport, group members are collected and arrive at the centre at 10.30 am. They are greeted by two members of staff and have about half an hour to have coffee and settle their babies. At 11.00 am the morning groupwork session begins and runs for an hour. The focus in this group is on the relationship between mother and child and issues relating to parenting such as feeding and sleeping problems, infant development etc. The structure used is to ask each member of the group in turn to talk about the past week from her baby's perspective. The purpose of this is to help the young women to see their baby as a separate entity and yet profoundly influenced by the attitude and feelings of its parent. For example, someone who may have experienced a stressful, difficult week may report that the baby has been 'a pain', constantly crying and difficult to placate.

At first it was the task of the facilitators to make the link between the mother's state and that of her baby; in time however, other members of the group were able to comment on the link and to see their own experiences, negative and positive, as influencing their babies' behaviour. The most difficult belief to challenge however was the prevailing view that the baby sometimes deliberately 'played up' to annoy the mother and therefore had to learn that this was unacceptable. The influence of grandparents and other family members reinforced this view; challenging this notion therefore has to be handled carefully in order not to alienate the young women or undermine their self confidence still further. Comments by the facilitators on the difficulties faced by all parents looking after a young baby is a useful tactic, but a long process. Normalising such behaviours as bouts of crying, food refusal, disturbed sleep patterns etc. also help the young women to see their own baby's 'difficult behaviour' in perspective. We are also aware of the additional stresses these young women are under in terms of lack of money, cramped housing conditions and lack of support from partners. As the group matured and friendships developed between members they would offer each other support outside the group e.g. meeting in the park, passing on pieces of equipment and clothes etc.

The morning group is co-facilitated by two workers (often male). During this time a duty worker is also available to see people individually to deal with practical problems e.g. benefits, housing, equipment etc. Lunch is provided by our cook project worker; it is an important part of the day and regarded as fundamental to the nurturing part of the work. After lunch, the young women meet together without their babies for their afternoon group. During this time the babies are cared for by creche workers, using a key worker system so that each baby has a named carer.

The afternoon group

The afternoon group is run by two female workers (one of whom is a worker from the Pregnancy Group) and provides a space for the young women away from their babies for an hour, where they can talk about their feelings and anxieties. Building on the trust created during their time in the Pregnancy Group, the young women exchange experiences and advice with each other. Initially, the group leaders facilitated this process by providing a similar structure to that of the Pregnancy Group, sitting in a circle, and taking turns to speak.

By the time the groupwork sessions at St Gabriel's begin, the young women have been working together for about three months. The structured groupwork model used at Marina House begins to shift away from turn-taking; instead the leaders take a much less 'parental' role, facilitating the interchange between group members, focusing on the immediate here and now feelings which become the material of the group.

As group leaders we have found that we need to relax and restrain our own wishes to be actively 'useful' and learn to assume a recessive role, i.e. partly to observe and partly facilitate, thus providing containment for the group. Our skill lies in deciding when to be active and when to let the group process unfold itself. The task is basically to help the group communicate more effectively. I have argued earlier in the article that structure in the group in the form of turn-taking is necessary in the early stages, but can be abandoned as the group matures.

I would like to illustrate how this process has enabled one individual to make changes in her life and how this has affected her behaviour in the group. K used to start every week by saying she had nothing to say, that 'nothing had happened', that it was all boring etc. Her attitude was extremely self-effacing and uncomplaining and yet she was always positive and responsive to other people's material. The group leaders were active in giving positive reinforcement to K and challenging her negative comments about herself. It was noticeable that in the first session where spontaneous interchange between members took place, K spoke more forcefully about her life and relationship with her partner, and went on over the next few weeks to challenge the nature of the relationship and to consider separating from him. She gradually stopped defending him and used quite abusive language to describe him. For the first time since their relationship began, she was able to see how his dependence on her was more like that of a child, rather than an adult in a mutually supportive relationship. She felt more able to challenge him and to stand up for herself. By speaking out she engendered more respect and support from the group. She has also recently expressed interest in joining the Peer Education Group made up of members of the group, who go into local schools to talk about the realities of being a teenage mother.

A brief review of the pregnancy groups and young mother's support group, content, methods and process

The first Pregnancy Group started in November 1991 and finished in March 1993. The second group began in the spring of 1993 and finished in July 1994:

> The people there were interested in what I had to say and did not try and push one point of view. They didn't tell me what to do but they did listen.

The above comment was made by one of the members of the first group we worked with; it encapsulates the principles of respect and trust which we believe are essential to the successful running of a support group in a day care setting. Much groupwork theory assumes as the norm an in-patient hospital setting where members have little contact outside the group, or an out-patient group where there is none. In a day care setting however, as has been demonstrated, the group members have contact both with each other and with the group facilitators, outside the therapeutic hour. While there is a specific personal development focus in the afternoon group, the support work is an ongoing process from the moment of arrival at the family centre.

Yalom (1975) cites research into adolescents in groups who 'overall, valued the therapeutic factors of universality and cohesiveness more highly than did adults'. Clearly, the additional factor of looking after a baby in difficult circumstances must increase the sense of universality for these young women. Being together with their infants, discussing and comparing common problems e.g. lack of sleep, relationships with partners and family etc., against a background of adult support and practical help, all contribute to the value of the programme. This is not to deny the difficulties that can arise if there are concerns about child protection. We encourage the young women to explain the circumstances if a baby should arrive at the centre with a bruise or injury. To date, we have not needed to take any action and the babies are generally well cared for and thriving.

Three monthly reviews

Every three months, each group member attends a review at the centre where all the issues relating to her own health and development and that of her baby are discussed together with any other outside professional such as a health visitor or social worker. It is also an opportunity for staff to evaluate how well the programme is working and to get feedback about the group from each individual. At the most recent reviews, all the young women said how much more they enjoyed the afternoon group since they had stopped taking it in turns to say how they were and truly could 'just talk about anything that came up'.

Engagement process

Engaging the young women after initial referral has been a learning process for us and one which was clearly influenced by the experience of the other agency, Marina House. St Gabriel's tends to give a large share of responsibility to its users for attendance. The initial referral is followed by a meeting with the professional who then goes back to the client with the offer of an appointment to visit the centre and meet staff. If the visit goes well, the family will be asked to visit again, this time to meet the other families with the possibility of joining the programme the following week. The final responsibility for attending however is left to the individual.

With referrals to the pregnancy group, however, young women are visited at home several times if necessary, or in a cafe or similar venue if appropriate. We have learnt that good attendance is dependent on early attachment and this may take a concentrated effort. For example, one young woman we visited, lived in a series of bed and breakfast rooms and was very reluctant to speak to us. At first she sat on the stairs and sucked her thumb while we explained what the Pregnancy Group could offer her. After several such visits she called in at Marina House one morning to ask for help with money. She eventually joined the group in the third week, the last opportunity before it became a closed group. Young pregnant women respond like many other adolescents; they need to feel cared for but are also resistant, hence the need to strike the right balance between caring, and respecting their independence. Once the group starts, we continue to make home visits if someone fails to attend one week. Currently, we are working with a young woman who attends very infrequently and who has only recently felt able to share that she often misses the group because she is worried about leaving her partner (who has serious mental health problems).

We recognise that for this individual, we need to be flexible, and consequently work extends beyond the group into frequent home visits and letters. When she does attend the group, however her presence is valued; she brings insight and maturity and relates well to the others.

Endings

Perhaps the most difficult aspect of the work is planning the end. When is the right time? We are constrained by time because we have to fit in with the needs of the other agency and the numbers of other young women who will form the next Pregnancy Group. We try to work towards integrating each member of the group into her local community by finding out what is going on, e.g. other groups or drop-ins, creche or nursery facilities, training courses etc.

A lesson learnt from the experience of running the first support group was that ending was an issue for the staff as much as for the young women. We were unprepared for the feelings of protectiveness and loss and were left with a sense that we could not do enough. This time, however, we planned the end more carefully and worked with the group on ways to enable them to continue to meet (something they said they very much wanted). To date this has meant offering them use of the building on a number of days during the summer, facilitated by one of the staff initially with a view to handing over the arrangements to them to continue if they wish.

We also maintain contact with the group in a different forum, i.e. the Peer Education Group. Our role here is to provide creche support while they meet to plan visits, and transport to and from local schools.

Another outcome of this piece of work with young mothers was a report, written with the full involvement of the group and published by the Children's Society (Norman and Wilks, 1993) at a time when teenage mothers were being criticised and blamed for the breakdown of family values. The report gives a positive account of the achievements of young mothers and calls for social policy changes which would help to alleviate some of the difficulties they face and provide opportunities for a better future. The process of involvement in the writing of the report was empowering for the young women who felt they were being given a voice and a chance to correct the negative assumptions made about them by the government and society. Empowerment has become a key phrase in social work in the nineties. As professionals we can and should act as advocates for individuals who experience powerlessness and alienation, but this should be alongside work which encourages self confidence and independence. Successful groupwork can and does empower individuals through a process of self discovery and growth, enabling them to regain control in their lives and make choices.

References

Anderson, J.D. (1979) 'Social work with groups in the generic base of social work practice', *Social Work with Groups*, 2(4), pp.281-293.

Norman, C. and Wilks, S. (1993) *A Fit State for Motherhood?*. The Children's Society.

Yalom, I.D. (1975) *The Theory and Practice of Group Psychotherapy*. Chapter 4, 'The therapeutic factors: an integration'. New York: Basic Books.

Groupwork for parents of young people in trouble: a proposal

Mark Drakeford

The rise of the 'justice model' in working with young offenders has included a withdrawal from traditional groupwork methods which has produced some unhelpful consequences. The 1991 Criminal Justice Act and subsequent Government announcements have targeted the parents of young people in trouble for official disapproval and punishment. This paper argues for a new, voluntary groupwork programme for parents in this position, sharing common concerns and drawing on common strengths. As a result, it suggests, benefits would accrue both to those taking part and to those concerned to manage youth justice systems on minimum intervention principles. Workers need to re-capture some groupwork skills and abilities in order to put such a programme into practice.

Introduction

This is a paper with a proposal. It does not have a piece of groupwork to report. It cannot make claims to any new or sophisticated understanding of process or theory. It does, however, make an urgent case for those who are interested both in social welfare and in groupwork to turn their attention in a new and hitherto neglected direction.

The area of social welfare practice with which this paper is concerned lies in criminal justice. To claim that groupwork is neglected in this context may seem perverse. In their introductory chapter to a recent collection of papers, *Groupwork with Offenders*, Brown and Caddick (1993) begin with the observation that 'There is a long tradition in the Probation Service, and elsewhere in the criminal justice system, of working with offenders in groups' (p.2) and cite evidence from Caddick's 1991 survey of groupwork in the Probation Service to conclude that 'the use of groups in the probation service - particularly in direct work with offenders - is now probably more extensive and more varied than it has ever been' (p.2).

Yet, this is not universally so. In the field of Youth Justice, groupwork has a more chequered and ambiguous history. On the

Groupwork Vol. 7(3), 1994, pp.236-247

one hand, the tradition of activity groups for adolescent young men has always been strong on the ground, even when its theoretical basis and practical achievements in affecting behaviour have been challenged (see, for example, Collins and Behan, 1981). On the other hand, the rise of a justice model in working with young offenders - discussed more fully below - has produced a new emphasis upon dealing with individual young people on the basis of their own behaviour alone, seeking to minimise intervention in their lives and where necessary working to eliminate unhelpful influences - such as peer groups - rather than engage with such influences directly. The result is a very mixed pattern indeed but includes many projects and workers for whom the idea of groupwork is unfamiliar in practice and, potentially, regarded with suspicion or hostility in principle.

Parents of young people in trouble: new departures

Within the field of youth justice, however, a new target for official intervention is emerging, where the requirements both of good practice and of efficient service delivery demand that groupwork should come again to the fore. Parents of young people in trouble have been identified by politicians for more than a decade as a source of their children's anti-social behaviour. Only in more recent times, however, has the rhetoric been turned into practical powers for courts to place sanctions upon parents who are seen, wilfully, to be neglectful of their duties. Because these are new departures, both the powers and the thinking behind them require a more detailed consideration here.

The Criminal Justice Act of 1991 sets out the powers to bind over the parents of young people who offend. While many of the changes introduced in the Act were controversial, its Youth Court provisions contained the potential to build upon and extend successful practice of the previous ten years. Indeed, as late as 1992 a group of respected commentators could begin a textbook of documents concerned with the introduction of the new Youth Court with a chapter entitled 'Juvenile justice - a decade of progress' and an opening sentence: 'The 1980s was a remarkable decade for juvenile justice practice in England and Wales' (Ashworth et al., 1992, p.20). Yet, less than a year after its practical implementation in October 1992 the Act had come under severe attack and had been, in significant measure, amended (Home Office, 1993). In the context of the new imperatives, particularly, the matter of parental 'binding over' took on a fresh importance because such powers were, from the outset, part of the coercive, rather than progressive, elements within the 1991 Act.

Indeed, the policy context of these specific powers now needs to be set out.

The policy context

Parental responsibility has been a theme of all Conservative administrations since 1979. In the earliest significant piece of legislation in the juvenile justice field, the Criminal Justice Act of 1982, new measures were introduced which, the Government said would 'reinforce parental authority' in the control of adolescent family members (Home Office, 1980). At this stage, however, Ministers were at pains to point out that the measures were designed only to assist 'conscientious parents' (Lord Elton, quoted in McEwan, 1983) and that the making of any Order could only follow the consent of both young offender and parent. In practice, powers such as Night Restriction Orders were almost never exercised. In response to a questionnaire sent out to all Probation areas in 1985 it was reported that 'there is virtually no take-up of restraining or negative conditions' (Jarvis et al., 1987, p.103). Practitioners declined to recommend them to courts who concurred in their lack of usefulness.

Despite these indifferent results, the notion of parental responsibility continued increasingly to exercise Government Ministers during the remainder of the 1980s. The justifications set out in the process leading up to the 1991 Criminal Justice Act are instructive. The White Paper which began the formal Parliamentary process was quite explicit. The power to bind over parents:

> ...could play an important part in ensuring that parents do all they can to stop their children reoffending. The knowledge that they may forfeit up to £1000 if they fail to meet the terms of the recognizance would be a strong incentive to improve their supervision of their children (Home Office, 1990, para.8.10).

The White Paper was followed by a Criminal Justice Bill. In Parliamentary debate the proposals surrounding parental responsibility attracted more attention that almost any other single issue. There were widespread calls, from Government backbenchers especially, for the new powers to be implemented and, often, widened.

The 1991 Act: new powers

The Act which followed proceeds on the basis that 'responsible' behaviour can only be promoted by the extension of the scope and the penalties of the criminal law so as to intervene directly upon the way in which parents act towards their children. Three distinct powers in the Act operate so as to identify parents more closely with the criminal activity of their children. For the purposes of this paper the most important lies in Section 58 which confers a completely new duty upon magistrates to bind over the parents of a child under 16 so as to 'take proper care and exercise proper control over the child' (s58(2)(b)). Unreasonable refusal to be bound over can result in a fine of up to £1000. A court must exercise its powers to bind over:

> ...if it is satisfied, having regard to the circumstances of the case, that their exercise would be desirable in the interests of preventing the commission by [the offender] of further offences (s28(1)(a)).

Should a court choose not to exercise its powers, reasons for that decision must be given in open court.

At the time of the Bill many commentators, including those from the Magistracy (see, for example, Thomson, 1990, and editorials in *The Magistrate* 1990, 1991) concluded that the powers in relation to parents would prove to be useless and therefore infrequently used. In fact, there is evidence to suggest that in practice, however useless, the powers may be more widely employed than anticipated and, certainly, in the proposals now before Parliament, a concerted attempt is underway to extend such powers further. A study by the present author of Youth Court practice within a South Wales county in a six month period in 1993 found that parental bindovers were employed in 16 per cent of cases within the county as a whole, and more than 21 per cent in one busy court. Parents are being penalised directly because of the behaviour of their children.

The proposals currently before Parliament look to extend these powers to penalise the parents of young offenders so as, for example, to be able to bind over parents in the sum of £1000 if community penalties given to their children are breached.

Implications for youth justice services: two problems

Why should local Social Services Departments take an interest in these developments? Firstly, and most generally, Departments will be faced with two very different and contradictory sets of legislative injunctions for dealing with parents of young people. On the one hand, Departments are obliged to operate within the requirements and the spirit of the 1989 Children Act, a piece of legislation which makes it clear that responsibility for child rearing has to be located with the parents rather than the state. As a leading commentator notes, political support for the proposals was accompanied by:

> ...the frequent suggestion that the reduction of control, or even

> supervision, over the way parents exercise their 'responsibility' will encourage them to behave more 'responsibly' towards their children (Eekelaar, 1991, p.49).

Minimum state intervention, as the Secretary of State argued, would lead directly to maximum parental responsibility: 'The Bill's emphasis on the primary function of parenthood will...highlight the obligation on parents to care for their children and bring them up properly' (House of Commons, 1988).

It is regularly claimed, and with justification, that the sections of the 1991 Criminal Justice Act which deal with young people must be viewed in conjunction with the provisions of the Children Act which had been contemporaneously part of the legislative programme of the same Government. David Faulkner, senior Home Office civil servant at the time, has described the two pieces of legislation as 'companion Acts' (Faulkner, 1992, p.133). In the words of Ashworth et al. (1992, p.18): 'The 1989 Act thus provides a crucial statutory backcloth to the new youth court'. Yet, nothing could be more different than the approach to parental responsibility adopted in the two Acts. Far from lauding the advantages of the minimalist state and, in sharp contradistinction to the idea that parents act most responsibly when most left alone, the Criminal Justice Act proceeds on the basis that 'responsible' behaviour can only be promoted by the extension of the scope and the penalties of the criminal law so as to punish parents for failed dealings with their children.

Social Services Departments will be left attempting to make practical sense of this dilemma. The parents to whom the contradictory approaches apply will very often be the same people, dealt with in one fashion when seeking a service delivered through the Children Act - partnership, empowerment, respect - and very differently when within the Youth Justice ambit.

A second difficulty for Departments then lies within the Youth Justice field itself. As noted at the start of this paper, during the 1980s a successful and concerted model of working with young people in trouble came to dominate social welfare practice. Summarising very briefly, the model was predicated upon the belief that formal intervention in the life of a young person was significantly more likely to do harm than good and that, as a consequence, the less interference in the lives of young offenders the better. Principles of maximum diversion, minimum intervention and systems management produced an impact upon the number of young people drawn into the most intrusive criminal justice penalties. (For an excellent critical summary of these developments see the introductory chapter to the Cambridge research into Intermediate Treatment, Bottoms et al., 1990.)

Youth Justice and the retreat from groupwork

Within the undoubted success of the model, however, a number of more problematic consequences have also emerged. John Pitts, for example, has effectively argued that the distaste for 'welfare'-inspired work with young people has led to a neglect of the very real needs of some very vulnerable individuals (in Dennington and Pitts, 1991). In those Youth Justice teams where hard-line, offence-focused approaches predominate this has produced two outcomes which are significant for the arguments of this paper. Firstly, it has led to a withdrawal from work within families. If a justice approach means work with an offender about their offending then even the immediate social circumstances of that individual have to take second place to the specific behaviour which has led to the intervention. Even where contact with the home does occur, it is likely to be confined directly to issues which surround court appearances and their outcomes. Secondly, Youth Justice, in contrast to work within the Probation Service with older offenders, has tended to withdraw from groupwork. A belief has taken hold that challenging, confronting and changing the behaviour which leads to a young person appearing before the courts is most effectively carried out on a one-to-one basis, rather than within groups where such behaviour is likely to be reinforced by the pressure of peers, the need to defend group norms or the opportunity to learn new tricks from more experienced offenders. At their most trenchant such views are to be found in articles such as that by Sue Ross (1984), 'The sacred cow of IT'. Here, amongst a reasonable account of the minimalist position, groupwork in particular is attacked as an especially insidious form of 'expansionist welfare intervention' (Ross, 1984, p.26). While the intervening years have not fulfilled Ross's final prediction that groupwork with young offenders was set to be 'reduced to a peripheral activity - merely a focus for filling time' (Ross, 1984, p.26) it is certainly true that youth justice services are unlikely now to meet the test set out by Brown and Caddick in their support of 'a work culture which validates working with people in groups as at least as 'natural' a method as working with them individually' (Brown and Caddick, 1993, p.9).

Amongst the greatest difficulties inherent in these generally questionable developments are the gaps which have been left in the ability of organisations and individual workers to respond to changed circumstances where new needs have to be addressed. In making this case, it is important to stress that the rationale for addressing the new powers which courts have to deal with parents of young offenders is entirely consistent with the major aims of contemporary youth justice practice. Put simply, the new powers pose a major danger of casting the net of the criminal justice system over a new and wider group. In doing so, the risks of such families, children as well as parents, becoming more deeply labelled and dealt with on the basis of that label will be similarly increased.

A groupwork solution

Finding a means of persuading the courts not to use their new powers in the damaging ways proposed through legislation is a proper and necessary task facing workers in this field. It is not adequate to act in the hope that, left alone, such measures will simply wither on the vine. However much practitioners and sentencers may doubt the practical efficacy of penalising parents in theory, in practice the powers have a seductive attractiveness. Therefore, if courts are not to treat parents in this way something will have to be put in place which will persuade them that the need does not arise. What is needed is a way of addressing the problems which the parents of adolescent offenders face which will be useful to them, capable of being carried out in a manner consistent with social work values and the spirit of partnership and which will be capable of being used within the criminal justice system as a means of persuading courts not to use their new powers.

The way in which these different objectives could best be met, it is argued here, is a groupwork programme for parents of young people in trouble. The history of groupwork with parents in Britain in recent years is patchy but examples of relevant activity in the field are to be found. Most often work has been reported with parents whose children have come to the attention of social workers for reasons which are not connected with offending: for example, because of health problems (Geirdal, 1989-90; Webb, 1990), behavioural problems (Gill, 1989; Robertson, 1990; Marchant, 1993), or concerns about level of parental care (Grealish, 1989; Wattley, 1992). The practice ideologies which underpin these different initiatives also vary in emphasis but with some common identifiable themes. Groupwork is chosen as a method of working with parents facing difficulties because it provides a medium through which such experiences may be shared and strength gained in finding new ways of proceeding.

Groupwork with parents of young people in trouble is far less reported, although the evidence includes the experience reported by Rogers et al. (1986) where parents' self-help groups complemented the work of local intermediate treatment projects (see McCaughan, 1988) and the long track record within the Probation Service of setting up support groups for the families of offenders generally, and in particular for the partners of people in prison. It is not, however, the intention here to suggest any prescriptive formula for a groupwork programme for parents of young people in trouble. Building on some of the ideas and principles of previous work, and applying them to the needs identified earlier, some characteristics may be suggested:

1. Parents of teenagers generally face issues which are not easy to negotiate, both because parents may not possess relevant information and because even when information is available, actions which follow are likely to involve ethical as well as factual considerations. Research cited by the Trust for the Study of Adolescence, for example, found that 'the self-confidence of parents increases slowly during the first ten or eleven years of a child's life. However, the arrival of teenage years leads to a dramatic drop in parental confidence. Mothers and fathers simply do not know what their role should be' (Coleman, 1993). A core curriculum swiftly suggests itself in which matters of drug and alcohol misuse, personal and sexual relations, divorce, school, accommodation, employment and intra-family matters all have an important place.
2. For these and further reasons, it follows that the Group would best be organised on an open basis, available to parents on an agency-wide and self-referral basis. The further reasons lie primarily in the contribution which this would make to the normalisation of parents' experience and an avoidance of a further intensification of the stigma which will already be their lot. There are more pragmatic reasons, also, which are highlighted by Rogers et al. in their account of work with parents of young people undergoing Intermediate Treatment programmes. Here, group membership progressively expanded from its criminal justice base, usually at the behest of parents themselves: 'from an early point in the group's life, the parents stressed that there must be other parents with similar needs for support and advice' (Rogers et al., 1986, p.28). At the end of the period covered in the account parents had established two self-help groups aiming to assist others who 'had experienced a

sense of isolation, and felt they had failed in some way as parents because of the problems their children presented' (Rogers et al., 1986, p.27).

3. In addition to these common concerns, parents introduced to a group through a criminal justice route will have an additional common and specific focus upon the concerns which arise when a young person is in trouble with the law. The emotional context which is part of this process - the powerful feelings of guilt, shame, resentment and anger, for example - will need to be addressed actively. While the group is likely to have a task focus - how to deal with common difficulties more effectively - there will be need to be an emphasis also upon the process of the group membership. In terms of the dichotomy identified by Paul Senior (1991) in his account of Probation Service groupwork in the 1990s - compulsory, pre-prepared, control-driven on the one hand, empowerment and anti-oppression on the other - the work with parents suggested here falls clearly into the latter mode.
4. Groups are an effective and efficient means of transmitting relevant information. The application of adult learning principles, particularly, mean that the participative learning which groups allow promote the discovery and retention of relevant material. Certainly, in the experience reported by Rogers et al., parents appear to have viewed their group in this manner: 'The group is seen by parents as a working forum, a source of advice about how to solve problems, and as a chance to meet other people' (Rogers et al., 1986, p.27).
5. Groups conducted according to certain principles allow, even more, for exploration of the social and ethical issues which surround the translation of information into practical action. Parents who attend such a group will be in receipt of powerful messages about their own failure to act successfully in this regard. Yet, many will have brought up other children without such difficulties and all will possess an expertise which is drawn from their experience of parenting. A worthwhile groupwork programme is therefore likely to emphasise the achievements of participants and the ways in which these can be built upon rather than assuming an unduly correctionalist ethos.

Successful examples exist of groups for parents where self-help and active participation are regarded as the most significant factors in enabling members to regain control over important areas of their lives and in lobbying for improved services to meet their needs (see, for example, Chesney and Chesler, 1993). In short, a social action approach (as set out, for example by Mullender and Ward, 1991 and, in the context of work with offenders by Bailey, 1992), although least common amongst those adopted in working within the criminal justice system, is likely to reap most benefits in this new sphere.

6. For these reasons it will be important that attendance at the group should be entirely voluntary. Workers would need to be confident enough of the relevance and accessibility of their product to command a place in the market. For those who operate primarily within the statutory climate of criminal justice work, such confidence is not always easy to generate, even though evidence exists that voluntarism results in at least as good attendance rates (see, for example Mistry, 1989; Ashe, 1991). Moreover, outside the statutory sector further evidence may be found that provided what is on offer is perceived to be sufficiently worthwhile and delivered in a way which promotes participation, involvement of service users will follow.
7. In terms of convincing courts, the intrinsic value of programmes on offer will, in the longer run, be the greatest guarantee of success. Cooperation rather than coercion remains a basis which can be convincingly advanced in such settings, provided it commands the self-belief of those putting forward the arguments and the evidence of usefulness of which voluntary participation is the greatest affirmation.

The detailed work which would be needed to translate such principles into practical operation lies outside the scope of this paper.

Conclusion

Increasingly coercive powers to intervene in the lives of parents of young offenders are set to cause difficulties in the field of Youth Justice over the coming years. Despite widespread agreement as to the lack of utility in these measures, courts are nevertheless likely to use their new powers in such a way as to draw more families into the ambit of the criminal justice system. Against that background, it is incumbent upon those organisations wishing to defend the principles of minimum intervention which have provided considerable benefits over the past decade to develop new ways of working, founded upon the same principles, in the new circumstances. Unfortunately, at the level of individual workers, the withdrawal of youth justice services from active involvement with families and a concentration upon the individual young person's pattern of offending, may have lowered levels of available skills both in working with parents and in using groupwork methods.

Nevertheless, a suitable groupwork programme for parents of young people in trouble would have double benefits. From a systems management perspective it would provide the courts with a means of addressing deficiencies or difficulties in parenting, without the attachment of a criminal justice sanction. For parents themselves, a social action group could provide both a source of much-needed information but also, and more importantly, a possible forum through which experiences with parents in a similar situation could be shared. The parents of young people in trouble are in danger of becoming a new moral folk-devil, a convenient scapegoat for the ills created in a deliberately unequal and divided society. The collective power to resist such stigmatising could yet turn out to be the best reason of all for groupwork to be the preferred method of practice in this new and deepening context.

References

Ashe, M. (1991) 'Meeting prisoners' needs through groupwork', *Groupwork*, 4(3), pp.277-283.

Ashworth, A., Cavadino, P., Gibson, B., Harding, J., Rutherford, A., Seago, P. and Whyte, L. (1992) *The Youth Court*. Winchester: Waterside Press.

Bailey, R., (1992) 'Perceptions of groupwork in the Probation Service', *Social Action*, 1(1), pp.10-14.

Bottoms, A., Brown, P., McWilliams, B., McWilliams, W. and Nellis, M. (1990) *Intermediate Treatment and Juvenile Justice*. London: HMSO.

Brown, A. and Caddick, B. (eds.) (1993) *Groupwork with Offenders*. London: Whiting and Birch.

Chesney, B.K. and Chestler, M.A. (1993) 'Activism through self-help group membership: reported life changes of parents of children with cancer', *Small Group Research*, 24(2), May 1993, pp.258-73.

Coleman, J. (1993) 'Parents of teenagers: how can we help?', *Community Education Network*, 13(6), p.8.

Collins and Behan (1981) *Social Work with Young Offenders*. London: Butterworth.

Dennington, J. and Pitts, J. (eds.) (1991) *Developing Services for Young People in Crisis*. London: Longman.

Eekelaar, J. (1991) 'Parental responsibility: state of nature or nature of the state?', *Journal of Social Welfare and Family Law*, 37(1), pp.37-50.

Faulkner, D. (1992) 'Seriousness, right or wrong', *Justice of the Peace*, 157(13).

Gill, A. (1989) 'Putting fun back into families', *Social Work Today*, 4 May, pp.14-5.
Geirdal, A.O. (1989-90) 'Supportive groupwork with young arthritic mothers', *Groupwork*, 2(3), pp.220-36.
Grealish, E.M. et al. (1989) 'A behavioural group procedure for parents of severely troubled and troubling youth', *Child and Youth Care Quarterly*, 18(1), pp.49-61.
Home Office (1980) *Young Offenders*. White Paper. Cmnd. 8045.
Home Office (1990) *Crime, Justice and Protecting the Public*. Cmnd. 965
Home Office (1993) *Criminal Justice Act 1993: Commencement of Certain Provisions on 16 August and 20 September 1993*. Circular 38.
House of Commons Debates (1988) *Hansard*, 151, col.1107.
Jarvis, G., Parker, H. and Sumner, M. (1987) 'An ambivalent service', *Probation Journal*, 34(3). pp.103-104.
Marchant, C. (1993) 'Hitting home', *Community Care*, 4 November, p.9.
McCaughan, N. (1988) 'Swimming upstream: a survey of articles on groupwork in social work journals 1986 - 87', *Groupwork*, 1(1), pp.77-89.
McEwan, J. (1983), 'In search of juvenile justice - the Criminal Justice Act 1982', *Journal of Social Welfare Law*, XX, pp.112-117.
Mistry, T. (1989), 'Establishing a feminist model of groupwork in the probation service', *Groupwork*, 2(2), pp.145-58.
Mullender, A. and Ward, D. (1991) *Self Directed Groupwork: Users Taking Action for Empowerment*. London: Whiting and Birch.
Robertson, R. (1990) 'Groupwork with parents of sleepless children', *Groupwork*, 3(3), pp.249-59.
Rogers, J.S.B., Thompson, B. and Brennan, A. (1986) 'Helping parents solve their children's problems', *Community Care*, 30 January.
Ross, S. (1984) 'The sacred cow of IT', *Community Care*, 16 February.
Senior, P. (1991) 'Groupwork in the Probation Service: care or control in the 1990s', *Groupwork*, 4(3), pp.284-295.
The Magistrate (1990) 'Editorial', 41(11), p.203.
The Magistrate (1991) 'Editorial', 47(6), p.109.
Thomson, R. (1990) 'Strong disagreement over some proposals for juveniles', *The Magistrate*, 46(8). p.41.
Wattley, R. (1992) 'Protecting children 'at risk': introducing a social action perspective', *Social Action*, 1(1), pp.5-9.
Webb, B. (1990) 'Mutual support for families of children with eye cancer', *Child: Care, Health and Development*, 16, pp.319-29.

A DRAMATIC VIEW OF GROUPWORK

JEREMY WEINSTEIN

Award winning films and novels can often provide more than just entertainment. The picture they offer of the experience of childhood or such traumas as mental breakdown or disablement can also offer important insights for social workers working with these client groups. This article examines four such films and / or books which seem to say something about the nature of groups and groupwork and suggests ways that they could be drawn upon primarily in our role as trainers but also in our direct work with groups. The subjects of the discussion are One Flew Over The Cuckoo's Nest , She'll Be Wearing Pink Pyjamas, Lord of the Flies *and* Dead Poets Society.

Introduction

The recent success of the Booker prize winner, *Paddy Clarke, Ha Ha Ha* (1993) by Roddy Doyle, follows in the tradition of other titles such as *The Colour Purple* (1982) by Alice Walker, and *Bone People* (1990) by Keri Hulme. Here novelists focus in on the world of a child coping with crisis and while not intended for the education of social workers these books beautifully complement the more traditional texts. The impact of such novels and autobiographies, especially if they are turned into feature films, can be considerable, helping shape new perspectives on social problems or social work practice. Other examples that spring to mind include the film *My Left Foot* (1989) on disablement; the novel *The Comfort of Madness* (1988) by Paul Sayers, on mental health; or *In the Ditch* (1972) and its sequels by Buchi Emecheta for the general experience of living on the knife edge of poverty. Developing this theme I want to use this article to discuss four other examples: *One Flew Over The Cuckoo's Nest* (book by Ken Kesey and the film); the film *She'll Be Wearing Pink Pyjamas* starring Julie Walters; *Lord of the Flies* (the book by William Golding and the 1990 film); and *Dead Poet's Society* the film starring Robin Williams. All of these provide entertaining, dramatic and moving insights into the world of groupwork and are relatively accessible in video hire shops or in the local library. They can be drawn upon as background reading or used in training sessions with students or with groups of clients but care needs to be taken: three of the examples focus exclusively on the experiences of men or boys and

Groupwork Vol. 7(3), 1994, pp.248-255

all assume the norms and values of white society to the neglect of the black experience. These points will need to be confronted in our work and the resulting discussion can help develop our understanding of anti-racist and anti-discriminatory practice.

One Flew Over the Cuckoo's Nest

I start with the influential work, *One Flew Over The Cuckoo's Nest,* which I have used very regularly while teaching groupwork to student social workers. This may, however, seem a strange and masochistic selection.

Certainly a therapy group, based on the ward of an American mental hospital, is a running theme throughout both the film and the book (Kesey, 1973) but most of the lessons of this formal group are startling.

Through the eyes of a new member, McMurphy, and, in the book, the watchful commentary of Chief Bromden, we see Nurse Ratched maintain her power through apparently working with the whole group but actually setting members against each other. McMurphy sharply describes this group process as resembling 'a bunch of chickens at a pecking party' (1973, p.49). Nurse Ratched's interventions draw each member into the group by exploiting and elaborating their weaknesses: this one's verbosity, another's sexual uncertainty, and then she sits back when they are attacked by other group members. The Big Nurse abuses confidential information, suddenly changes the rules (the membership of the group is expanded to include the 'chronics' when she might otherwise lose a vote) and should the challenge grow too strong she can rely on the system to physically control the offender through ECT or, ultimately, a lobotomy. The fact that McMurphy does not initially realise that such sanctions exist is a powerful lesson that every new member has to learn the stated and unstated rules of the group. For all the above, however, *One Flew Over The Cuckoo's Nest* is not just an object lesson in 'what not to do', rather it can act as a wonderful celebration of the potential of groups. In my teaching sessions I start shortly into the film, as the ward group starts with some desultory 'warm ups', and I finish with the episode where McMurphy gathers his companions around him to watch the World Series on an empty TV screen. Within these 45 minutes there is a profusion of material. Students are asked to take notes as the film progresses for a subsequent discussion comparing and contrasting the formal therapy group of Nurse Ratched and the informal group which McMurphy gathers around himself whether in the card games or the exercise yard or on the ward generally. This very much focuses on differing styles of leadership. The impact and growing influence of McMurphy can be measured in his continuing commitment and reaching out to those around him. In a host of carefully observed incidents the film shows how he appreciates and works with each individual's idiosyncrasies. Something about this urge for contact transcending McMurphy's gambling instincts is shown by the energy he invests in attempting to teach basketball to the apparently mute and unresponsive Chief Bromden. Interestingly a key moment in both the book and the film focuses on McMurphy attempting, and failing, to lift a solid marble control panel. It is when McMurphy shows his vulnerability that he makes his most important impact.

One Flew Over The Cuckoo's Nest cannot be used uncritically, however. On one level we cheer with McMurphy as the other patients, individually and collectively, find the confidence to challenge their own image as 'nutters' and failures. But if this is empowerment it is at the expense of both the black ward orderlies and the female Nurse Ratched. McMurphy's flow of speech has a spontaneity and authenticity so much in contrast to the words as weapon approach of the formal groupwork sessions, but the wit and energy is shot through with sexist and racist language and assumptions. Whenever we use this film we need to make time to explore how we develop a language that is as equally vivid, immediate, humorous *and* anti-oppressive. In my own discussions we have looked to how a change of group membership, to include just a single black member or a significant minority of black members, might shift the atmosphere. We have explored concepts of masculinity and drawn on groupwork with male sex offenders to explore how the negative aspects can be challenged. We have also examined the way that institutional racism and sexism is played out within the hospital and serves to encourage a divide and rule approach exemplified by McMurphy. The discussions are never easy but the film is a provocative way into the issues and something new can be discovered on every showing.

She'll Be Wearing Pink Pyjamas

Similar issues but from a different perspective emerge from *She'll Be Wearing Pink Pyjamas* which is a less dramatic but humorous and celebratory film which could be shown as both entertainment and learning to groups of students or clients. The story follows eight women in their various exploits at an Outward Bound centre set in the British countryside. The group is relatively mixed, certainly in terms of ages (including a mother and adult daughter) but they are all white and middle class, e.g. headmistress, antiques dealer or graphic designer, with just one fairly tokenistic working class woman, an ex-dinner lady in what she describes as her first 'real' job in an office. Judging from the banter in the shower room they are all heterosexual.

What is emphasised throughout is that this is the first women only course and questions are raised from the male observers at the centre and, at crucial points, from the women themselves as to whether the course is 'too hard'? It is predictable, I think, that the film will allow them to win through but the dramatic tension is nevertheless maintained as we watch the particular ways that the group comes together. In almost the first scene they are left at night in the woods to find their way back: one member suggests that they elect a leader and is met with the sharp response that they don't need any 'male hierarchy nonsense'. This, then, is very much about women working together as women. Through the mountain trekking, canoeing and mountain climbing etc they support each other, will each other on with humour, shared confidences, songs and hugs although there is also a sharp edge in the competitiveness and in the sadness of some of the sexual banter. For the women the outward bound course is about their learning to respect first themselves and then each other. Caring enough to scale the next cliff face will help them to brave the hazards in the rest of their lives once the week is over. When one of the women shouts out 'life isn't a rehearsal, this is it', she makes a powerful point which could be taken back to discussion with your own group. I am struck that this is my only example which puts women at the centre of its interest. In the other films/books discussed in this article the women are either totally absent (*Lord of the Flies*), marginal (*Dead Poets Society*) or the enemy (*One Flew Over The Cuckoo's Nest*). The Big Screen seems more concerned with women as friends (*Fried Green Tomatoes at the Whistle Stop Cafe*, 1991; or *Steel Magnolias*, 1989). This can be used as a way of opening up an important discussion about perceived differences in groups between 'male bonding' and women's friendships. The film is a useful illustration of the way that women use groups for 'support, validation and strength and a growing sense of personal awareness' (Butler and Wintram, 1991, p.1) and there is now a growing literature to help elaborate and ground our learning in feminist approaches to groupwork.

Lord of the Flies

The next example, *Lord of the Flies*, may seem a surprising choice for this paper since it is, at heart, deeply pessimistic about the potential of groups. The story features a collection of boys who, stranded on a desert island, split into warring factions and slowly, and apparently inevitably, descend into anarchy. The power and popularity of this classic makes the novel worth re-reading at the very least as background reading for those involved in training to become groupworkers. Certainly the first section of the book is startling. In the space of less than twenty finely written pages it brings alive all the textbook writings of the initial stages of group formation. We watch the boys slowly coming together, the tentativeness of the first meeting, the establishing of new rules in a world turned upside down and the jockeying for leadership:

> ...the clamour changed from the general wish for a chief to an election by acclaim of Ralph himself. None of the boys could have found good reason for this; what intelligence had been shown was traceable to Piggy while the most obvious leader was Jack. But there was a stillness about Ralph as he sat that marked him out: there was his size, and attractive appearance; and most obscurely, yet most powerfully, there was the conch (Golding, 1962, p.30).

The symbolic impact of the conch has resonated through many groups that I have known, members have consciously created their own version of this symbolic shell used to control meetings since only the person holding the conch is allowed to speak. In the *Gamesters Handbook* (Brandes and Phillips, 1989, p.S15) it is suggested that 'the conch' can be any sort of everyday object and that as a variation the glove or set of keys can be tossed quickly from person to person with members having to speak when s/he is in possession.

Other themes which are central to the story, and provide insights for groupworkers, include roles in groups, especially focusing on the scapegoating of Piggy, a process much encouraged by his clumsiness, his disabilities (asthma and short sightedness) and his more modest class origins.

Also crucial to the plot is the way the group splits along the lines of rivalries between actual and aspiring leaders. This is then fought out between those who wish to stick with the requirement to keep the fire alight as a signal, and those who go for the excitement and fun of hunting the pigs, a fascinating playing out of task versus process in groups. These last two themes are reflected clearly in the most recent film adaptation of *Lord of the Flies*, and the one most readily available from video hire shops. Where the film is less satisfying from our perspective is the way it marginalises the key issues of group formation and competition for leadership. Thus in this version the boys arrive together on a life raft and already know each other since they all come from the same school, a US military academy where a sharp hierarchy of command is already established. It is the novel then that I would recommend with a wealth of material to bring alive discussion of groupwork issues, while Golding's bleak outlook provides plenty of controversy.

Dead Poets Society

Schoolboys are the theme also of the film *Dead Poets Society* although the basic political assumptions behind the film are very different and provide a different focus for groupworkers.

The film follows a few months in the lives of a group of seventeen year olds in a school committed to the traditional values of middle America in the 1950s. The appearance of John Keating, a charismatic English teacher, poses a fundamental challenge to the boys and to the system and the film explores these tensions to great effect. For me the film works on several levels. The first is where it portrays the development of the boys from a loose group shifting between resignation to, and grumbled rebellion against, the norms of the school, to their growing involvement in *The Dead Poets Society*, a group which is underground both literally (it meets in a cave) and symbolically since they sneak out of school at midnight for its meetings. For some of the members the Society is a peripheral piece of daring, a place to smoke and impress girls, and they betray it readily at the point of crisis. For others it provides a safe space in which to continue their rehearsals in their new ways of being and which they can take out to the wider world. Still others seem to drift into the group almost failing to recognise its importance until it is taken away from them. This is well portrayed making an interesting statement about the shifting significance of a group for its members.

The film switches from the ordinary and becomes really important, however, when it draws out the influence of Keating. In his teaching he uses his whole self, with humour and enthusiasm and personal risk taking, and several brief but brilliantly acted set pieces stay in the mind. During one such scene, where he is asking individual pupils to read out their own poems, it would be useful to stop the video in our own class and discuss his methods for working with resistance. Another episode shows him with a class exploring issues of conformity and individuality in the simple exercise of walking around the courtyard. This could be repeated in any number of social work and personal growth groups and could lead to a useful discussion about how games and exercises can engage the whole person in groups in a way that 'just talking' often fails to do.

Central to the film, however, is the way that his direct leadership in the class room also impacts on the boys outside the school in the Dead Poets Society. One interpretation of the film is that Keating allows the boys to act out his own rebellion or relive his past in proxy without him fully recognising that he is setting up the boys for a collision course with the stronger system of the institution. The film finishes with a continuing act of defiance by some of the group but Keating walks away while the cost to the boys includes one suicide and one expulsion and the apparent survival of the system. Again this provides excellent material for a class discussion about styles of leadership. Keating is a classic example of the impact on vulnerable people of a charismatic but careless leader using all his skills and charm as an encouragement to empowerment while working within a system which retains most or all of its power to control and oppress.

This is a powerful endorsement of Brown's warning that in day and residential settings:

> ...the internal climate...will profoundly affect every group and grouping that meets there. This underlines the importance of having some agreed general principles and values which prevail throughout (Brown, 1992, p.139).

In conclusion

In conclusion it needs to be noted that in recent years training videos have joined the more traditional methods for teaching groupwork and shown themselves to be effective and versatile. Thus one video uses role plays taken from carefully contrasted groups to explore particular issues such as handling conflict in groups, supervision, or techniques such as the hot seat. Supported by a handbook this is a useful addition to the trainer's repertoire (University of Bristol, 1984). The films I describe above have not been made with groupwork training in mind so need greater care in being adapted to our more specific needs. In my view only one of the films discussed above, *One Flew Over the Cuckoos' Nest* lends itself to being shown as an extract so if the other films are to be used adequate time needs to be given for both a full viewing and the subsequent discussion. Whatever the medium, participants will need some sort of careful preparation, such as a list of learning points to look out for, to keep them to the task and prevent them getting caught up in the wider issues of the film or novel and so losing the specific groupwork focus.

Last but not least we need to remind ourselves of a serious difficulty and dilemma. While I am clear about the potential of popular fiction and film as a way of helping us learn more about the drama of groupwork, a central problem remains. The preoccupations of the commercial cinema and publishers, the latter to a lesser extent perhaps, reflect rather than challenge the racism and sexism of the wider society. I have indicated ways that we can acknowledge and confront these themes in the examples I have drawn upon and we can complement that with the discussion which is beginning to emerge in the groupwork texts. But one response to this article may be to encourage a wider search of novels and films which we could use without any such reservations to affirm the anti-oppressive practice which is inherent in groups.

References

Books

Brandes, D. and Phillips, H. (1989) *Gamesters' Handbook: 140 Games for Teachers and Group Leaders*. London: Hutchinson.

Brown, A. (1992) *Groupwork*. Aldershot: Ashgate.

Butler, S. and Wintram, C. (1991) *Feminist Groupwork*. London; Sage.

Doyle, R. (1993) *Paddy Clarke Ha Ha Ha*. London: Secker and Warburg.

Emecheta, B. (1973) *In the Ditch*. London: Pan.

Golding, W. (1962) *Lord of the Flies*. London: Faber and Faber.

Hulme, K. (1990) *Bone People*. London: Hodder.

Kesey, K. (1973) *One Flew Over the Cuckoo's Nest*. London: Picador.

Sayers, P. (1988) *The Comforts of Madness*. London: Hodder and Stoughton.

Videos

Aunet, John (1990) *Fried Green Tomatoes at the Whistle Stop Cafe.*

Forman, Milos (1975) *One Flew Over the Cuckoo's Nest.*

Goldschmidt, John (1984) *She'll Be Wearing Pink Pyjamas.*

Hook, Harry (1990) *Lord of the Flies.*

Ross, Herbert (1989) *Steel Magnolias.*

Sheridan, Jim (1989) *My Left Foot.*

University of Bristol (1984) *Developing Your Groupwork Skills.*

Wier, Peter (1989) *Dead Poets Society.*

Anger management groupwork with prisoners: an empirical evaluation

Graham J. Towl and Polly Dexter

In this paper, we focus on evaluating anger management groupwork in prisons. We give the background to, and an update of, prison based anger management groupwork, and outline some of the difficulties of evaluating this type of groupwork. We present the results of a psychometric evaluation of a set of anger management courses (N=50), and finally, we suggest some new research directions.

Background

In recent years a number of forensic psychologists in prisons have been involved in the development and application of anger management groupwork programmes. The application of such programmes was largely a response to the needs of prison managers (Towl, 1994). For example, in young offender institutions, young offenders who received high rates of 'Governor's Reports' for various types of disruptive behaviour were identified as a priority group for such interventions. Programmes were applied in young offender settings (e.g. McDougall et al., 1987) and in adult settings (e.g. Towl and Jennings, 1990). By 1991, 15 adult prisons and six young offender institutions reported running anger management groups (Towl, 1993). In May 1992, under the auspices of the Directorate of Inmate Programmes, training for prison officers in running the national anger management treatment package commenced. Since then about 40 prison officer teams (of about 5) have been trained in using the package. Thus we may assume that about 40 prisons have the potential to run anger management programmes.

The approach

The approach is based upon a cognitive-behavioural account of anger. A hallmark of a cognitive-behavioural perspective is the importance placed upon the link between our thoughts and behaviour. This link is applied in cognitive-behavioural intervention methods with, for example, self-reflection and self-monitoring of our thoughts about events. Related to a cognitive-behavioural perspective is a cognitive-physiological arousal theory of emotion.

Groupwork Vol. 7(3), 1994, pp.256-269

The premise here is that two things are necessary for such an emotion to be experienced; physiological arousal and a labelling of the aroused state. This premise is reflected in anger control interventions with an emphasis upon developing an awareness of signs of increased bodily arousal and practising relaxation training techniques.

The structure and content of the programmes

There are typically about eight modules in anger management treatment programmes in prisons, each lasting about two hours. It is recommended that modules are run at the rate of about two per week. Institutional and regime constraints in prisons sometimes make this impossible. In practice, sessions are sometimes more widely spaced or run over four consecutive days. If there is a high 'turnover' of prisoners going in and out of a prison the scope for spacing sessions is reduced. Staff availability for running the groups can be an important factor in influencing the spacing of sessions. The group requires a continuity in facilitators, shift patterns may militate against this.

The structure of the groupwork may be conceptualised as involving three stages. First, the general exploration of anger ; second, an individual examination of personal experiences of anger; third, the examination, selection and practice of a number of anger management methods (Towl, 1993).

The first two stages involve the facilitators making an assessment of the anger management difficulties that group members report experiencing. At these stages of the programme the facilitators attempt to examine the degree of insight, motivation and capacity for change that each individual appears to have. The facilitators attempt to examine (and facilitate) the group's psychological resources as an aid to helping individuals within it. By stage three the group critically examines various anger management methods with a view to addressing the problems that group members have brought to the group.

Below we give a number of examples taken from parts of anger management modules to give the reader a flavour of the work. The examples are presented sequentially from each stage of the programme.

A commonly used exercise involves 'brainstorming' the positive and negative consequences of having lost control over anger. The idea here is to help establish and enhance motivation for change when it becomes evident during the module, that the negative consequences of a loss of control over anger, by far outweigh the positive.

Another example. Group members are asked to work in pairs and recount to each other an example of where they have lost control over their anger (and regretted it later). Each group member talks through their 'partner's' story to the rest of the reconvened group. Group members are invited to comment upon accounts. The group is facilitated in asking questions such as, at what point was there no turning back? could he have done anything else? were there other ways of dealing with the problem?

In the final stage of the programme, anger management methods are examined in detail in terms of their applicability and helpfulness for individuals in the group. One widely helpful method is to monitor and adjust the things we say to ourselves in anger provoking situations. Examples of helpful 'self-statements' which prisoners have brought up on the groups are 'its not worth getting into trouble for', 'he's not worth it', 'I won't let him wind me up', and 'I won't let my temper get the better of me'.

For a discussion of the common themes and dynamics in anger management groupwork in prisons the reader is referred to Towl's (1993)*Anger Control Groupwork in Practice.* This may be of practical use to practitioners who are considering facilitating anger management groupwork.

Evaluation issues

The effective evaluation of groupwork is fraught with difficulties. Two major problems underpin a number of such difficulties. First, the problem of defining and measuring change. Second, the problem of establishing whether or not any change is a direct product of participation in the group rather than the result of other events.

Evaluation methods of anger management groupwork have included; Governor's reports, behavioural checklists and psychometric questionnaires. The establishment and achievement of group aims and objectives for individual participants have also been used as an outcome measure (Towl, 1994).

Each of these methods of evaluation have their own strengths and weaknesses, some of these for each 'measure' are briefly discussed below:

1. 'Governor's reports' or 'adjudications' have the strength that they are a clear measure of reported behaviour often linked with anger management difficulties. A statistical weakness of this measure is the 'regression to the mean' problem. If prisoners are selected for the programme largely because of a very high rate of 'reporting', such 'peaks' are liable to lower whether or not there is an intervention.

2. Behavioural checklists have the strength that they focus on observable behaviour. However, there can be difficulties in establishing the reliability and validity of such measures. For example, those administering the checklist require training to ensure inter-rater reliability of observed behaviour. Also, often individual items on (generic) behavioural checklists may not be germane in particular institutional settings.
3. Psychometric questionnaires provide quantifiable measures of self-reported change, however they do not demonstrate behavioural change.
4. Group aims and objectives may be adequately assessed on the basis of the agreed views of facilitators and prisoners. Just as with psychometric testing, they do not demonstrate behavioural change.

Currently, probably one of the major obstacles to the effective evaluation of anger management groupwork is the very varied selection procedures for group members. Some prisoners present anger management difficulties in prisons and hence are referred to the groups. Other prisoners report having anger management difficulties, or their conviction history indicates that they may have difficulties in this area and they are sometimes referred to the groups. Still other prisoners may be instrumentally aggressive and they in turn may be referred to anger management groups, even though their aggressive behaviour is not necessarily directly linked to anger management difficulties. Thus in this typology we have three groups; those who have anger management difficulties 'inside' (prisons), outside (prisons) and those who are instrumentally aggressive but not necessarily angry.

Each of the three 'types' listed above serve to illustrate the point that the selection of prisoners for anger management groupwork will have critical relevance for the most appropriate type of evaluation.

There is no reason to assume that those who fall into the 'aggressive' group will benefit from anger management groups. Those who have anger management difficulties either inside or outside prison may well benefit. However, the types of evaluation for these two groups will differ. Related to these general points it is questionable whether or not it is useful to have prisoners from the 'inside' and 'outside' groups on the same programme.

For those with anger management difficulties in prisons a combination of numbers of 'adjudications'/'Governor's reports', behavioural checklists and prisoner anger diaries may be used to contribute to the evaluation of such programmes. For those with anger management difficulties outside prison, evaluation methods can rarely be so focused and are outside the direct purview of prison staff. Psychometric questionnaires may be useful as exploratory evaluative tools for both groups.

One major benefit of psychometric testing is that the data obtained from such studies may usually be compared with normative data. Psychometric measures are probably amongst the most sophisticated of self-report methods. One major criticism of self-report measures is the response bias problem.

Two factors which may impact on response bias effects are what may be termed 'contingency-explicitness' and 'sanction scope'. For example, in a prison setting a prisoner may be informed that if he attends x group then a 'good report' will result which may very well contribute to his early release. In this example the contingency, group attendance with early release, is very explicit, early release is also a very positive sanction.

In practice, it is probably axiomatic to state that engagement in constructive structured activities in prisons, by prisoners, is generally positively sanctioned. Thus it is reasonable to suppose that the prisoners engaged in our groupwork may well have had a general expectancy that this was so. However, it was made clear to (potential) candidates for our groups that their individual psychometric scores would be confidential. The contingencies within the prison may have resulted in a bias to 'motivate' prisoners to attend. However, crucially, psychometric scores were not linked with positive (or negative) sanctions.

Below we outline the results of an exploratory evaluation of an anger management group using the State Trait Anger Expression Inventory (STAXI).

A psychometric evaluation of anger control groupwork using the State Trait Anger Expression Inventory

STAXI data was collected over nine anger management courses run between February 1991 and September 1993 (8 courses were run in a security category C prison and 1 at a security category B prison). All courses were co-facilitated by a Psychologist and a Probation Officer. Prisoners attending the courses were asked to complete the STAXI prior to, and 7 to 14 days after completion of the course. A further, later, follow-up would have been desirable but regrettably not feasible. The STAXI was used as a measure to assess self-reported changes in the prisoners' experience and expression of anger. Approximately a hundred prisoners were referred for the groupwork, about 40 of these were deemed unsuitable or, for logistical reasons, unable to attend for the full programme. Of the remaining 60 prisoners who commenced the groups, 50 prisoners completed the programme and filled in 'before' and 'after' STAXIs. Only prisoners who had attended the course and completed both 'before' and 'after' measures were included in this evaluation (N=50).

The STAXI

The STAXI consists of 44 items, forming six scales and two sub-scales to measure the experience and expression of anger.

The experience of anger, as measured by the STAXI, is conceptualised as having two major components:

1. State anger - defined as an emotional state marked by subjective feelings which vary in intensity over time, according to frustration experienced or perceived injustice, attack or unfair treatment. The STAXI includes a 10 item 'state anger' scale which measures the intensity of angry feelings at a particular time.
2. Trait anger - defined as the disposition to perceive a wide range of situations as annoying or frustrating, with a tendency to respond to these situations with elevations in state anger. A 10 item 'trait anger' scale measures individual differences in the disposition to experience anger. This scale has two sub-scales:
   a. Angry temperament - a four item sub-scale measuring the general propensity to experience and express anger without specific provocation.
   b. Angry reaction - a four item sub-scale measuring individual differences in the disposition to express anger when criticised or treated unfairly by others.

Anger expression, as measured by the STAXI, is conceptualised as having three key components:

1. Anger-in - which involves anger directed inward (i.e. anger which is held in or suppressed). The eight item 'anger-in' scale measures the frequency with which angry feelings are suppressed.
2. Anger-out - which involves the expression of anger towards people or objects in the environment. The 8 item 'anger-out' scales measures the frequency with which angry feelings are expressed in this way.
3. Anger control - which refers to individual differences in the

extent to which attempts are made to control the expression of anger. The eight item 'anger control' scale measures the frequency with which an individual attempts to control their expression of anger.

The STAXI also consists of an 'Anger Expression' scale which is based on the responses to the 'anger-in', 'anger-out' and 'anger control' scales. This scale provides a general index of the frequency that anger is expressed, regardless of the direction of expression (Spielberger, 1988).

At present, there is no normative STAXI data from the general British prison population available to assist in the interpretation of the STAXI scores. The STAXI professional manual (Spielberger, 1988) provides normative data based on the responses of American male prisoners. Means, standard deviations and tables of percentiles derived from the frequency distributions of the normative sample are provided. We feel that these are the most appropriate set of normative data available, although we would add a cautionary caveat insofar as there will be cultural differences between the two groups.

Results

In the present evaluation, means and standard deviations were calculated for the pre and post course scores, on each of the six scales and two sub-scales. For details, see Table 1, which also provides the means and standard deviations from the normative data. A t-test for related samples was carried out on the scores for each of the STAXI scales to determine whether there were any significant differences between the pre and post-course scores. Table 2 shows the value and the level of significance for each of these analyses.

Data analyses

Individuals who score above the 75th percentile on the STAXI scales are more likely to experience anger to the extent that it may interfere with their optimal functioning. Individuals scoring between the 25th percentile and 75th percentile may be considered to be within the 'normal' range (Spielberger, 1988).

Separate analyses were carried out for those prisoners scoring between the 25th and 75th percentile (Group 1), and those scoring above the 75th percentile (Group 2) for each of the STAXI scales for which percentiles are available (state anger, trait anger, angry temperament, angry reaction, anger-in and anger-out). Table 3 provides the means and standard deviations for groups 1 and 2 on each of these scales, pre and post-course.

TABLE 1 - DESCRIPTIVE STATISTICS: STAXI - NORMATIVE DATA AND PRE AND POST-COURSE DATA

SCALE	NORMATIVE DATA		PRE-COURSE (N = 50)		POST-COURSE (N = 50)	
	MEAN	STANDARD DEVIATION	MEAN	STANDARD DEVIATION	MEAN	STANDARD DEVIATION
STATE ANGER	15.06	6.55	13.14	5.95	11.34	3.08
TRAIT ANGER	21.66	6.71	23.82	7.01	20.38	7.01
ANGRY TEMPERAMENT	7.25	3.27	9.74	3.20	8.40	3.01
ANGRY REACTION	9.59	3.02	9.26	3.51	8.36	3.23
ANGER-IN	18.06	4.61	18.98	4.47	17.54	5.21
ANGER-OUT	16.52	4.96	19.40	5.34	18.32	4.60
ANGER CONTROL	24.79	4.98	17.26	5.44	19.38	6.23
ANGER EXPRESSION	NOT AVAILABLE		37.10	11.16	32.50	11.11

TABLE 2 - T-TESTS: STAXI - PRE AND POST-COURSE ANALYSES

SCALE	ALL SUBJECTS			GROUP 1 - SUBJECTS SCORING < 75TH PERCENTILE			GROUP 2 - SUBJECTS SCORING > 75TH PERCENTILE		
	N.	T-VALUE	LEVEL OF SIGNIFICANCE	N.	T-VALUE	LEVEL OF SIGNIFICANCE	N.	T-VALUE	LEVEL OF SIGNIFICANCE
STATE ANGER	50	2.25	<0.025	44	1.19	NS	6	2.61	<0.025
TRAIT ANGER	50	3.77	<0.001	33	2.37	<0.025	17	3.32	<0.005
ANGRY TEMPERAMENT	50	3.29	<0.01	20	0.36	NS	30	3.54	<0.005
ANGRY REACTION	50	1.94	<0.05	34	-0.08	NS	16	2.86	<0.005
ANGER-IN	50	3.38	<0.005	27	2.49	<0.025	23	2.25	<0.025
ANGER-OUT	50	1.37	NS	25	-1.08	NS	24	2.71	<0.01
ANGER CONTROL	50	-3.35	<0.005	PERCENTILES NOT AVAILABLE					
ANGER EXPRESSION	50	4.09	<0.001						

TABLE 3 - DESCRIPTIVE STATISTICS FOR GROUPS 1 & 2 ON STAXI SCALES: PRE AND POST-COURSE

SCALE	PRE - COURSE				POST - COURSE			
	GROUP 1 < 75TH PERCENTILE		GROUP 2 > 75TH PERCENTILE		GROUP 1 < 75TH PERCENTILE		GROUP 2 > 75TH PERCENTILE	
	MEAN	STANDARD DEVIATION	MEAN	STANDARD DEVIATION	MEAN	STANDARD DEVIATION	MEAN	STANDARD DEVIATION
STATE ANGER	11.29	1.81	26.67	7.91	10.89	2.47	14.67	4.68
TRAIT ANGER	19.54	3.63	32.12	3.80	18.09	4.52	26.00	7.44
ANGRY TEMPERAMENT	6.65	1.56	11.73	2.20	6.55	1.75	9.63	3.04
ANGRY REACTION	7.21	1.81	13.62	1.87	7.32	2.53	10.56	3.64
ANGER-IN	15.55	2.56	23.00	2.39	14.59	4.31	21.00	3.87
ANGER-OUT	15.12	2.42	23.68	3.81	15.96	3.43	20.72	4.38

Table 2 shows the T value and level of significance derived from tests carried out separately on groups 1 and 2 for each of the scales.

Discussion of results

The results will be discussed for each individual scale:

State anger

The results indicate a significant reduction in the intensity of angry feelings which prisoners were experiencing following the course. However, the breakdown of analyses according to percentiles indicates that the significance of the decrease is accounted for by the scores of the six prisoners, falling above the 75th percentile before the course. It is possible that these six prisoners' angry feelings were situationally determined and their situation had changed between 'test' times. Alternatively, their high scores may reflect chronic anger which they were managing more effectively after the course. To what extent the changes were linked to the course cannot be firmly established. The finding that there was no significant decrease in the scores for the majority of prisoners may be a consequence of there being little opportunity for the scores to decrease (i.e. a large proportion (N=23) scored the minimum for this scale both 'before' and 'after' the course).

Trait anger

The results indicate a significant reduction in the scores for prisoners scoring both above and below the 75th percentile (although the level of significance is higher for prisoners scoring above the 75th percentile). It may be that the programme, on a general level, helped prisoners to assess and deal more effectively with anger provoking situations and their experience of anger and frustration within these situations.

For the two sub-scales of this scale, significant reductions in the scores of the whole group were found:

1. Angry temperament - this sub-scale changed significantly for group 2 but not group 1. The course may have helped some prisoners who had a propensity to experience and express anger without specific provocation, by increasing their understanding of their own anger and its manifestations.
2. Angry reaction - This sub-scale changed significantly for group 2 but not group 1: for prisoners who were highly sensitive to criticism or perceived affronts, the course's cognitive focus on evaluating and dealing with difficult situations and considering

the consequences of any actions may have reduced the likelihood of them expressing anger in such situations.

Anger-in

The results indicate a significant reduction in the 'anger-in' scores, whether or not they fell above the 75th percentile. The emphasis within the programme that anger is a 'normal' emotion and can be expressed constructively with assertive behaviour, may have contributed to the general reduction in scores.

Anger-out

Although there was not a significant decrease in the 'anger-out' scores overall, there was a significant reduction in scores falling above the 75th percentile. It appears the course was helpful for those prisoners who frequently expressed anger in aggressive behaviour, in reducing the frequency of this behaviour.

Anger control

A significant increase in 'anger control' scores overall was found, indicating prisoners were investing more energy into monitoring and preventing their experience and expression of anger. Unfortunately, it was not possible to breakdown the analyses according to the score percentiles, as normative data for this scale and the 'anger-expression' scale was not available.

Anger expression

Unsurprisingly (in view of the results from the 'anger-in', 'anger-out' and 'anger control' scale scores) there was a significant reduction in the prisoners' scores on this scale (i.e. the frequency with which prisoners reported expressing their anger decreased).

Some limitations of our evaluation

The STAXI is a self-report measure rather than a behavioural measure. In other words, our evaluation is based on what people say that they do, rather than what we have observed them doing. Self-report measures are frequently criticised for this reason. Behavioural checklist models also rely on similar levels of observations, but of others rather than the self.

Our interpretation of the results is limited by a number of factors: first, the lack of control data and normative data derived from the UK prison population. Second, the lack of follow-up data or information on offence type, age, length of sentence, reason for attending course and nature of perceived difficulties for those prisoners included in the evaluation. Thirdly, our lack of information on prisoners who did not complete the course or declined to complete the STAXI.

Conclusions

These results add to the growing body of psychometric evidence to suggest that cognitive behaviourally based anger management groupwork interventions in prisons do work. However, our conclusions can only be tentative in the light of the manifold conceptual complexities and methodological difficulties associated with the effective evaluation of anger management groupwork. Inevitably in the prison environment, researchers are limited in the methodological purity of their research. Our results may be a statistical artefact of the use of multiple t-tests. We believe that our results are encouraging, but that further data analyses may be warranted. Indeed, if we can improve future data sets, opportunities for more comprehensive multi-variate analyses exist and may well prove fruitful.

We find these results promising but inconclusive, and below we make a number of recommendations about research design for future evaluations.

Recommendations for future evaluative research

1. There is a need to conduct a qualitative evaluation of the experiences of prisoners in relation to their anger before and after the interventions.
2. There is a need to take biographic information on prisoners who participate e.g. age, offence type.
3. There is a need to establish behavioural outcomes of anger management interventions.

Point number one is important because it may help us to understand *what* is 'working' in the interventions. Point number two may help us in understanding who it is working for. Finally, point number three would give us considerably increased confidence that participants had got to grips with effectively controlling their anger.

Note

The views expressed in this paper are those of the authors and they may not necessarily represent the views of the prison service.

References

Copestake, S. (1993) *An Evaluation of the National Anger Management Programme* (of the Prison Service). Unpublished MSc Research Project. From Prison Service Psychology, Home Office, Prison Department.

Law, K. (1993) *Use of Behaviour Monitoring Checklists in the Evaluation of Anger Management Course*. Unpublished Research Paper. From Prison Service Psychology, Home Office, Prison Department.

McDougall, C., Thomas, M. and Wilson, J. (1987) 'Cognitive control of anger' in McGurk, B., Thornton, D. and Williams, M. (eds.) *Applying Psychology to Imprisonment*. London: HMSO.

Novaco, R.W. (1975) *Anger Control: The Development and Evaluation of an Experimental Treatment*. Lexington, Mass: D.C. Heath.

Novaco, R.W. (1985) *Anger, Stress and Coping with Provocation; An Instructional Manual.* University of California, Irvine.

Speilberger, C.D. (1988) *State Trait Anger Expression Inventory: STAXI Professional Manual.* Psychological Assessment Resources, Inc. Florida, USA.

Towl, G.J. and Jennings, M. (1990) *An Anger Control Course at HMP.* Highpoint: DPS Series 2, 177, Home Office, Prison Service.

Towl, G.J. (1993) 'Anger Control Groupwork in Practice' in Clark, N.K. and Stephenson, G.M. (eds.) *Children, Evidence and Procedure.* Issues in Criminological and Legal Psychology, No 20. Leicester: British Psychological Society, DCLP.

Towl, G.J. (1994) 'Anger control groupwork in prisons' in *Perspectives On Violence*. The Howard League, Quartet Publishers.

REVIEWS

Group Participation: Techniques for Leaders and Members
HARVEY J. BERTCHER
Sage Publications Ltd, 1994, pp.197, price: £29.50 (hbk) £13.95 (pbk)
ISBN 0-8039-5213-9 (hbk) 0-8039-5214-7 (pbk)

I received the request to review this book at just the time I was preparing a training programme in groupwork skills for an English social services department. I have run the programme for a few years and felt that it was due for an overhaul, especially since there will be a new assessed component. In describing the audiences for his book, Bertcher includes 'students of small group theory who want to learn about groups through participation in one'. I thought it would be a useful testing ground for the book to consider it in relation to my groupwork training programme.

Before commenting on this, let us have a clear and detailed idea of the book's content. Bertcher describes the differences between the first edition and this new one, which has been updated in response to comments from three faculty members around the US and the students of one of the faculty members. Each of twelve groupwork techniques has its own chapter, with the same basic structure:

1. How do you describe the technique in question?
2. When do you use the technique?
3. How do you manage the technique?
4. How do you know you have used the technique correctly?
5. Oppression and empowerment in relation to the technique*
6. An example of the technique (this is a transcript from a different group for each technique)
6. An exercise (to help students learn more about the technique)
7. Postscript: issues in this technique*
8. In preparation* (a brief section to help students to prepare for the next chapter)

Sections marked with an * are new to the second edition, as is the final chapter which looks at five different types of group. The introductory chapter on the nature of the small group has been updated and enlarged.

Since the book's raison d'etre lies in the 12 groupwork techniques which Bertcher identifies, it is worth giving a brief description of his definitions (some are direct quotes):

Attending is letting a group member know that you are paying close attention to what he or she is saying or doing so that he or she will be encouraged to continue.

Seeking information and giving information are self-explanatory, though Bertcher considers that they are often poorly handled.

Contract negotiation refers first to an explicitly stated or written agreement to keep to certain expectations of behaviour in the group and, secondly, to specific goals that the group as a whole and/or its individual members hope to achieve through their participation in the group.

Rewarding is any action that tells an individual or the group that they have done something to help move the group towards its goal.

Responding to feelings is the verbal or nonverbal action by which group leaders or members communicate empathic understanding, an ability to sense how people feel.

Focusing means calling the group's attention to something that has been said or that has happened to highlight or clarify it so that the group will be more aware of it, or to bring the discussion back to the agreed-upon business of the group.

Summarising is the process of drawing together and briefly restating a number of prior responses into one statement, then seeking agreement or correction from other group members until an agreed summary statement has been produced.

Gatekeeping is behaviour that helps all members of the group participate more or less equally by limiting those members who monopolise the discussion and by encouraging low participators to talk more.

Confrontation is when people are informed of an inconsistency between something they have said or done, and something else they have said or done; or an inconsistency between the facts and something they have said or done.

Modelling occurs when a group participant demonstrates behaviour in such a way that another person can imitate it. Modelling is a conscious focusing of something that is happening in an unfocused way all the time in groups.

Mediating involves putting yourself in a neutral position between opponents in order to avoid or resolve a disagreement that is keeping the group from reaching its goals. The timing of the mediation is particularly important.

Starting refers to the activities and behaviours used to begin a group meeting or to introduce a new topic during the session.

It is always possible to quibble over taxonomies (for example, it could be argued that Ending requires its own unique combination of skills, similar to but not the same as summarising). However, I found the twelve techniques a convincing and comprehensive list. Any groupworker who could employ these techniques appropriately would be working at a highly skilled level.

There are two important factors to bear in mind when reading the book. The first, acknowledged by the author, is that the book is a supplemental and not a core text on groupwork. By focusing exclusively on techniques, it does not pretend to do the work of a classic like Allan Brown's *Groupwork* (1992) or Lawrence Shulman's *The Skills of Helping Individuals and Groups* (1984). The second factor, not explicit, is the 'American-ness' of the book. This is most evident in the examples used to illustrate each technique, which are both the strongest and weakest element in the book. The transcripts of extracts from groups, with a commentary running alongside the transcript, are a helpful illustration of groups at work, but they are also a vivid reminder of how specific they are to American culture. Any reader not versed in the American Way might find it a struggle. European taste will find the extract used to illustrate the Rewarding technique particularly teeth-stripping.

Finally, to return to my plans for the training programme. The book has stimulated me to focus more on techniques, and I intend to use a few of the learning exercises. It also helped my consideration of issues of oppression and empowerment, but I have a note of caution about the tendency to see anti-oppressive practice as kicking into gear only when people from oppressed groups are present, and a sense that mixed groups are seen as a 'problem' to be managed by group leaders. This view of oppression and empowerment needs broadening in the third edition.

Mark Doel, Lecturer in Social Work Studies and Co-Director of Practice Teaching Studies at the University of Sheffield, and Independent Training Consultant

References

Brown, A. (1992) *Groupwork*. Third Edition. Aldershot: Ashgate.

Shulman, L. (1984) *The Skills of Helping Individuals and Groups*. Second Edition. Illinois: F E Peacock.

The Psyche and the Social World: Developments in Group-Analytic Theory
DENNIS BROWN AND LOUIS ZINKIN (EDS.)
Routledge, London, 1994, ISBN 0-415-08708-2 (hbk), 0-415-08709-0 (pbk)

This collection of papers is an attempt to map out the theoretical basis of group analysis as it is practised today. All but one of the contributors are members of the Institute of Group Analysis. The founder of group analysis was S.H. Foulkes (originally Fuchs, 1898-1976), who was one of the pioneers of psychoanalysis who came to England from Nazi Germany in the 1930s. Foulkes had the heretical idea of bringing his patients together in groups, in the belief that they would contribute to each other's therapy, and that the group would provide access to the conflicts of many people more readily than the one-to-one meeting of analyst and analysand. This move estranged him from many of his psychoanalytic colleagues. The editors and contributors demonstrated this belief in the group by meeting to discuss each other's papers while the book was in preparation.

It has been to the impoverishment of many like me, who have worked within the Tavistock tradition of group theory initiated by Wilfred Bion, that we have heard little or nothing about Foulkes and group analysis, unless we have literally or metaphorically turned left out of the Tavistock Centre and knocked on the neighbours' door in 1 Daleham Gardens where the Institute of Group Analysis is based. Foulkes is acknowledged to have been less than brilliant at articulating the ideas implicit in his work: they were however 'leading edge' ideas in their time, and remain the core of group-analytic practice today.

Like Bion, Foulkes conceived of the group as functioning as an integrated whole, or as what we would now call a system. He called this system the 'matrix'. His underlying metaphor is that of the brain. He wrote:

> The...matrix can be thought of as a network in quite the same way as

> the brain is a network of fibres and cells which together form a complex unit...(quoted p.13).
>
> The network of all individual mental processes, the psychological medium in which they meet, communicate and interact, can be called the matrix...Inside this network, the individual is conceived as a nodal point (quoted p.11).

So for Foulkes the isolated individual is an abstraction. Biologically we are separate individuals, but socially and psychologically we are 'nodal points' in the network of communication in language which creates us as subjects. Something like that.

So the group (he says) in which each member speaks and acts out of a shared pool of language, images and fantasy. This group matrix intersects with the personal matrix of each member, the network of relations which make up his or her individual psyche. And all these matrices are embedded in the larger social matrix (which Foulkes called the 'foundation matrix') constituted by the culture of which they are a part.

The book is not an easy read, for two reasons. First, it requires historical imagination to appreciate the distinctiveness of Foulkes's position, reading thirty years after it was formulated, when this holistic view of persons and groups is now around in many guises. Secondly, we can be bewildered if we do not appreciate that we are listening to recent exchanges in a conversation which has been going on since Freud and before. The contributors are not writing for the man on, or waiting for, the Clapham omnibus, but for group analysts and others who are party to this conversation. I have the same experience reading some essays in this book as I have looking at some twentieth century paintings: I feel excluded, and realise that this is because they are the outcome of a long conversation on canvas which has been going on since Giotto and before, a conversation which has generated questions which are not my questions.

The book will therefore be of greatest interest to group analysts and to others engaged in psychodynamic work with groups. I also recommend it to anyone who aspires to a general education in group theory and who has missed out on group-analytic thinking. It is a book to dip into. In particular I would go for Dick Blackwell's paper, 'The psyche and the system', which takes up a critical position in relation not only to group analysis but to open systems theory, family therapy, and 'second order' systems thinking. Blackwell takes seriously the concept of the foundation matrix. Everything we say (he says) - all our theories, hypotheses and interpretations - are shaped by our position in the social matrix, and come from an address which is not politically neutral. They are flawed and potentially oppressive, to the extent that they do not look back upon themselves and scrutinise where they have come from.

This larger matrix is illuminatingly discussed by the Belgian contributor Jack Le Roy, drawing upon a Lacanian analysis, the work of the European Association for Transcultural Analysis, and anthropological work in Central Africa. Le Roy asserts that complete individuation is an illusion; we are always defined and contained by our family, and by our social and institutional groups. In this light he examines the consequences of migration, war, totalitarianism, and rapid social change.

I also recommend John Schlapoborsky's paper on 'The language of the group', in which he illustrates the idea that, if all goes well, the group member progresses from monologue, through dialogue, to participation in a discourse encompassing the whole group. 'To understand the group we should have to consider the texture of this discourse rather than merely the text of its narrative' (p.223). Other contributors examine the concept of the group-as-a-whole (Malcolm Pines), larger groups (Patrick de Mare), gender (Barbara Elliott), the influence of fantasies about the primal scene (Maurice Nitsun), resonances with John Bowlby's attachment theory (Mario Marrone), and other themes.

How successful is this book in providing a statement of where group analytic theory has got to since Foulkes - if I have not already disqualified myself from offering a judgement about this? The compilers' task is paradoxical, since group analysis, like the individual, is not an isolated object, but a node in a larger network of thought, conversation and practice. Group analysis does not exist: it comes into being for me as I draw a boundary round a cluster of ideas and practices, which includes what Foulkes himself did and said, and excludes many other things that have been done with, and said about, groups. In their conclusion the editors say:

> As editors reviewing the book as a whole, we have similar problem to that facing the group conductor trying to understand the group-as-a-whole. We can see both a unity and a great diversity (p.233).

Wisely, therefore, they scan the contributions both for differences and divergences, and for what is held in common. They acknowledge that contributions draw upon a range of theoretical systems, and that they were unable to agree whether these could be brought together in 'some all-encompassing mega-theory', or whether this would be desirable anyway. They thus approach the question of what constitutes group analytic theory by examining the dilemmas inherent in trying to answer that question. That they do this is for me one of the successes of the book. The book itself puts a hard- or paper-back boundary round the thinking of some of the leading lights in group analysis, with its limitations and contradictions, and so provides us with a provisional synthesis. Inevitably they will have left out ideas which do not seem significant now, but which might prove to be so in the future. In any case we might say that the unity of group analysis is in the practice of group analysts, and not in the theories; or that it is in practice and theory together. Foulkes after all created group analysis through an innovation in practice. The theory on its own - even with clinical examples - is inevitably no more than a figure in a ground we cannot see.

Barry Palmer, Independent Consultant, co-author with Nano McCaughan of *Systems Thinking for Harassed Managers* (Karnac, 1994).

Group Treatment of Adult Incest Survivors
M.A. DONALDSON AND S. CORDES-GREEN
Sage Publications, price: £31.95 (hbk) £14.95 (pbk)
ISBN 0-8039-6165-0 (hbk) 0-8-39-6166-9 (pbk)

This is a very lucid, well organised and approachable handbook that would serve as an excellent preparation for anyone undertaking this kind of work. It might have been appropriate for anyone undertaking this kind of work. It might have been appropriate to show in the title that the book addresses women clients only, since the treatment described does not include males who have been sexually abused, but the groupwork model put forward is clear, cogent and, it would appear, flexible enough to be adapted to other settings. The heart of the book is the experience of the co-authors and their colleagues on the Incest Treatment Programme at the Village Family Service Centre in North Dakota. The result is a lively description of the development of a programme that is geared to the emotional needs of its clients. A great deal of common sense and practical advice is here presented on the stages of preparation of the service, the conceptual basis of the therapeutic model and some useful discussions of the sorts of problems that can arise in the group work.

Included also is an overview of the literature on the long-term effects of childhood sexual abuse on the victims, including sexual difficulties, self-destructive behaviours, low self-esteem, depression, and so on. In this review, however, there is a notable absence of psychodynamic references, and this seems to be connected with another slant in the approach of the book, which is to see the effects of CSA only in terms of victimisation. If the work of psychoanalytic writers such as Estela Welldon had been included then the authors might have looked differently at repetitions of abuse that occurred with their clients own children.

On the question of clinical outcome studies the authors acknowledge the lack of systematic data from controlled studies, though the programme described in this book has been evaluated: in the one hundred and seventy nine patients assessed and treated, a general amelioration and stabilisation of symptoms was evident after only six to seven months of treatment. Practitioners should note, however, that in the early stages of treatment there as frequently an increase in the number and severity of symptoms.

It is interesting to see the careful preparations of clients for the therapy group; there are individual sessions, (which may continue during the group programme), 'education' groups, and 'pretherapy' groups. The net effect of these seems to be to maximise the clients ability to use the group constructively. There is consequently an absence of the expressions of frustration, anger, and mystification which are usually apparent when people suddenly find themselves (as is often the case) part of a group.

The group therapeutic model is based on that of Yalom, adapted by the authors to provide a very positive framework for clients in the group. Sometimes this seems idealistic; for example, the Four Rs, (respect, reflect, respond, receive), seems to leave too little room for more difficult feelings. Anger, pain and sadness are of course, recognised by the therapists but quickly transformed into the PGI (Power, Goodness and Importance) framework. Clients in the group are encouraged to relate any difficult feelings to the goals of acquiring Power, Goodness and Importance. On the other hand the many vignettes of the group process demonstrate the readiness of the therapists in this programme to work with the frequently traumatised emotions of group members. Something I found particularly useful to follow was the way in which flashbacks can be worked with in the group.

For group therapists there are some helpful pointers to the effective management of the group setting. Another mnemonic, the Four Ms, is intended to aid the therapist in distinguishing between different functions that the therapist can be seen to have in the group. As messenger, the therapist gives information, about theory and the therapeutic process, and also models empathy, boundaries etc for the group members to emulate. As monitor she maintains accurate observation of the group interaction, and analyses in terms of the PGI model. As mediator the therapist enables interactions to take place constructively in the group, and as member, the therapist needs to take into account the effects on her that the group has and to find what she can learn from the process.

What shines through the detailed descriptions of groupwork is the commitment that the therapists have in staying with the client when she is reliving painful experiences, (no 'false' memories here). Using the group as a support for the client is fundamental to this capability. Nevertheless the strain of this work on the therapist is seen to be very real. Frequent mentions are made of the support of the team but there is little detail on just how this would operate, and nor is there much on the question of supervision. Work with sexual abuse is notoriously productive of splits and dissension among workers, leading sometimes to traumatic experiences in the workers themselves. Like the absence of male workers (who might 'unintentionally revictimise clients' p.28) there is an impression that the positive gains in this therapy are achieved by denial of certain difficulties. Groupwork with spouses is mentioned in passing and I found I wanted to know more about this aspect of the programme. Were the men concerned seen as only abusers, or as the only ones who abuse? From such an apparently successful treatment model as the one described in this book, it would have been helpful to have had these more complex aspects addressed.

John Woods, Psychotherapist, Young Abusers Project, Tavistock Centre

Reference

Weldon, E.V. (1988) *Mother, Madonna, Whore; The Idealisation and Denigration of Motherhood*. London: Free Association Books.

Appendix: Contents of *Groupwork* Volumes 1-13

Volume 1 (ISBN 9781861770554)
Groupwork practice with hard to reach clients: A modality of choice Lawrence Shulman
The worker and the group process: A dilemma revisited Ken Heap
Race and groupwork: Some experiences in practice and training Ros Muston and Jeremy Weinstein
A group for white women with black children Clare Rhule
Structured activities with adolescent boys Rod Craig
Supporting voices: Groupwork with people suffering from schizophrenia Lynda Randall and Wendy Walker
Groupwork books published in Britain 1980-86 Harold Marchant
Swimming upstream: Articles on groupwork in social work journals 1986-87 Nano McCaughan
Preparing the client for social groupwork: An illustrated framework Oded Manor
Groups for older people in residential and day-care: The other groupworkers Lorraine Bernard, John Burton, Phyllis Kyne and June Simon
'But I don't want to lead a group!' Some common problems of social workers leading groups Ken Reid
Programming skills in social groupwork. Sue Ross and Andy Thorpe
A model for evaluating groupwork Michael Preston-shoot
Groupwork as the method of choice with black children in white foster homes Audrey Mullender
Short term groupwork in the treatment of chronic sorrow. A Norwegian experience Gerd Kramm Engebrigtsen and Ken Heap
Revisiting open groups Michael Henry
Social action groupwork as negotiation: Contradictions in the process of empowerment Eamonn Keenan and John Pinkerton
'Nowt to do and always getting into trouble'. The Bulwell Neighbourhood Project: A social action response Bill Badham, Michael Bente and Pauline Hall
A team development exercise John Taylor, Di Miles and John Eastgate
'The brothers and sisters group': A group for siblings of children with physical disabilities Anne Badger
Groupwork with adolescents: Abstracts Alison Skinner

Volume 2 (ISBN 9781861770561)
Challenging familiar assumptions: Preparing for and initiating a self-directed group Audrey Mullender and David Ward
Doing something with our lives when we're inside: Self-directive groupwork in a youth custody centre. Bill Badham (Ed.). Bob Blatchford, Steph Mcartney and Malcolm Nicholas
Using contracts in groupwork Michael Preston-shoot
Targeted activities in group contexts: The analysis of activities to meet consumer need Julie Phillips
Designing cancer groups for maximum effectiveness Barry M. Daste
Decision-making in therapeutic groups Marian F. Fatout
Confronting human finitude. Groupwork with people with AIDS George S. Getzel and Kevin F. Mahony
Organising accountability for social groupwork: More choices Oded Manor
A group for black and white sexually abused children Marie Lebacq and Zaffira Shah
Learning about groupwork. Jenny Lumley and Harold Marchant
Establishing a feminist model of groupwork in the Probation Service Tara Mistry
A way forward: A group for refugee women Rachel Tribe and Jane Shackman
Searching the literature on women's groups Cathrine Fitzgerald
Open grief groups: the resolution of complicated loss Marianne Davidsen-Nielsen and Nini Leick
Groupwork with the spouses of seriously ill patients Janine Favier
Supportive groupwork for dialysis patients Lizzie Bollmann
Supportive groupwork with young arthritic mothers Amy Østertun Geirdal
Staff development through groupwork in Polish

community agencies: 'The Centres Of Culture' Jerzy Szmagalski
Self-help groups as basic care in psychotherapy and social work Jürgen Matzat
Family group treatment in drug abuse Anna Casanova Torras
Groupwork As Early Intervention In High Risk Families Rigmor Grette Moe

Volume 3 (ISBN 9781861770578)
Social work with groups in multicultural contexts Kenneth L. Chau
Siblings in groups: Children of separated/divorced parents Sandra Regan and Jan Young
Groupwork techniques in a residential primary school for emotionally disturbed boys Peter Clarke and Amanda Aimable
The role of groupwork in research with people with learning difficulties Jan Walmsley
Groupwork training: A case study Andrew Kerslake
Beulah Rothman: An appreciation Oded Manor
Starting the journey: Enhancing the therapeutic elements of groupwork for adolescent female child sexual abuse victims Eileen Craig
Evaluating success in groupwork: Why not measure the obvious? Anne Peake and Olive Otway
Investigating groupwork: A Case study using a group approach in the initial stages of child sexual abuse investigation Sarah Allum
The Forgotten parent: Groupwork with mothers of sexually abused children Helen Masson and Marcus Erooga
Work with male sex offenders in groups Malcolm Cowburn
Protection, control, treatment: Groupwork with child sexual abuse perpetrators Marcus Erooga, Paul Clark and Mai Bentley
Group treatment for women sex offenders against children Sharon Barnett. Francesca Corder and Derek Jehu
Selected article abstracts on child sexual abuse and groupwork Julia Cramp and Helen Armstrong
Self help groups: A minefield for professionals Ulla Habermann
Facing the challenge of developing group services for high risk families Alice Home and Lise Darveau-Fournier
Groupwork with parents of sleepless children Rona Robertson
Culture' groups in prison Graham Towl
Groupwork with a difference: The group 'mosaic' in residential day centre settings Allan Brown
Groupwork in residential settings for elderly people Audrey Mullender

Volume 4 (ISBN 9781861770585)
Empowerment through mutual aid groups: A practice grounded conceptual framework Judith AB. Lee
Making authority accountable: The experience of a statutory based women's group Helen Bodinham and Jeremy Weinstein
Towards a model of social groupwork practice with marginalised populations Margot Breton
Working creatively with children Eugene Clerkin and Belinda Knaggs
The termination phase in groupwork: Tasks for the groupworker Sue Ross
Miami, October 1990 Oded Manor and Dave Ward
Black/white co-working in groups Tara Mistry And Allan Brown
Groupwork and oral history: Raising the consciousness of young people during social transition Sandra Drower
The use of photographs as a projective and facilitative technique in groups Merav DeVere And Ossi Rhonne
Facilitation in self-directed groupwork Dave Ward and Audrey Mullender
Evaluative study of groupwork for stress and anxiety Rhona Birrell Weisen
A long-term support group for chronic schizophrenic outpatients: A quantitative and qualitative evaluation Julie Cwikel And Adina Oron
Using groups in working with offenders: A survey of groupwork in the Probation Service of England and Wales Brian Caddick
A Miskin Model of groupwork with women offenders Marion jones, Mary Mordecai, Frances Rutter and Linda Thomas
Evolution and accountability Ten years of groups in a day centre for offenders Judith Earnshaw
The Telford Motoring Offenders Education Project Kathryn Hutchins
Groupwork in the Luton Probation And Bail Hostel Catherine Mulvie
The Newcastle intensive probation programme A centralised approach to groupwork Jane Mackintosh

Meeting prisoners' needs through groupwork Mike Ashe
Groupwork in the Probation Service: Care or control in the 1990s Paul Senior
Selected abstracts on groupwork with offenders John Hodge
Derek Carter 1934-1991

Volume 5 (ISBN 9781861770592)
Groupwork from across the Atlantic: Its identity and diffusion Catherine Pappell
Groupwork in Europe: Past, Present, Future Ken Heap, Diakonhjemmet School of Social Work, Oslo
The groupwork consultant's role in facilitating work groups Alan Turkie, Independent
Evaluation For The Improvement Of Groupwork Practice Kenneth H Gordon, School of Social Work, King's College, Western Ontario
Groupwork in a residential home for older people: Building on the positive aspects of group living Gun Lewis, Officer in Charge
Groupwork with Youth Gangs in Hong Kong T Wing Lo, City Polytechnic, Hong Kong
On empowerment, partnership and authority in groupwork practice: A training contribution Michael Preston-Shoot, School of Social Work, University of Manchester
Groupwork with involuntary clients: Remotivating strategies Cyrus S Behroozi, Indiana University School of Social Work
Handling conflict: Groupwork with violent offenders Rob Canton, Carolyn Mack and Jeff Smith, Nottinghamshire Probation
The dream in groupwork practice Iain Edgar, Dept of Social Work, University of Northumbria
Support groups for older people: Is homogeneity or heterogeneity the answer? Susan Rice and Catherine Goodman, Dept of Social Work, California State University, Long Beach
The group turns inward: A consideration of some group phenomena as reflective of the Northern Irish situation Jarlath Benson, Psychotherapeutic Groupworker, Belfast
Groupwork with bereaved children Nuala Harmey and Bernie Price, Medical Social Work, Temple Street Children's Hospital, Dublin
Reminiscence groupwork with older people Faith Gibson, Dept of Social Work, University of Ulster, Coleraine
Social workers and psychologists as facilitators of groupwork with adults with a learning difficulty: A survey of current practice Heno Schonfield and Mary C Morrissey, Senior Social Workers, Dublin
Groupwork with teenage cancer patients Nicola Martin Medical Social Worker in Oncology, and Eddie O'Neill, Paediatric Oncology Social Worker, Mater Hospital, Dublin
Bereaved by suicide: Setting up an 'ideal' therapy group in a real world Imogen O'Connor, Therapist, Dublin Rape Crisis Centre

Volume 6 (ISBN 9781861770608)
Groupwork versus casework in a group Roselle Kurland and Robert Salmon, Hunter School of Social Work, New York
Why groupwork is not put into practice: Reflections on the social work scene in Denmark Ulla Habermann, Director, Volunteer Centre, Denmark
Away with the experts? Self-help groupwork in Germany Jürgen Matzat, Psychologist, Klinik für Psychosomatik und Psychotherapie, Justus-Liebig-Universität, Gießen
Groupwork with siblings of children with special needs: A pilot study Georgina Ferraro and Julie Tucker, Senior Family Project Workers
Neutralisation of group control in youth gangs T Wing Lo, City Polytechnic, Hong Kong
The large group: The heart of the system in group care Adrian Ward, Dept of Social Work, University of Reading
Working with a family group of bereaved children Sheila Finlayson, Child Advisory Social Work Service, City of Birmingham Education Dept
A comparative study of four family bereavement groups Estelle Hopmeyer, and Annette Werk, McGill School of Social Work, Montréal
An asian mothers' group Lynne Muir Director, MEd Programme in Community Education and Hardev Notta, Acorns Hospice for Children, Birmingham
A Cruse family circle Joyce Rimmer, Birmingham Cruse
Coping with trauma Frank Parkinson, former Army chaplain
From group meeting to therapeutic group Bernadette Duffy, Social Care Worker, Dublin and Brian McCarthy, Lecturer in Psychology, Dublin Institute of Technology
Group therapy with adults with learning difficulties who have committed sexual offences Elisabeth

Cormack, Young People's Centre , Northern Ireland

Critical incident analysis and its application in groupwork David Henchman and Susan Walton, Avon Probation Service

Life history work with a group of people with learning disabilities Dorothy Atkinson, School of Health, Welfare and Community Education, Open University

Art therapy: Creative groupwork for women. Olive Otway, Lecturer in Social Work, University of Keele

Groupwork with parents of learning disabled adolescents. Helen Gobat, Independent Social Worker

Groupwork with deaf people. Kavita Kohli, Social Worker, Hounslow Social Services s

Combining activities and growth games: A systems approach Oded Manor, Middlesex University, and Miriam Dumbleton, Care Manager, Westminster Social Services

Volume 7 (ISBN 9781861770615)

The linguistic and cultural barriers to cross-national groupwork Paul Taylor, Lecturer in Community Education, University of Tours, France

Partnership in training and practice with refugees Jill Reynolds, School of Health, Welfare and Community Education, Open University and Jane Shackman, Social Worker, The Medical Foundation for Care of Victims of Torture

Men working with men in groups: masculinity and crime John Benstead, Gloucester Probation, Allan Brown, School of Social Work, Bristol University, Carlton Forbes, and Rick Wall, Avon Probation Centre

Working *with religious communities* Geraldine Grindley, Dublin City University

Issues of empowerment: Anti-oppressive groupwork by disabled people in Ireland Maire Ni Chorcora and Eddie Jennings, DET and Nuala Lordan, Dept of Applied Social Studies, University College Cork

A Psychotherapeutic group for boys who have been sexually abused Gary Dixon formerly South London FSU and Michelle Phillips, Clinical Nurse Specialist, Camberwell Child Guidance Centre

Groupwork and black women: Viewing networks as groups Marcia Francis-Spence Centre for Applied Social Studies, University of Durham

Staying alive in difficult times: The experience of groupwork with mothers of children who have been sexually abused Deb Dobbin and Sarah Evans, Independent Social Workers

A time for women: An account of a group for women on an out of city housing development in Leicester Claire Wintram, Independent Trainer, Kerry Chamberlain, National Health Service Administrator, Marlene Kuhn, Midwife and Jo Smith, Woman with a Disability active in support and campaign groups , Leicester

Groupwork for mental health: Providers utilising the enchanted self concept Barbara Becker Holstein, Psychologist, Long Branch, New Jersey, and Doreen Laperdon-Addison, Movement Educator and Professional Dancer

Promoting positive images:. The role of groupwork in promoting women managers within organisations Judy Fawcett, Independent Consultant and Trainer

Using a facilitated self help group for women whose children have been sexually abused Olive Otway, Dept of Social Work, Keele University, and Anne Peak, Principal Psychologist, Oxfordshire

'All I've got in my purse is mothballs' the social action women's group Sandra Butler, Dept of Social Work, University of Nottingham

Silence in working across difference: Groupwork in a youth and community work training context Janet Batsleer, Youth and Community Work Section, Manchester Metropolitan University

Ourselves and others Helen Gobat, Independent Social Worker

Groupwork with young mothers Caroline Norman, Project Worker, St Gabriels Family Centre, Brighton

Groupwork for parents of young people in trouble: A proposal Mark Drakeford, Dept of Applied Social Studies, University of Wales, Swansea

A dramatic view of groupwork Jeremy Weinstein, Dept of Social Work, South Bank University

Anger management groupwork with prisoners: An empirical evaluation Graham J Towl and Polly Dexter, Forensic Psychologists, HM Prison Service

Volume 8 (ISBN 9781861770622)

'Cycling Over Everest' Groupwork with depressed women Pamela Trevithick, Dept of Social Work, Bristol University

Groupwork in Croatia: Experiences with older refugees Marina Adjukovic, School of Social Work, University of Zagreb, Milena Cevcizovic

and Ksenija Kontak, Psychologists, Society for Psychological Assistance, Croatia
Group dialogue within prisons Peter Garrett, Centre for Action Research in Professional Practice, School of Management, University of Bath
Establishing community meetings in a children's home Adrian Ward, Dept of Social Work, University of Reading
Groups for children who have lived with domestic violence: Learning from North America Audrey Mullender, Centre for Applied Social Studies, University of Durham
Facilitating enquiry and action learning groups for social work education Hilary Burgess and Imogen Taylor, School for Policy Studies, University of Bristol
Developing critical conversations about practice Mark K Smith, Research Fellow and Tutor, YMCA George Williams College
Dialogue and reparation in the large whole group Alan Turkie, Independent and Lecturer in Youth and Community Work, Goldsmiths' College
Using groupwork methods in social work education Margaret O'Dee, Social Work Studies, Salford University
An outdoor treatment programme for a group of first year sixth formers Derrick Rowland Coverdale consultant
A Strategy for groupwork education and training in a social work agency Mark Doel, University of Sheffield and Catherine Sawdon, Training Officer, Wakefield Social Services
Managing the tension between being task-centred and being anti-oppressive Marcia Francis Spence and Beverley Prevatt-Goldstein, Centre for Applied Social Studies, University of Durham
Teachers, learning, ego and groups Leslie Silverlock and Marion Silverlock 'Groups Work'
Creative short term group therapy in a managed care environment Barry M Daste, Louisiana State University School of Social Work
Groupwork to facilitate family reconstitution: A social work response Jan Hadlow, Keynes College
Social groupwork practice in Hong Kong: Application of western ideas in an asian population Debbie O B Lam, University of Hong Kong
Time and space to grieve: A bereavement group for children Sister Margaret Pennels, Northampton General Hospital NHS Trust
An integrated feminist-socioeducational model: Groupwork with nurses in Hong Kong Elaine Au Liu, City University of Hong Kong

Volume 9 (ISBN 9781861770639)
Living with loss: A bereavement support group Sheila Thompson, School of Social Work, McGill University
A collaborative group approach for urban parents Mary McKernan McKay, Teresa Garcia, Joseph Scally and Lori Martinez, Institute for Juvenile Research, University of Illinois, Chicago
Groupwork with male 'domestic' abusers: Models and dilemmas Audrey Mullender, Professor in Social Work, University of Warwick
'Without the group, I'd still be eating half the Co-op': An example of groupwork with women who use food Jill Ball and Annemarie Norman, , Northern Initiative on Women and Food, Newcastle
The use of sculpt in social groupwork education Nuala Lordan, University College, Cork
Groupwork into the future: Some personal reflections Allan Brown, formerly University of Bristol
Ethical issues in practice: Participatory social research and groups George Taylor, Dept of Social and Community Studies, De Montfort University
Enhancing research usefulness with adapted focus groups Alice M. Home, Professor of Social Work, University of Ottawa
Focus groups and familiar social work skills: Their contribution to practitioner research Pat Walton, Lecturer in Post-Qualifying Studies (Child Care)
Focusing on groups in social policy research Paul Swift, Project Researcher, School for Policy Studies, University of Bristol
Exploitation or empowerment? Gaining access to young people's reflections on crime prevention Strategies Alan France, Research Fellow, University of Warwick University
A youth and community work approach to practitioner research into sensitive issues Steve Kenny, Dept of Applied Community Studies, Manchester Metropolitan University
Black community members-as-researchers: Working with community groups in the research process Simon Dyson and Mark Harrison, Director, Centre for Social Action, de Montfort University,
Empowering research process: Using groups in research to empower the people Asnarulkhadi

Abu-Samah, Doctoral student, University of Nottingham

Storming as transformation: A case study of group relationships Oded Manor, Middlesex University

An art therapy group for young people with eating difficulties Janet Fitzsimmons, Social Worker and Rosemary Levy, Art Therapist, Barnet Social Services Children and Families Health related Social Work Team

Intervention in the decision-making of youth gangs Francis W L Lee, Dept of Social Work, Chinese University of Hong Kong, T. Wing Lo and Dennis S W Wong, Dept of Applied Social Studies, City University of Hong Kong

Support groups for families of confused elders: Issues surrounding open peer-led groups Elizabeth Hughes Schneewind, Independent Social Worker

Drama and groupwork: Overcoming the 'double whammy' Philip Moore, Actor and Groupworker, Cumbria Probation

Psychosocial assistance to refugee and displaced women in Croatia Nina Pecnik, School of Social Work, University of Zagreb and Mira Miskulin, Programme for Refugee Women, 'Sunflower' Centre for Grassroots Relief, Zagreb

Volume 10 (ISBN 9781861770646)

Teleconferencing group counselling: Pre-group public phase Sandra Regan, Senior Lecturer in Groupwork, School of Social Work, University of New South Wales,

Suddenly the light went on: Using groupwork to empower returning students Roni Berger, Assistant Professor, School of Social Work, Adelphi University

A group's journey through separation and loss: Therapeutic groupwork with children as a social work intervention Maria Neary and Geraldine Brandon, Thamesmead Family Service Unit

Implementing a novel groupwork model: Application of an innovation-developmental process Jerome R. Kolbo, University of S Mississippi, Kimberly Horn, W Virginia University and Elizabeth Randall, University of S Mississippi

Applying a strengths, competence and empowerment model Anna Nosko, Family Services Association of Toronto and Margot Breton, University of Toronto

Effective groupwork packages and the importance of process David Henchman and Susan Walton, Freelance Trainers and Probation Officers

Using the sensory orientation group with a frail elder population Norma Thomas, Professor, Center for Social Work, Widener University, Pennsylvania and Suzanne Coleman, Social Worker, Bryn Mawr Terrace Nursing Home, Pennsylvania

Research into practice does go: Integrating research within programme development Rob Harry, Staff Dev't Manager, Patricia Heggarty, Probation Officer, Cathy Lisles, Freelance Researcher, Richard Thurston, Research Mgr, Mid-Glams Probation and Maurice Vanstone, Lecturer, University of Wales, Swansea

Brief group therapy and the use of metaphor Christian C Sunderland, Clinical Social Worker, Cardston Clinic, Alberta

We'd like you to come back Hilary Hopkin, Social Worker, Royal Liverpool University Hospital

The use of music in group work with out-patient alcoholic couples: A pilot investigation Wilfred A Gallant, Assoc. Professor of Social Work, Melanie D Galant, Research Asst Human Services Research Unit, Kevin M Gorey, Assoc. Professor of Social Work, Michael J Holosko, Professor of Social Work and Sammi Siegel, Director of Music Therapy, University of Windsor, Ontario

Exploring worker responses to critical incidents Marian F Fatout, Professor, School of Social Work, Louisiana State University, Baton Rouge

A Critical analysis of a support and clinical supervision group for interpreters working with refugees located in Britain Rachel Tribe, Senior Lecturer, Psychology Dept, University of East London, Romford

Feminist groupwork with lesbian survivors of incest Patricia A Groves, Director of Social Work Program and Connie Schondel, formerly Associate Professor, , University of Toledo, Ohio

Don't worry, it's just a stage he's going through: A reappraisal of the stage theory of group work as applied to an open model treatment group for men who abuse women Tom Caplan, Adj. Professor and Director, and Harle Thomas, Clinical and Groupworker, McGill University Domestic Violence Clinic

Active learning programmes to promote cognitive change Siu-Kau Cheung, Principal Lecturer,

Division of Social Studies, City University of Hong Kong

Volume 11 (ISBN 9781861770653)

Crossing bridges: Groupwork in Guyana Judith A B Lee, Professor, Dept of Social Work, Florida Gulf Coast University

Working with polarities, roles and timespirits: A process oriented approach to emotions in the Group Bogna Szymkiewicz-Komalska, Asst Professor, Inst of Applied Social Sciences, Warsaw University

It ain't (just) what you do: It's the way that you do it: Working towards effective practice in probation groupwork Alan Hayden, Jonathan Hopkinson, Janeen Sengendo and Elisabeth von Rabenau, Probation Officers, Cambridgeshire Probation

A Group intervention for children of incarcerated parents: Initial blunders and subsequent solutions David W Springer, Asst Professor, Elizabeth C Pomeroy, Asst Professor and Toni Johnson, Doctoral Student, School of Social Work, University of Texas, Austin

Expressing our anger: Hindrance or help in groupwork with adolescents? Andrew Malekoff, Director or Program Development, North Shore Child and Family Guidance Center, Roslyn Heights, New York

Technical errors or missed alternatives: An interview with Catherine Pappell

Groupwork with the mothers of teenage mothers Catherine Dennison, Research Psychologist and Helen Ingledew, Family Centre Worker, Trust for the Study of Adolescence

Men united: Fathers' voices Jennie Fleming, Research Fellow, Centre for Social Action, de Montfort University and Zbyszek Luczynski, Broader Initiatives Development Worker, Nottingham City Council

Parent education groups: Using cultural literature during engagement phase Gwenelle Styles O'Neal, Assoc Professor of Social Work, West Chester University, Pennsylvania and Janis Coombs Reid, Vice President of Academic Affairs, Atlanta Metropolitan College, Georgia

Action methods and interpersonal processes in groups: An exploration of psychodramatic concepts Annie Huntington, Lecturer, Dept of Social Work, Salford University

Building solutions in groupwork with parents John Sharry, Senior Social Worker, Dept of Child and Family Psychiatry, Mater Hospital, Dublin

Crossing the great gap: Groupwork for personal growth John Rowan, Group and Individual Psychotherapist

When actions speak louder: Groupwork in occupational therapy Linda Finlay, Associate Lecturer in Social Psychology, the Open University, Leeds

Help as mutual aid: Groupwork in mental health Oded Manor, Principal Lecturer in Social Work, School of Social Science, Middlesex University

No Group is an island: Groupwork in a social work agency Mark Doel, Professor of Social Work School of Social Work and RNIB Rehabilitation Studies, University of Central England and Catherine Sawdon, Training Officer, Wakefield Social Services

Breaking the culture of silence: Groupwork and community development Jacky Drysdale, Lecturer in Social Work and Rod Purcell, Lecturer in Community Development and Adult Education, University of Glasgow

Values as Context: Groupwork and social action Mark Harrison, Director, Centre for Social Action and Dave Ward, Professor and Head, Dept of Social and Community Studies, De Montfort University

Volume 12 (ISBN 9781861770660)

Punishment and the question of ownership: Groupwork in the criminal justice system Liz Dixon, Senior Lecturer in Criminal Justice Studies, University of Hertfordshire and Probation Officer, ILPS

Picking up the Pieces: Groupwork in Palliative Care Pam Firth, Senior Social Worker/Head of Family Support, Isabel Hospice, Welwyn Garden City

Developing the professionals: Groupwork for health promotion Ellen E Reverand, Senior Manager (Learning and Professional Development) and Louis B Levy, Acting Director, Health First, London

Learning beyond the classroom: A role for groupwork? Marion Silverlock, Education and Training Consultant, Somerset

Evolving the curriculum: Groupwork and community based learning Lynne Muir, Course Director, MA in Community Based Learning. , Centre for Education Development, Coventry

Using workshops on loss for adults with learning

disabilities Sue Read, Vicky Papakosta-Harvey and Sal Bower

Groupwork with schizophrenia: Clinical aspects Susan E. Mason, Associate Professor of Social Work, Wurzweiler School of Social Work, Yeshiva University, New York

Multi-family group interventions with schizophrenia Jane Hanvey Phillips, Doctoral Candidate, and Jacqueline Corcoran, Assistant Professor, School of Social Work, University of Texas, Arlington

The mixed-based nature of self-help groups in Finland Marianne Nylund, Researcher, Doctor of Social Sciences, Dept of Social Policy, University of Helsinky

Teenagers' experiences of a health promotion project Frances Maggs-Rapport, Senior Research Fellow, Mary Seacole Research Centre, De Montfort University

Working with natural groups of youth-at-risk: An RGC approach Francis Wing-lin Lee Assistant Professor, Dept of Social Work, University of Hong Kong

The strengths perspective in reminiscence groupwork with depressed older adults Alison C. Rishty Advanced Standing MSW Candidate in Clinical Practice, Columbia University

Using fieldwork experience as a tool for teaching: A multi-layered approach Barbara Worden, Assoc. Professor of Social Work, Southern Conecticut State University

Volume 13 (ISBN 9781861770677)

Using technologies in groupwork . Part I: Face-to-face groups, and *Part II: Technology-based groups* Paul R. Smokowski, Director of Distance Education, Maeda Galinsky, Kenan Distinguished Professor, School of Social Work, University of North Carolina at Chapel Hill, and Kristin Harlow, Social Work Practitioner

Researching our own practice: Single system design for groupwork Paul Johnson, Asst Professor, Dept of Social Work, University of S. Maine. Aaron Beckerman, Professor Emeritus and Charles Auerbach, Professor, Wurzweiler School of Social Work, Yeshiva University

Facilitating group beginnings. I: A practice model, and *Part II: From basic to working engagement* Alf Lizzio, Lecturer, and Keithia Wilson, Senior Lecturer, School of Applied Psychology, Griffiths University, Brisbane

To share or not to share: Dilemmas of facilitators who share the problem of group members Marian Maram, Assistant Director of Field Education, and Susan Rice, Professor and Undergraduate Program Coordinator, Dept of Social Work, California State University, Long Beach

In their own voices: Play activities and art with traumatised children Bruce St. Thomas, Psychotherapist/Art Therapist, Westbrook Street Psychotherapy Associates, Portland, and Paul Johnson, Assistant Professor, Dept of Social Work, University of S. Maine

Groupwork with children and adolescents using lifegames Isabelle C. Streng, Chartered Clinical Psychologist, Erasmus Medical Centre, Rotterdam, The Netherlands

Closing a cultural divide: Enhancing mutual aid while working with groups in Hong Kong Fanny L.W.C. Liu, Senior Lecturer, Division of Social Studies, City University of Hong Kong

Strengths and weaknesses of self-help groups in mental health: The case of Grow Kam-shing Yip, Associate Professor, Dept of Applied Social Studies, Hong Kong Polytechnic University

Using groupwork in community mental health: Practitioners' views Ben Papps, Lecturer in Clinical Psychology, Institute of Psychiatry, London., Oded Manor, Principal Lecturer in Social Work, Middlesex University and Jerome Carson, Senior Lecturer in Clinical Psychology, Institute of Psychiatry, London

Hearing voices: Learning to engage the group Terry Conway, Senior Social Worker, Kneesworth House Hospital, Royston

An isle full of noises: Enhancing mental health through the Music Workshop Project Tony Gillam, Early Interventions Team Leader, Merdian Family Interventions Programme, South Worcestershire Early Interventions Service

Henderson Hospital: Greater than the sum of its sub-groups Dr Kingsley Norton, Director, Henderson Hospital and Reader in Psychotherapy, St George's Hospital Medical School

Groupwork fit for purpose? An inclusive framework for mental health Oded Manor, Principal Lecturer in Social Work, School of Health and Social Sciences, Middlesex University

Authors' professional affiliations are those at the time of original publication

www.ingramcontent.com/pod-product-compliance
Lightning Source LLC
LaVergne TN
LVHW101442200926
848483LV00001B/29
9781861770615